Harry:—

I am convinced (at 82) that the average American is *not* particularly interested in *good* government. They are apathetic and indifferent about politics. They seem willing to sit by complacently and let the politicians (many of whom are dishonest if not mentally retarded) pick their pockets. Most of the citizens and voters don't do their "home work" ~~before~~ voting. They seem to be much more interested in Revenue Sharing, Social Security etc. They seem only interested in "a Free Lunch", although the controversial Economist Milton Friedman says "There's No Such Thing as a Free Lunch."

Best Regards John W Conrad

11/22/77

There's No Such Thing as a Free Lunch

There's No Such Thing as a Free Lunch

Milton Friedman

Open Court   LaSalle, Illinois

Also published as AN ECONOMIST'S PROTEST 2nd Edition by Thomas Horton, Glen Ridge, N.J.

Published by the Open Court Publishing Company in 1975.

Business and Society Review interview copyright *Business and Society Review,* 1972. Reprinted with permission.

"Using Escalators to Help Fight Inflation" copyright *Fortune* Magazine, 1974. Reprinted with permission.

Newsweek columns copyright Newsweek, Inc., 1966, 1967, 1968, 1969, 1970, 1971, 1972, 1973, 1974. Reprinted with permission.

"Morality and Controls I & II" copyright *The New York Times,* 1971. Reprinted with permission.

"The Voucher Idea" copyright © 1973 by *The New York Times* Company. Reprinted with permission.

Playboy interview originally appeared in *Playboy* Magazine; copyright © 1973 by Playboy. Reprinted with permission.

Printed in the United States of America.

Library of Congress Cataloging in Publication Data.

Friedman, Milton, 1912-
   There's no such thing as a free lunch.

   1. United States—Economic policy—1961-   —Addresses, essays, lectures. I. Title. HC106.6.F77   330.9'73'092   74-20959
ISBN 0-87548-310-0
ISBN 0-87548-297-X pbk.

Contents

Preface

In a book published in 1891, John Neville Keynes, the father of the more famous John Maynard Keynes, wrote: ". . . People think themselves competent to reason about economic problems, however complex, without any such preparatory scientific training as would be universally considered essential in other departments of enquiry. This temptation to discuss economic questions without adequate scientific preparation is all the greater because economic conditions exert so powerful an influence upon men's material interests. 'Few men,' says General Walker [a famous American economist of the nineteenth century], 'are presumptuous enough to dispute with the chemist or mechanician upon points connected with the studies and labours of his life; but almost any man who can read and write feels himself at liberty to form and maintain opinions of his own upon trade and money.' The economic literature of every succeeding year embraces works conceived in the true scientific spirit, and works exhibiting the most vulgar ignorance of economic history, and the most flagrant contempt for the conditions of economic investigation. It is much as if astrology were being pursued side by side with astronomy, or alchemy with chemistry."

I often send this quotation as part of a response to letters from earnest, sincere, well-intentioned, but economically illiterate, correspondents offering their own economic panaceas, or criticising my views, who display an utter lack of comprehension that economics is a serious subject with a hard core of sophisticated analysis that is widely accepted by professional economists of every political persuasion and that the chances against a rank amateur stumbling on a profound—and true—law are millions to one.

Let me hasten to add that the correspondents are not wholly to blame. Economists, like other scientists, do not write a great deal about the part of their subject that is taken for granted—that is taught in the schools and enshrined in advanced textbooks. They write mostly about the frontiers of the subject, the areas about which there is controversy. More important, economists, to a far greater extent than most other scientists, and precisely for the reasons John Neville Keynes stressed, are likely to be concerned with broad public issues in which technical economic analysis is only one element, and in which personal values and political beliefs—with respect to which the authors are not experts— play a vital role. The general public is far more likely to be exposed to the writings of economists on such subjects than to their more technical publications. Further, the writings that demand least in the way of hard thought and that appeal most to emotion and prejudice are likely to command the widest readership.

There is no satisfactory solution to the dilemma posed by the propositions: (1) there is a body of "positive" economics that can be applied to specific problems and that can yield reliable predictions of the consequences of change; (2) there are "experts" in positive economics; (3) differences about the desirability of governmental policies often reflect different beliefs about the consequences of the policies—conclusions of positive economics—rather than different values; (4) there is no simple litmus test by which a citizen can decide who is an "expert" and who is a "quack"; yet (5) even though the patient is incompetent to choose the physician, there is no alternative in a free society.

This book offers the reader no prescription for choosing among experts.

As was the case in my former book *An Economist's Protest*, the present volume consists primarily of columns which I have been contributing to *Newsweek* once every three weeks over the past eight years. Some of the columns of the previous book have been retained as still pertinent and new columns published in the past two years, along with a few other significant items, have been added. However, the basic themes remain the same and are dual: First, to offer persuasive evidence that there is a valuable body of positive economic analysis that can yield reliable results when applied to specific problems and that has important implications for both the consequences and the desirability of public policies. (We are today paying heavily for having neglected this simple proposition.) Second, to present an evaluation of current policies in light of a fervent belief that the promotion of individual freedom should be the prime objective of social arrangements.

To further the first theme, I have tried, as in the earlier book, to attach footnotes to all predictions indicating whether they were confirmed or contradicted. On the whole, the batting average of positive economics is excellent.

To further the second theme, I have included as the first item in the book a lengthy interview initially published in *Playboy* magazine. I am grateful to *Playboy* for permitting republication and especially to Michael Lawrence and Geoffrey Norman, the *Playboy* editors who conducted the interview. They devoted much effort to planning the questions and editing and organizing the answers. Their friendly skepticism, intellectual acuteness, and fine command of style contributed greatly to the effectiveness of the interview.

With the same objective I have replaced in the present Chapter Eleven an article that I wrote for the *New York Times Magazine* on "Social Responsibility of Business" with an interview published in *Business and Society Review*, which covers the same subject but also ranges more widely. I am indebted to the *Review* and especially to John McClaughry, who conducted the interview and wrestled a very much longer initial transcript into a readable final form.

In addition to these interviews and the new columns, I have added two other items: in Chapter Six, in which I have drawn together items about indexing, a piece first published in *Fortune* magazine urging the widespread adoption of escalator clauses; and in Chapter Twelve, an updated analysis of the voucher scheme for schooling, written for the *New York Times Magazine*.

We are indebted to these publications as well as to *Newsweek* for permission to reprint. I am indebted also to Barry Keating of Virginia Polytechnic Institute; Gerald Gunderson of the University of Massachusetts, E. Barry Solomon of George Mason University, Lawrence B. Smith of Grossmont College, and James G. Witte of Indiana University, for comments on the first volume that were extremely helpful in preparing this revised volume. My secretary, Gloria Valentine, contributed to this revised volume with the efficiency and good-will that I have been so fortunate as to be able to take for granted. This indebtedness is an addition to, not a substitute for, the debts acknowledged in the earlier book. As I face my mounting intellectual debt, I am reassured by the absence of any maturity date—else, I would be a hopeless bankrupt.

MILTON FRIEDMAN
Ely, Vermont
August 2, 1974

There's No Such Thing as a Free Lunch

Introduction
Playboy Interview

[February, 1973]

Playboy: In every public debate on an issue involving economics, there seem to be nearly as many conflicting opinions as there are economists. Why can't you people get together?

Friedman: We do. But that seldom makes news. It's our disagreements that receive attention. For example, how much attention is paid to agreement between Galbraith and myself in opposing a draft and favoring an all-volunteer armed force, or in opposing tariffs and favoring free trade, or on a host of other issues? What is newsworthy is that Galbraith endorses wage and price controls, while I oppose them.

Playboy: Yet in the past election, you supported Nixon despite his imposition of controls. Have you changed your mind?

Friedman: I haven't—and neither has Nixon. I'm still opposed to wage and price controls, and so is he. Incidentally, going back to Galbraith, in a note that I wrote to him shortly after Nixon imposed the controls, I said, "You must be as chagrined as I am to have Nixon for your disciple." So far, he hasn't replied.

I regret that he imposed them; yet in doing so, I think he behaved the only way a responsible leader of a democracy could. He resisted controls for nearly three years when there was strong pressure for their introduction. He tried to make the case against controls, to educate the people about the causes of inflation, and the best methods of fighting it—namely, reduced monetary growth and lower federal spending. But he failed, and finally gave in to the popular demand for some kind of immediate and extreme measure to halt rising prices, and controls were the measure most people seemed to agree on. As a leader, that was a proper thing for him to do, even though he felt it was the wrong solution. He behaved the same way with regard to the war.

Playboy: Aren't you saying that there's been a large element of political opportunism in Nixon's reversals?

Friedman: One man's opportunism is another's statesmanship. There is a very delicate balance between the two in our society. Good politics is what we should demand from our politicians—to a degree. We don't want our leaders to charge off in every direction trying to satisfy the latest public whim, but neither do we want them to completely ignore the will of the people. I think Nixon acted properly. The real problem is educating the public, and there he was unsuccessful.

Playboy: Isn't it possible that Nixon was wrong? Wasn't inflation at a level that demanded drastic action such as controls?

Friedman: No. Inflation was already tapering off as a result of earlier monetary and fiscal measures when the President imposed controls. In any event, controls are the wrong way to ease inflation.

Playboy: Why?

Friedman: Because they never work. We've seen that throughout history, ever since the time of the Emperor Diocletian. If controls are administered with any real zeal, people find ways to get around them. The current controls cover only about one-third of all prices. Suppose those prices were kept down by controls. That would simply mean people would have more money to spend on the products represented by the other two-thirds and would drive up the prices of those goods and services.

In the case of wages, there are any number of ways of getting around the controls. If an employer wants, for some reason, to pay a higher wage, he can promote the wage earner, offer him fringe benefits, give him a car—all sorts of things. This takes place especially at the higher income levels, with corporate executives, and so forth. So the people who are hurt most by wage controls are those the program is said to protect: the hourly wage earner, the employee on a low salary—production-line workers and secretaries.

If the controls are tightened or expanded, people will find new and more ingenious ways of getting around them. And as the power of enforcement increases, you move farther and farther from a free society; this is the most damaging effect of controls. The apparatus required to make them effective in even a limited way will be unpopular in a free society. We saw that in World War Two; even then, when there was fairly broad agreement on the need for controls, there was resentment and there were black markets.

Playboy: Why does inflation seem to be such a perennially insoluble problem?

Friedman: Technically, inflation isn't terribly difficult to stop. The real problem is that the favorable effects of inflation come early, the bad effects late. In a way, it's like drink. The first few months or years of inflation, like the first few drinks, seem just fine. Everyone has more money to spend and prices aren't rising quite as fast as the money that's available. The hangover comes when prices start to catch up. And, of course, some people are hurt worse than others by inflation. Usually people without much political voice—the poor and retired people on fixed incomes. Some people aren't hurt at all. And others profit enormously.

When you start to take some action *against* inflation, on the other hand, the bad effects are felt right away. People are out of work. Interest rates go up. Money gets tight. It's unpleasant. Only later do the good effects of an end to rising prices show up. The problem is getting through the painful cure without wanting another drink. The greatest difficulty in curtailing inflation is that, after a while, people begin to think they'd rather have the sickness than the cure. What they don't realize is that once the cure has taken effect, it's possible to have both economic growth and price stability. But as we saw with Nixon, there is terrible public pressure to junk the cure and go back to being sick—or drunk, to continue the metaphor.

Playboy: Why is it so difficult to make the public understand this?

Friedman: That has to do with the rather complex causes of inflation. When a shopper goes to the grocery store and sees that the price of meat has gone up 10 percent or so, she screams bloody murder and demands that something be done about it. She writes her congressman. Well, perhaps she's been admonishing that same congressman to vote for Medicare and increased Social Security and federal housing assistance—and, naturally, for no increase in the income tax. The congressman has voted for all these things and the Federal Reserve Board has made it possible for her congressman to pay for these measures, without increasing taxes, by expanding the money supply. Those are the basic sources of inflation and they are hidden. The shopper thinks the butcher is stealing and she wants it stopped. The butcher thinks his landlord is stealing when he increases the rent by 15 percent. The landlord, in turn, is upset about the increased costs of maintaining his building, and so on.

Playboy: But why have costs and prices risen?

Friedman: Not because of greedy wage earners or avaricious business-men. Prices have risen by 25 percent in the past five years because of what nineteen identifiable men, sitting around a table in Washington, did with respect to such arcane subjects as reserve requirements, dis-count rates, and purchases on the open market.

Playboy: You're talking about the Federal Reserve Board?

Friedman: Of course. Now, I'm not talking about any kind of conspiracy, or even dereliction of duty. These men did what they thought best for the country. They would have acted differently had government expenditures gone up less rapidly, had the deficits been lower.

Playboy: But how does the Federal Reserve System cause inflation? Isn't it simply the government's bank?

Friedman: That "simply" covers a lot of ground. The Fed, because it's the government's bank, has the power to create—to print—money, and it's too much money that causes inflation. For a rudimentary understand-ing of how the Federal Reserve System causes inflation, it's necessary to know what it has the power to do. It can print paper money; almost all the bills you have in your pocket are federal reserve notes. It can create deposits that can be held by commercial banks, which is equivalent to printing notes. It can extend credit to banks. It can set the reserve re-quirements of its member banks—that is, how much a bank must hold in cash or on deposit with the Federal Reserve Bank for every dollar of de-posits. The higher the reserve requirement, the less the bank can lend, and conversely.

These powers enable the Fed to determine how much money—cur-rency plus deposits—there is in the country and to increase or decrease that amount. The men with this power are appointed by the President and approved by the Senate and are leading financial experts. But this is tremendous authority for any small group of men to have. These men have attempted for the past sixty years to predict where the economy is headed and to keep it on an even path of growth. I have studied the mon-etary history of the United States and written a book on the subject, and it's my opinion that there have been more severe crises in the years since we've had a Federal Reserve System than in the years from the Civil War until 1914. Even if you leave out the years covered by the two world wars, the Fed seems to have failed in its mission of keeping the economy on a steady plane.

Playboy: Why?

Friedman: Basically, I think because it's a system of men and not of rules, and men are fallible. The decisions of the people who run the Fed, as I said, are made in good faith. They want to do the right thing. But the state of our knowledge is incomplete. Often they don't have all the facts or they see one particular phenomenon out of proportion. In the Great Depression, they managed to shrink the total money stock by a third. They did this for the most honorable of reasons, but it was exactly the wrong thing to do. Just as banks all around the country were closing, the Fed raised the discount rate; that's the rate they charge for loans to banks. Bank failures consequently increased spectacularly. We might have had an economic downturn in the thirties anyway, but in the absence of the Federal Reserve System—with its enormous power to make a bad situation worse—it wouldn't have been on anything like the scale we experienced.

Playboy: Has the Fed's recent record been this bad, or have we learned from past mistakes?

Friedman: We've learned a great deal from past mistakes. Two decades ago, I argued that the U.S. was depression-proof because the monetary authorities would never again permit a collapse of the monetary system like the one that occurred from 1929 to 1933. But I went on to say that the danger now was a swing in the other direction, that in attempting to avoid recession and unemployment, the system would overreact and produce inflation. Unfortunately, that is exactly what's occurred. Even so, the record for the post-World War Two period as a whole is enormously better than for the prewar period. We've had a quarter of a century without a really serious recession or depression, and our inflation, while we regard it as serious, has so far been mild by world standards. We've done better, but not as well as we easily could have done.

Playboy: What's the answer? Should we junk the Federal Reserve System and go back to private banking?

Friedman: No. But we can take some of the discretionary power away from the Fed and make it into a system that operates according to rules. If we're going to have economic growth without inflation, the stock of money should increase at a steady rate of about 4 percent per year— roughly matching the growth in goods and services. The Fed should be required to take the kind of limited action that would ensure this sort of monetary expansion.

Playboy: Wouldn't the Fed lose its emergency powers—powers that would be useful in a crisis?

Friedman: Most so-called crises will correct themselves if left alone. History suggests that the real problem is to keep the Fed, operating on the wrong premises, from doing precisely the *wrong* thing, from pouring gas on a fire. One reason we've so many government programs is that people are afraid to leave things alone when that is the best course of action. There is a notion—what I've called the Devil Theory—that's often behind a lot of this. The Fed was supposed to take power out the hands of the conniving bankers, who were supposed to profit when the economy fluctuated wildly. The idea is to pass a law and do something about it. Put good men in charge; that's one line. The competing line is that there are problems in the world not only because of bad men but also because it's an imperfect world. People are imperfect. There are scarcities. Shortages. You can let things work themselves out or try to do something about them by passing a law. Of course, you know which idea is easier to sell.

Playboy: But you prefer the *laissez-faire*—free-enterprise—approach.

Friedman: Generally. Because I think the government solution to a problem is usually as bad as the problem and very often makes the problem worse. Take, for example, the minimum wage, which has the effect of making the poor people at the bottom of the wage scale—those it was designed to help—worse off than before.

Playboy: How so?

Friedman: If you really want to get a feeling about the minimum wage, there's nothing more instructive than going to the congressional documents to read the proposals to raise the minimum wage and see who testifies. You very seldom find poor people testifying in favor of the minimum wage. The people who do are those who receive or pay wages much higher than the minimum. Frequently Northern textile manufacturers. John F. Kennedy, when he was in Congress, said explicitly that he was testifying in favor of a rise in the minimum wage because he wanted protection for the New England textile industry against competition from the so-called cheap labor of the South. But now look at it from the point of that cheap labor. If a high minimum wage makes unfeasible an otherwise feasible venture in the South, are people in the South benefited or harmed? Clearly harmed, because jobs otherwise available for them are no longer available. A minimum-wage law is, in reality, a law that makes it illegal for an employer to hire a person with limited skills.

Playboy: Isn't it, rather, a law that requires employers to pay a fair and livable wage?

Friedman: How is a person better off unemployed at a dollar sixty an hour than employed at a dollar fifty? No hours a week at a dollar sixty comes to nothing. Let's suppose there's a teen-ager whom you as an employer would be perfectly willing to hire for a dollar fifty an hour. But the law says, no, it's illegal for you to hire him at a dollar fifty an hour. You must hire him at a dollar sixty. Now, if you hire him at a dollar sixty, you're really engaging in an act of charity. You're paying a dollar fifty for his services and you're giving him a gift of ten cents. That's something few employers, quite naturally, are willing to do or can *afford* to do without being put out of business by less generous competitors. As a result, the effect of a minimum-wage law is to produce unemployment among people with low skills. And who are the people with low skills? In the main, they tend to be teen-agers and blacks, and women who have no special skills or have been out of the labor force and are coming back. This is why there are abnormally high unemployment rates among these groups.

Playboy: How can you be sure that the minimum-wage law is the cause?

Friedman: In 1956, I think, the minimum was raised from seventy-five cents to a dollar—a very substantial rise. In the early fifties, the unemployment rate among male teen-agers was about the same for blacks as for whites. Both were about 8 percent when the over-all unemployment rate was about 4 percent. In the late fifties, after the minimum-wage rate was raised from seventy-five cents to a dollar, the unemployment rate of black teen-agers shot up from 8 percent to something like 20 to 25 percent. For white teen-agers, it shot up to something like 13 percent. From that day to this, the rates for both black and white teen-agers have been higher than before 1956. When they start to decline, a new rise in the minimum-wage rate comes along and pushes them up again. The black teen-age rate has been very much higher than the white teen-age rate, for reasons that are highly regrettable and that we ought to be doing something about: blacks get less schooling and are less skilled than whites. Therefore, the minimum-wage rate hits them particularly hard. I've often said the minimum-wage rate is the most anti-Negro law on the books.

Playboy: Couldn't those who are hurt by minimum-wage legislation be trained for more skilled jobs at better wages?

Friedman: The minimum wage destroys the best kind of training programs we've ever had: on-the-job training. The main way people have risen in the labor force is by getting unskilled jobs and learning things. Not merely technical skills: they learn such things as being at a job on time, spending eight hours a day at a job rather than standing around on street corners, having a certain element of responsibility, letting their employer know when they're not going to come in. All of those traits are very important. In an attempt to repair the damage that the minimum wage has done to traditional on-the-job training, you now have a whole collection of programs designed to take up the slack. The great proliferation of governmental programs in which employers are subsidized to provide on-the-job training gives employers an incentive to hire people and then *fire* them in order to get other people for whom they can get more subsidies.

Playboy: Even if minimum-wage laws have been as counterproductive as you say, isn't there a need for some government intervention on behalf of the poor? *Laissez faire,* after all, has long been synonymous with sweatshops and child labor—conditions that were eliminated only by social legislation.

Friedman: Sweatshops and child labor were conditions that resulted more from poverty than from *laissez-faire* economics. Wretched working conditions still exist in nations with all sorts of enlightened social legislation but where poverty is still extreme. We in the United States no longer suffer that kind of poverty because the free-enterprise system has allowed us to become wealthy.

Everybody does take the line that *laissez faire* is heartless. But when do you suppose we had the highest level of private charitable activity in this country? In the nineteenth century. That's when we had the great movement toward private nonprofit hospitals. The missions abroad. The library movement. Even the Society for Prevention of Cruelty to Animals. That was also the era in which the ordinary man, the low-income man, achieved the greatest improvement in his standard of living and his status. During that period, millions of penniless immigrants came in from abroad, with nothing but their hands, and enjoyed an enormous rise in their standard of living.

My mother came to this country when she was fourteen years old. She worked in a sweatshop as a seamstress, and it was only because there *was* such a sweatshop in which she could get a job that she was able to come to the U.S. But she didn't stay in the sweatshop and neither did most of the others. It was a way station for them, and a far better one than anything available to them in the old country. And she never thought it was anything else. I must say that I find it slightly revolting that people sneer at a system that's made it possible for them to sneer at it. If we'd had minimum-wage laws and all the other trappings of the welfare state in the nineteenth century, half the readers of *Playboy* would either not exist at all or be citizens of Poland, Hungary or some other country. And there would be no *Playboy* for them to read.

Playboy: Aren't there any government programs that can successfully improve the lot of the poor?

Friedman: The actual outcome of almost all programs that are sold in the name of helping the poor—and not only the minimum-wage rate—is to make the poor worse off. You can take one program after another and demonstrate that this is the fact. Indeed, by now, I'm getting a lot more company than I used to have on this point. In a recent Brookings Institution report, the authors of Great Society programs such as the War on Poverty now admit that those programs spent a lot of money but accomplished very little except to create employment for a lot of high-priced poverty fighters. Sometimes these programs have been well-meaning—those who are naive about the laws of economics think the best way to help the poor is to vote them higher wages—but often they are out right subsidies to the middle class and the rich at the expense of the poor.

Playboy: Please explain.

Friedman: Take aid to higher education. In my opinion, that's one of the country's greatest scandals. There is an enormous amount of empirical evidence that subsidies to higher education impose taxes on low-income people and benefit high-income people. In the state of California, over 50 percent of the students in government-financed institutions of higher learning—the University of California, the state universities, junior colleges and all the rest—come from the upper 25 percent of families by income. Fewer than 5 percent come from the lower 25 percent. But even that understates the situation, because what really matters is what the incomes of the people who go through college will be after they get out of college. If you have two young men, one middle class, who goes to the university, and the other poor, who doesn't—who goes to work as, say, a garage mechanic—the one who goes to college will obviously make more money over his lifetime. But the man in the garage will be paying taxes to support that other man's education—and perhaps his draft deferment. When I'm being demagogic about this, I say that the system in California is one in which you tax the people of Watts to send children from Beverly Hills to college.

Playboy: There are probably liberals who would agree that some well-intentioned government programs aimed at helping the poor don't work and are demeaning or unfair to the people they're supposed to help. Would you agree with *them* that the government has a responsibility to protect the public—via consumer protection, for example—from the excesses of capitalism?

Friedman: The basic premise of the consumer "crusade" is that unless the government moves in with inspectors and agencies, consumers will be defrauded by unethical producers and sellers. I can't accept that kind of solution. If a consumer finds he's being sold rotten meat at the grocery store, he has the very best protection agency available: the market. He simply stops trading at that store and moves to another. Eventually, the first seller gets the message and offers good meat or he goes out of business.

Playboy: Isn't the issue more complex than that? One of the most serious consumer problems is mislabeling and misrepresentation of products that only the most sophisticated shopper can spot.

Friedman: Yes, it's more complex, but the model is valid. If there is devious misrepresentation—which isn't likely, because the return isn't that great—a few shoppers will spot it. Producers work on a margin, like everybody else. If the 5 percent of shoppers who are careful spot a clever misrepresentation, they'll leave the store. That's enough pressure on the store owner. The infrequent shopper assumes this when he goes to a store that's popular. There has to be a reason for its popularity, he decides. The reason is that it appeals to those who are very careful about measures and labels and that sort of thing.

Playboy: Without some kind of consumer safeguards, how is the public to be protected from such things as injuries caused by faulty products?

Friedman: You sue. That's why we have courts. But in the case of a consumer-protection agency, that might not be so simple. Do you sue the manufacturer or the agency that didn't find the error and approved the product? I think most people would rather be able to sue General Motors than an agency of the government.

Playboy: But there *are* consumer frauds and there are dangerous goods put thoughtlessly on the market. Isn't there a way to prevent that rather than inflict punishment after the fact?

Friedman: The most effective deterrent a producer can feel is loss of profits. He's going to be careful about what he puts on the market because he doesn't want to lose business. He doesn't want to be sued, either. People like Ralph Nader are always talking about misleading advertising and mislabeling, but I believe it would be very hard to find any examples of mislabeling that can approach what is practiced by those of us who write for the public at large. We're the worst advertisers of the lot. We screech about how important our own products are, how good they are, how they'll cure every ill, and yet some of us complain when businessmen do the same thing. We don't want an agency to assure the public that we do or don't measure up to our claims. Critics and consumers do that.

One of the most dramatic failures of government has been the case of the regulatory agencies. Even the strongest critics of the market and the warmest supporters of government will agree that these organizations have become the servants of those they were supposed to protect the public *from.* Yet there is now a demand for a federal consumer-protection agency. We never learn.

Playboy: Do you discount the possibility that John Gardner or Ralph Nader might put together an honest-to-God consumer coalition—outside the government—that would get effective legislation passed?

Friedman: Do I discount the possibility that water can run uphill? They're working against the fundamental nature of things. The interests of consumers are diverse and diffuse. You buy a thousand things, but you make your living producing a single product let's say a magazine—and you spend the income from that on the thousand different things. When the chips are down, your willingness to promote your interest as a consumer of the thousand things will be far less than your willingness to engage in something that will promote your interest as a producer. You're going to lobby for postal subsidies for magazines, and you're going to make a much harder case than the people who only *read* magazines. That's in the nature of things.

Playboy: You're talking about the assertion of individual self-interest. But you also seem to feel that it's in the nature of things for a governmental agency—even one specifically created to protect the public from corporate self-interest—to put the welfare of industry before that of the consumer. Why?

Friedman: Because it's in the clear and immediate interest of the regulated industry or industries to either neutralize the effect of that agency or use it to their advantage. Since the interest of an industry is direct and focused, it will spend a lot more time, money and energy to accomplish its goal than the public will to protect its interests. The public's interest is diffuse, as I said. A consumer-protection agency might work for a brief period of time, but after the initial, faddish interest in the project dies down, the producers will move in with pressure for exemptions and other special rulings.

Take the historical example of the Interstate Commerce Commission, which was established to protect the consumer from exploitation by monopolistic railroads. In actual effect, this created a tight cartel that was able to keep rates up. The railroad people themselves had been trying to set rates, to establish a cartel, but every time they got an agreement, some chiseler would break it and they'd be back in competition again. So the ICC was created, and its initial effect was to enable the railroads to keep rates up and competition out.

Then trucking came along, which would have competed with the railroads. There was no monopoly argument whatsoever for including trucking under government regulations. Nobody ever argued that, because there was an enormous amount of competition in the trucking business. Yet trucking was brought under the ICC on the claim that consumers had to be protected from unscrupulous truckers. Of course, the real reason for bringing trucking under the ICC was to protect the railroads from competition.

Or consider the control of air fares by the Civil Aeronautics Board. Now, it's perfectly clear that if you didn't have governmental price fixing, air fares would be roughly 60 percent of what they are now. We know that because California is big enough to support rather a sizable airline, within the limits of the state. It is, therefore, not controlled by the CAB. If you compare the fares from Los Angeles to San Francisco on Pacific Southwest Airlines with the CAB-controlled fares from Los Angeles to Reno or Phoenix, which are roughly the same distance—or even with the earlier CAB-mandated fares between Los Angeles and San Francisco—you will find that the Pacific Southwest Airlines fares are roughly 60 percent of CAB fares.

Playboy: Do P. S. A. and the other federally unregulated airlines make a profit?

Friedman: P. S. A.'s rate of return on capital is as high as, and I believe higher than, that of the other airlines. It's clear that a large part of the effect of higher fares is simply to cause the commercial airlines to waste money. Since they can't compete on fares, they compete with free drinks, fancy meals, attractive hostesses and, most important, with service—all of which keeps the fares up, which means half-empty planes. If you look at the occupancy rate on P. S. A., it consistently averages much higher than that of the main-airline planes on similar heavily traveled routes.

Playboy: So the CAB-regulated airlines aren't really benefiting from higher fares?

Friedman: Most of this "benefit" is eaten up in higher operating costs. But let's suppose some of it does trickle through. Where does it trickle through to? It trickles through to airline profits. Who owns the airline stock? The same income class of people that does most of the flying. Perhaps they don't realize it, but all they're doing is taking ten dollars out of their left-hand pocket in order to put one dollar into their right-hand pocket.

Playboy: What about areas in which there is nearly a universal public interest? The regulation of television, for instance? Shouldn't the government have some authority over the airwaves?

Friedman: TV is a more complicated case. The Federal Communications Commission has tremendous power over the networks, which are few in number, and the broadcasters have an ultimate interest in the decisions of the FCC. Consequently, they can and do exert influence on that agency. And the FCC has done a great deal to keep the big networks in business and to protect them from competition. Many liberals want stronger FCC regulation to improve programing and reduce advertising. Yet cable television would allow people to watch Shakespeare uninterruptedly if they were willing to pay enough so that a producer could make a profit by supplying it to them. But the FCC has held up cable TV with regulations and delaying tactics that are completely acceptable to the big networks, which make their money through advertising. If you want to watch television, you watch what the networks provide—complete with the advertisements. So, in a way, the advertisers are being federally subsidized. Of course, there are still substitutes. You can read or go to the movies. And even in television, which has been shackled by government regulation, the free market is close to surmounting the problem. Technology spurred by competition will soon make video cassettes available. Since they don't require use of the public airwaves, they won't be subject to federal regulation.

Playboy: Do you think there's a constructive purpose to *any* governmental regulation of commerce?

Friedman: No, I don't. All of these interferences with the market are justified as protection of the public interest, but, in fact, they endanger the public interest. In the absence of regulation and protection, we are told, we would be exploited and overcharged for shoddy service and unsafe products, degrading the quality of our lives and jeopardizing our safety. I've always found it amusing and paradoxical to behold the enormous success Nader has had in selling the idea that capitalism degrades quality.

Picture one of these dupes whom Nader feels for walking into his home and turning on his magnificent hi-fi set. Stop and think about the improvements that have taken place in electronics and hi-fi and ask yourself whether that was through governmental action, whether it was due to regulation, whether it was due to standards set up by the government. The answer is no. It was due to straight private competition. He turns on his fancy stereo FM—which is living proof of a proposition contrary to Nader's—and listens to Nader telling a Senate subcommittee how production under capitalism, by business enterprises, is synonymous with reduction in quality, with shoddy goods. If Nader tried to carry that same message through letters handled by that efficient government monopoly, the U. S. Postal Service, he would never be heard.

Playboy: Why *do* we have such poor postal service?

Friedman: Precisely because it *is* a government monopoly—and performs exactly like one. But we can't eliminate it, because a very strong interest group lobbies against its elimination. And that group, like all interest groups, has a focused interest as opposed to the diffuse, general interest. We've seen in the case of parcel delivery, which can be undertaken by private firms, that there is an opportunity for profitable and efficient delivery. United Parcel Service makes a profit and provides good service. But the postal union and the government employees in the Postal Service aren't going to give up their monopoly on first-class mail.

Playboy: How do you feel about *private* monopolies? Should they be either broken up or closely regulated by the government?

Friedman: The problem in this kind of discussion is making a distinction between the real world and the ideal world. For an ideal free market, you want a large number of producers. For an ideal government, you want a saint. In the absence of both, you have three choices: unregulated private monopoly, private monopoly regulated by government and government monopoly. All three are bad, but, in my opinion, the best of the bad lot is unregulated private monopoly. The ICC and the railroads provide a good example of regulated private monopoly; the Postal Service is a good example of public monopoly. Those aren't really appealing cases.

Playboy: Is there an unregulated private monopoly in existence?

Friedman: A recent historical example would be the stock exchange before 1934. You have so much regulation now that you'd have to take a total industry to find a good example. Iron and steel, perhaps. But there really is no such thing as pure monopoly, since everything has substitutes. Even iron and steel. The telephone is a monopoly, but it has substitutes in the other forms of communication.

There's never been anything like the monopoly domination of the economy that some people claim exists. It's a matter of relative size. While some people point to the automobile industry as a giant monopoly that disproportionately influences the economy, they don't recognize that the wholesale-trade industry is twice the size of the automobile industry. Studies of labor unions indicate, similarly, that their influence is relatively small and unimportant—though obviously some of them have great power in limited areas.

Perfect competition is a theoretical concept like the Euclidean line, which has no width and no depth. Just as we've never seen that line, there has never been truly free enterprise. But the examples of monopoly that can be found in this country are nothing like the threat to our imperfect free-enterprise system posed by the government's attempts to control monopoly "in the public interest." The examples we've been talking about are a case in point. Another very good example is the whole system of agricultural programs. Agriculture would be entirely competitive if it weren't for government control of prices, which has hurt the consumer without benefiting the farmer.

One final thing on this subject: free enterprise isn't necessarily strongly supported by one group in our economy and denounced by another. Both business and labor would like exemptions that would work to their advantage and against the public good. Both would like to behave as monopolies and receive special government considerations. The oil industry fights hard for import quotas to keep foreign supplies out and its own prices high. All the while preaching the virtues of free enterprise. Tariffs are supported by certain elements of labor for the same reason. The essence of the problem is that once we begin to allow exceptions for special interests, we move from a system of private arrangements to a political system where everyone's freedom is limited and government becomes a matter of trying to balance those interests. Nobody really wins under these terms.

Playboy: If consumer protection—even from monopoly—isn't an area that is legitimately the province of government, what about pollution?

Friedman: Even the most ardent environmentalist doesn't really want to stop pollution. If he thinks about it and doesn't just talk about it, he wants to have the *right amount* of pollution. We can't really *afford* to eliminate it—not without abandoning all the benefits of technology that we not only enjoy but on which we depend. So the answer is to allow only pollution that's worth what it costs, and not any pollution that isn't worth what it costs. The problem is to make sure that people bear the costs for which they are responsible. A market system rests fundamentally on such an arrangement. If you hit me with your car and you damage me, you are obligated to pay me—at least until we have no-fault insurance. The problem of pollution is that if you emit noxious smoke that damages me, it's difficult for me to know who's done the damage and to require you to be responsible for it. The reason the market doesn't do it is that it's hard to do. The resolution does have to be through governmental arrangements, but in the form of effluent taxes rather than emission standards. I prefer such taxes to emission standards because taxes are more flexible. If it's more expensive for a company to pay the tax than emit the pollutant, it will very quickly raise its own emission standards.

Playboy: At its own expense or the consumer's?

Friedman: The consumer's, of course. There is a romantic notion that by cracking down on the producers, we will somehow end pollution without any increase in prices. Nonsense. We've already seen some firms go out of business because of antipollution legislation. They couldn't afford to stay in production. Why shouldn't consumers bear the increased costs of a company's effluent tax or of antipollution devices? They themselves are the only real producers of pollution. There is pollution from steel mills because people—consumers—desire steel. Otherwise, it wouldn't be produced. So those who desire steel are responsible for the pollution that's caused by its production, and they should bear the cost of reducing that pollution.

Playboy: Suppose the effluent tax on, say, a paper mill isn't as high as the cost of reducing water pollution. Won't the customer pay higher prices for the paper—and won't the water still be dirty?

Friedman: Not necessarily. That depends on how the government uses the revenue from the tax. The money could be spent on treatment plants—cleaning the water. Insofar as it's feasible, the effluent taxes collected could also be paid back as a tax reduction to the people who are harmed, if it can be proved who did what to whom. Which is preferable depends on whether people would rather have the money or the clean water.

Playboy: Then the tax isn't really a solution?

Friedman: There *is* no perfect solution. It's a fact of life that there are hard, nasty problems that can be mitigated but not eliminated. This is one of them. The tax is the best—or, if you prefer, least bad—of the ways to mitigate pollution. Let me add that there are some ways in which the market works to resolve the problem of pollution, or at least to lessen its effects. Take a town like Gary, Indiana. To the extent that the pollution caused by the U. S. Steel plant there is confined to that city and people generally are truly concerned about the problem, it's to the company's advantage to do something about it. Why? Because if it doesn't, workers will prefer to live where there is less pollution, and U. S. Steel will have to pay them more to live in Gary.

Playboy: Quite apart from emission standards and effluent taxes, shouldn't corporate officials take action to stop pollution out of a sense of social responsibility?

Friedman: I wouldn't buy stock in a company that hired that kind of leadership. A corporate executive's responsibility is to make as much money for the stockholders as possible, as long as he operates within the rules of the game. When an executive decides to take action for reasons of social responsibility, he is taking money from someone else—from the stockholders, in the form of lower dividends; from the employees, in the form of lower wages; or from the consumer, in the form of higher prices. The responsibility of a corporate executive is to fulfill the terms of his contract. If he can't do that in good conscience, then he should quit his job and find another way to do good. He has the right to promote what he regards as desirable moral objectives only with his own money. If, on the other hand, the executives of U. S. Steel undertake to reduce pollution in Gary for the purpose of making the town attractive to employees and thus lowering labor costs, then they are doing the stockholders' bidding. And everybody benefits: the stockholders get higher dividends; the customer gets cheaper steel; the workers get more in return for their labor. That's the beauty of free enterprise.

Playboy: We've been discussing government programs aimed at protecting the public. Do you reject the kind of programs by which the government attempts to aid individuals directly? Social Security, for instance?

Friedman: If you talk about misleading labeling, Social Security is about as misleading as you can get. It has nothing to do with social and it has nothing to do with the security of society. What's called Social Security is a program that links together a particular set of taxes and a particular set of benefits. It involves an 11.7 percent tax on wages up to a maximum that is now $10,800. The employer and the employee each supposedly pay 5.85 percent, but since the employer's half is part of his total wage cost, it's the employee who's really paying the whole bill. So here you have a regressive payroll tax.

On the other side of that, you have a benefit structure under which people above a certain age receive certain amounts. There are many things that can be said about it, but let me try to say the most important first: is it a good buy? The answer is, if you take the law as it now stands, it's a very good buy for people in the older age groups, and it's a very lousy buy for people in lower age groups. If a person below about forty-five invested the same amount of money in a private annuity or just put it in the bank and let it accumulate interest, he would end up with a much larger annuity than he is now being promised by Social Security. On the other hand, older people are getting a larger annuity than their taxes would have paid for. They're getting it partly because many of them didn't pay during the whole of their working lives, since Social Security is a relatively new thing. The number of people who have been paying taxes has been growing more rapidly than the number of people receiving benefits. Also, when they started paying, the tax rates were much lower than they are now.

In addition to the old/young discrepancy, which is the most serious, there is also a poor/rich discrepancy that works to the benefit of the rich. People who have high incomes from property don't lose their Social Security benefits when they reach the age of sixty-five, while those who have to keep working lose all or a part until they reach seventy-two. But there's a much more important bias. The lower-income person will be likely to go to work and start paying taxes at something like seventeen or eighteen years of age, while the upper-income person might go from college to graduate school and not start working and paying taxes until he's twenty-three or twenty-four. That means the low-income person will pay taxes for more years and, when you take account of the effect of compound interest, he will pay the economic equivalent of roughly a third more than the well-to-do person.

It's also an established fact of demography that upper-class people live longer than lower-class people, so the lower-class person not only starts paying earlier but he's less likely to receive benefits and, if he does, it will be for fewer years. So he pays more taxes and gets less in benefits. This biases the whole program in favor of the well to do, who don't need the money, as opposed to the poor, who do. This is offset only somewhat by the fact that the benefit schedule is biased in favor of low-income people.

Finally, it really is misleading to think of Social Security as an individual purchase of insurance, as if your payments were buying your benefits. There is almost no relationship between what you pay and what you get. What we have in Social Security is a tax system and a separate benefits system. I don't know anyone—whatever his political persuasion—who thinks that a flat-rate wage tax with a maximum on the amount of wages taxed is a good tax. It's equally hard to find anybody who would accept it as a satisfactory benefit system. If somebody happens not to have worked in a covered industry, for example, he gets nothing, no matter how severe his need. A man over sixty-five who is qualified can have an income of $1 million from investments and still get his full benefits. A man of the same age, with no income from property, who works and earns over a certain amount, gets nothing. To add insult to injury, he has to keep paying the taxes. It's always been a funny thing to me that people who don't have a good thing to say about Social Security as a tax system or a benefit system regard it as a sacred cow when you tie the two together.

Playboy: Would you be in favor of a Social Security system that eliminated the inequities by linking payments more closely to benefits?

Friedman: Let me accept, for the sake of argument, the false claim made for this system: that it really is an insurance program. There are still two strong reasons for objecting to it. One is that it involves *compulsory* purchase of retirement. Second, it involves compulsory purchase of that retirement *from the government.* Suppose you're a young man of thirty, but it so happens you come from a family that has a very short life span. Everybody in your family has inherited cancer, heart disease and what not and you look forward and say, "Hell, I'm not going to live beyond fifty." Is it irrational for you to decide that you want to spend your money on living now and not put it aside for retirement at the age of sixty-five? What justification is there for the government to say it won't let you do that? On the other hand, say you're going to live a long time—at least you think you are—but you just enjoy the present and you'd rather live it up now, knowing full well that this may put you into difficulty later on. The argument is that when you get into difficulty later on, you'll be a charge of the state. But you'll only be a charge of the state if the state wants to take you as a charge. If you decide to live it up now and take the consequences later, it seems to me that should be your right.

Playboy: Realistically, the state would probably take care of someone under those circumstances.

Friedman: All right, let's suppose we're going to compel him to provide for his old age. Here I've got two people. Mr. X, a saving type, is going to be accumulating wealth and is buying a retirement annuity on his own. Mr. Y is not. Why, in addition to what X is doing on his own, should he have to buy it through the government? If you're going to have compulsory retirement, shouldn't the government specify that every individual in the community must demonstrate to the satisfaction of the authorities that he's providing for a retirement benefit of a certain kind, then let him do it however he wants? If you want government to be in the business, let's require it to compete with private enterprise. Let it offer the terms on which it's willing to give a retirement benefit and let it be a self-supporting concern.

Playboy: Even if your objections to Social Security were shared by a majority of the voters, don't we have too much at stake to abandon it for the program you suggest?

Friedman: We have too much at stake *not* to abandon Social Security. Replacing it would take some time, of course; we couldn't in good conscience renege on the obligations we've already undertaken. I have outlined elsewhere a program that would get the government out of the business of providing for people's retirement while, at the same time, honoring present commitments. It's an involved program, however, too complex to get into here, but entirely feasible.

One final thing: like any number of government programs, Social Security was conceived as a method of dealing with special problems involving the poor. Like the other programs, it has expanded—as we've become wealthier as a nation—more rapidly than the nation's wealth. There is a reason for this. There is a particular group with a strong interest in maintaining and strengthening Social Security: the people who administer that program. As poverty declines, the pressure for more and more poverty programs increases. That pressure comes from the people who administer the programs more than from the poor themselves. This is just one more reason I propose a simple solution—a negative income tax—for the problem of poverty. It would eliminate this whole business of special categories and special programs.

Playboy: Before we deal with the negative income tax, let's talk about your more fundamental suggestions for reform on the income tax itself.

Friedman: Well, I'd like to move toward an enormously simplified income tax, by eliminating all present deductions except for a personal exemption and substituting a flat-rate tax for the current graduated schedule. Let's consider the deductions first. I would eliminate *all* personal deductions, except for strictly occupational expenses. There would be no more tax deductions for charitable contributions, for interest payments, for real-estate taxes; no more special treatment for capital-gains income, for oil depletion or for all the rest. The income tax would then be based on what it was supposed to be based on all along: individual income.

From this figure, representing his total receipts in excess of business costs, each taxpayer would be entitled to deduct a sum—a personal exemption—that reasonably reflects the cost of a survival existence in the 1970s. When the income tax was enacted, the personal exemption was supposed to assure that there would be no tax whatever on people with very low incomes. The assumption was that everybody deserved a subsistence income before he was taxed. But today, this concept has become a joke. We still have a personal exemption, but—considering the effects of inflation—it's lower now that it's ever been. I would double the present personal exemption, to $1,500, or $1,600 per person.

Playboy: At what percentage of income would you place the flat-rate tax?

Friedman: If you eliminate the present deductions and retain the present personal exemption, you could scrap the current graduated rates—which run from 14 percent up to 70 percent—and raise the same amount of revenue with a flat-rate tax of around 16 percent. This sounds unbelievable, but it's true. Our current graduated rates, while they supposedly go from 14 up to 70 percent, are fraudulent. Very few people pay taxes in the higher brackets, largely because of the loopholes we've heard so much about.

Playboy: According to the conventional wisdom, the graduated tax is a good way to democratically redistribute wealth by allocating the revenues to social programs. Doesn't it do that?

Friedman: The graduated tax, to the extent that it works, doesn't redistribute wealth. Not only does most of the tax revenue from the higher income brackets not go to the poor in the form of social programs, the graduated tax also *protects* rather than redistributes wealth. It is, in effect, a tax on *becoming* wealthy. It doesn't affect people who are already wealthy. All it does is protect them from the competition of those who would share the wealth with them.

Playboy: Do you think a confiscatory inheritance tax would better solve the problem?

Friedman: There's no such thing as an effective inheritance tax. People will always find a way around it. If you can't pass $100,000 on to your children, you can set them up in a profitable business; if you can't do that, you can spend the money educating them to be physicians or lawyers or whatever. A society that tries to eliminate inheritance only forces inheritance to take different forms. The human desire to improve the lot of one's children isn't going to be eliminated by any government in this world. And it would be a terrible thing if it were, because the desire of parents to do things for their children is one of the major sources of the energy and the striving that make all of us better off. Even an effective inheritance tax, if one could be concocted, wouldn't prevent the transmission of wealth, but it would put an enormous damper on progress. I've never been able to understand the merit of the sort of equality that would chop the tall trees down to the level of the low ones. The equality I would like to see brings the low ones up.

Playboy: Would your flat-rate tax bring the low ones up or would it —at the expense of those in the lower brackets—benefit primarily those who would pay less under your system than they do now?

Friedman: I think it would be fairer to almost everyone than the present system, assuming you eliminated the loopholes. After all, loopholes are nothing more than devices that allow people with relatively large incomes to avoid high taxation. The Brookings Institution, which has been looking into this, estimates that if you eliminated all the loopholes, you would increase total taxable income by something like 35 percent. Given a 21 or 22 percent average tax rate on the current base to collect current revenues, you can see that on a base a third again as large, a flat-rate tax of around 16 percent would raise the same amount of money. Personally, I can't imagine many people saying that such a tax would be unfair. As you suggest, people who are very poor might make such a claim, with some justification. That's why I'd also like to double the size of the present personal exemption. Then it would take a flat-rate tax of around 20 percent to yield the same amount of revenue that the current system raises.

Playboy: You make it sound almost simple. Yet few knowledgeable people besides yourself have ever seriously considered such a proposal.

Friedman: That's not necessarily an indictment of the soundness of the idea. But you have a point. The current system, with all its loopholes, makes many taxpayers—especially the influential ones, who have a large voice in government policy—think they have a vested interest in the status quo. Probably most present taxpayers would prefer the current system of taxation to the one I've proposed. Yet the one I propose would probably save everybody money.

Playboy: But tax reform can't save *everyone* money; the revenue has to come from somewhere. Surely the rich people who pay little or no taxes under the present system wouldn't benefit by the elimination of tax loopholes.

Friedman: You're wrong. You're not taking into account what it costs people to avoid taxes. This is one of the most important—and most overlooked—points in the whole field of taxation. Let me give you the simplest case: municipal bonds. As you know, the income from municipal bonds is tax-free. You're not even required to report it. For this reason, municipal bonds pay a much lower return; if corporate bonds are paying 8 percent, municipals might be paying 5. Suppose you buy some municipal bonds. You get the income from them, yet on the government books, no taxes on this income are recorded. But still, you *do* pay a tax. You pay three dollars in eight—the difference between what you could have got if you had bought corporate bonds at 8 percent and what you did get buying municipals at 5. That's a 37.5 percent tax. It's not recorded, but you're still paying it. What happens, in effect, is that as a buyer of municipal bonds, you pay a 37.5 percent tax to the federal government, which turns your money immediately over to the municipality.

A better example is the oil-depletion allowance. A man drills for oil. It costs him $100,000 to drill the hole, but he expects to find only $50,000 worth of oil. Still, he drills the hole because of the tax advantage of being able to deduct the drilling cost from other income. That makes it worth while to drill. But understand, he's not really drilling for oil, he's drilling for tax advantage. If it weren't for the tax laws, nobody would spend $100,000 to find $50,000 worth of oil. So there's $50,000 of pure waste in such an undertaking. Businessmen call it buying a tax shelter.

Playboy: Who actually bears this cost—the entrepreneur or taxpayers at large?

Friedman: A good question, and one not easily answered. Individuals enter such transactions, obviously, because they think others will bear most of the burden. If they thought they'd have to pay the cost themselves, they would probably never get involved. But when you have a whole nation of entrepreneurs, each seeking tax advantage, it's impossible to say just who pays the bill. In essence, we all do. All you can say is that when a man pays $100,000 to drill a hole that will produce $50,000 in oil, $50,000 has been wasted. Given a better tax system, this waste would not have occurred. And that alone justifies changing the tax system.

Playboy: The oil companies defend the depletion allowance on the ground that it encourages exploration for new oil reserves in the U.S.— reserves that might be crucial in a national emergency.

Friedman: They do, but have you ever seen them give an estimate of how much it costs to provide emergency reserves by this device rather than by others? Two different questions are involved here. First, do considerations of national defense require a large oil reserve for emergencies? Second, what is the best and cheapest way to provide such a reserve? The answer to the first question is far from clear, given the likelihood that any major war involving nuclear weapons would be extremely short. But even if the answer is yes, there are ways of providing a reserve that would be far cheaper than requiring consumers year after year to pay unnecessarily high prices for oil in order to finance exploration for additional wells, and then using the oil from these wells for current consumption, so you have to explore for still more wells.

But I'm getting away from the question you raised: whether the rich could benefit from getting rid of the loopholes. My main point is that all these wasted expenditures, tax shelters—whatever you might label these evasive maneuvers by the well-to-do few—are largely at their own expense. True, they reduce the taxes they pay, but only at a high cost. Philip Stern wrote an article in the *New York Times Magazine* a few months ago entitled "Uncle Sam's Welfare Program—For the Rich."

His argument went like this: people like H. L. Hunt, let's say, pay $2 million a year in taxes. But if the loopholes were closed, he'd pay $20 million. Therefore, Stern said, the current system is the equivalent of Congress' enacting an $18 million welfare grant for Mr. Hunt, paid for by the public. This is sheer demagogic nonsense, because it completely neglects what it costs Mr. Hunt to avoid the taxes. Maybe Mr. Hunt, to avoid paying $20 million in taxes, paid $16 million—by buying municipal bonds, digging uneconomical holes, paying high-priced tax lawyers to find new loopholes. There probably *is* an element of welfare for the rich, but it's much less than many people imagine.

Joseph Pechman of the Brookings Institution has estimated that the loopholes reduce tax collections by seventy-seven billion dollars a year. My guess—and it's just a guess—is that this seventy-seven-billion-dollar loss in taxes through the loopholes produces no more than twenty-five billion dollars for the people who use them. In fact, I'd be surprised if it produced that much. The rest, as I've tried to explain, is simply wasted.

Playboy: Under the graduated-tax system, the wealthy pay far more—in theory, at least—than those in any other income bracket. Under your proposed flat-rate system, they and everyone else would have to pay only 20 percent. But with all the loopholes at their disposal—even though you say they save less then they think by using them—don't the rich stand to lose more than anyone else under your system, with its no-loopholes stipulation?

Friedman: Not necessarily. If I were Howard Hughes, I'd rather pay 25 percent in taxes than buy a tax shelter that costs me 50 cents on the dollar. Wouldn't you? The only people this change would actually hurt are those who make their living by providing tax shelters for others. Statistically, these are a tiny minority. Moreover, money would be more economically invested than it is now, and these better investments would create more wealth, and thus generate more taxes, all up and down the line.

Playboy: Most people would have less quarrel with the flat-rate tax than with the elimination of all personal deductions other than provable business expenses. Doesn't a man who's hit, say, with tremendous medical expenses one year deserve a tax break?

Friedman: I have a good deal of sympathy for the deductibility of catastrophic medical expenses—more than I do for almost any other deduction. Medical expenses are a sort of occupational expense—the cost of earning an income. But for the sake of this proposal, I'd eliminate *all* deductions. For any income tax to really work, it's got to be simple and straightforward—something you can fill out on one side of one page without too much trouble. Admit one loophole and you admit them all.

As for how to cope with medical expenses if they're nondeductible, the solution is a simple one: buy insurance. When a man buys medical insurance, he's betting the price of the premium that he's going to get sick and the insurance company is betting the cost of his medical bills that he won't. If he wins, he gets his bills paid for; if he loses, he's out the premium. But it was his own decision—and responsibility—to buy the insurance. If he *doesn't* buy insurance, on the other hand, he's betting that he's not going to get sick. If he loses, my question is: why should the rest of us have to pick up his expenses by paying in taxes for the medical bills he deducts from his return? Let *him* pay the bills; that's what he risked when he bet.

Playboy: But you assume that this man is a gambler, that he makes a calculated decision not to buy insurance. Don't most people fail to buy insurance because of either ignorance or poverty?

Friedman: We're not talking about poverty-stricken people here, we're talking about taxpayers. As for ignorance, that's not a valid argument. My fundamental belief is that you've got to hold people individually responsible for their actions.

Playboy: Even as nontaxpayers, the poor can afford neither insurance nor medical expenses. Would you hold them individually responsible for such costs?

Friedman: Obviously, it bothers me, as it bothers anyone else, to see people destitute, whether through their own fault or not. That's why I'm strongly in favor of charitable activities, whether individual or joint. One of the worst features of the current system of Social Security and welfare arrangements is that it has drastically reduced the feeling of obligation that members of society traditionally felt toward others. Children today feel far less obligation toward their parents than they did fifty years ago. If the state is going to take care of the parents, why should the children worry? Similarly with the poor. Who feels a personal obligation to help the poor? That's the government's job now.

Playboy: To return to the point you raised earlier, you think a negative income tax will change this?

Friedman: I hope it will. But before we really get into that, let me stress one thing. If we were starting with a clean slate—if we had no government welfare programs, no Social Security, etc.—I'm not sure I would be in favor of a negative income tax. But, unfortunately, we don't have a *tabula rasa*. Instead, we have this extraordinary mess of welfare arrangements, and the problem is: how do you get out of them? You can't simply abolish them, because when we enacted these programs, we assumed an obligation to those who are now being helped by them. In fact, we have *induced* people to come under the protection of these programs.

Playboy: What do you mean?

Friedman: I mean that the law of supply and demand works very generally. If there is a demand for poor people, the supply of poor people will rise to meet the demand. In setting up programs such as Aid to Dependent Children and all the other welfare programs, we have created a demand for poor people. Don't misunderstand me. I'm not blaming poor people. You can hardly blame them for acting in their own interest. Take a poor family in the South, working hard for a very low income. They learn that in New York City they can get $300 a month—or whatever it is—without working. Who can blame such a family for moving to New York to get that income? The blame falls on those of us who set up the incentives in the first place. The blame also falls on us for creating a system that not only induces people to seek its benefits but forces them to stay in the program once they're enrolled and demeans them terribly in the process of helping them.

I remember how impressed I was, six or eight years ago, when a young man who was writing a book on welfare programs in Harlem came to see me. He said, "You know, I've been reading *Capitalism and Freedom*, where you talk about the extent to which government bureaucracy interferes with the freedom of individuals. You really don't know the extent of this. *Your* freedom hasn't been much interfered with; *my* freedom hasn't been much interfered with. When do *we* meet a government bureaucrat? Maybe when we get a parking ticket or talk about our income taxes. The people you should have been talking about," he said to me, "are those poor suckers on welfare. They're the people whose freedom is really being interfered with by government officials. They can't move from one place to another without the permission of their welfare worker. They can't buy dishes for their kitchen without getting a purchase order. Their whole lives are controlled by the welfare workers." And he was absolutely right. The freedom of welfare recipients is terribly restricted. Whether we're doing this for good purposes or bad, it's not a wise thing to do. Not if we believe that individuals should be responsible for their own actions.

Playboy: For those who don't know how it works, would you explain how welfare forces people to stay on the dole once they're enrolled?

Friedman: If someone on welfare finds a job and gets off welfare, and then the job disappears—as so many marginal jobs do—it's going to take him some time to go through all the red tape to get back onto the program. This discourages job seeking. In the second place, if he gets a job that pays him, say, $50 or $75 a week, he's going to lose most of that extra money, because his welfare check will be reduced accordingly —assuming he's honest and reports it. Since he gets to keep only a small fraction of his additional earnings, there's small incentive for him to earn.

Also, the present setup has encouraged fathers, even responsible fathers, to leave their families. Again, it's a matter of incentives. If a man is working and has an income above the minimum, he's not entitled to welfare. But if he deserts his family, *they* can receive welfare. That way, he can continue to earn his income and contribute it to his family, in addition to the welfare they get. Many ADC families are actually created by fake desertions. Of course, you have real desertions, too. If a deserted woman is going to be immediately eligible for welfare, the incentive for the family to stick together is not increased, to put it mildly. So the problem is: how do you get out of all this? And this brings us back to the question you asked a moment ago. I see the negative income tax as the only device yet suggested, by anybody, that would bring us out of the current welfare mess and still meet our responsibilities to the people whom the program has got in trouble.

Playboy: How would the negative tax work?

Friedman: It would be tied in with the positive income tax. The two are similar. Ideally, I'd like to see a flat-rate tax above and below an exemption. I've already discussed the flat-rate tax above an exemption. The tax on income below the exemption would be a negative one. Instead of paying money, the low-income person would receive it. Consider the current tax system. If you're the head of a family of four, with an income of roughly $4,000, your personal exemptions, plus automatic deductions, plus low-income allowance, will mean that you pay no tax. Suppose you're the same family of four with an income of $6,000; you'd end up with a taxable income of $2,000—that is, $6,000 minus $4,000—and you'd pay a fraction of that $2,000 in taxes. Now suppose you had the same family of four with an income of $2,000, you'd have a taxable income of minus $2,000—that is, $2,000 minus $4,000. But under present law, with a taxable income of minus $2,000, you pay no tax and that ends the business.

With a negative income tax, an income of $2,000 would be subject to negative taxation. Instead of paying taxes, you'd *get* some money. Just how much would depend on the negative tax rate. If the negative tax rate were 20 percent, you'd get $400. If the rate were 50 percent, you'd get $1,000. The 50 percent negative tax rate is simplest, so it's the one I always like to use for illustration. If you have no income at all, for example, you would have a negative taxable income of $4,000—that is, zero minus $4,000. You would be entitled to receive 50 percent of that: $2,000

Playboy: In other words, your system would amount to a guaranteed annual income of $2,000 for a family of four?

Friedman: Yes. But it's very important, in all systems like this, to keep in mind you're talking about two different numbers: the minimum income, which would be guaranteed to every family or taxpayer; and the break-even point, which is the point at which people would stop receiving money and start paying it. In the example I just gave, $2,000 is the base—the amount you'd receive from the government if you earned nothing at all. On the way between the base and the break-even point, which is $4,000 in this example, you would receive 50 cents less from the government for every extra dollar you earned, so you'd get to keep 50 cents. This provides a consistent incentive for additional earnings. Above $4,000, you'd be on your own. You'd receive nothing extra. In fact, you'd have to start *paying* taxes, partly to help those who are less fortunate than you.

Playboy: Do you think your negative tax program would be an adequate substitute for our present welfare programs—Aid to Dependent Children, food stamps and the rest?

Friedman: I believe it would be far superior to the present programs—superior from the point of view of the recipients and also of the taxpayers. But you asked whether it would be adequate. I really don't think you can discuss negative taxation in terms of adequacy or fairness. You have to ask a different question: how much are you and I willing to tax ourselves in order to benefit someone else? The great fallacy in these discussions is

the assumption that somehow somebody else is going to pay the bill.
Early in his campaign, Senator McGovern came out with a proposal to
give a grant of $1,000 to every person in the country. That was really a
form of negative income tax, but one on a very high level. Essentially,
what McGovern proposed was a $4,000 guarantee for a family of four,
with a $12,000 break-even point. The result would have been to sharply
reduce the incentive to work for people in a very wide income range. It
would have reduced the incentives for people making between $4,000
and $12,000 by enabling them to collect from the government rather
than pay taxes; and it would have reduced incentives for people making
more than $12,000 by requiring them to pay much higher taxes. And
much of the extra money collected from people making above $12,000
would have gone not to the desperately poor but to people with middle-
class incomes.

We have to ask not only how much the recipients get but also who
pays for it. Can you really justify taxing people receiving $13,000 a year
in order to raise the income of people receiving $11,000 a year? So while
I'm in favor of a negative income tax, I don't favor *any* negative income
tax. I want one that has both the guarantee and the break-even point low
enough so that the public will be willing to pay the bill, and one where
the marginal tax rate, between the guarantee and the break-even point,
will be 50 percent or so, low enough to give people a substantial and consistent incentive to earn their way out of the program.

Playboy: Do you think any of these proposals you've been discussing—
on taxes, welfare, and so on—has a chance of public acceptance?

Friedman: There have been some hopeful signs. Some things I've been
saying for a number of years now are receiving a little more attention.
Some of the proposals I've made concerning international financial arrangements, for instance. Also, the negative income tax has become a
fairly respectable notion. But you see, the problem is twofold. First, you
have to sell your ideas, to convince people that government programs generally do the opposite of what their well-meaning proponents intend—
that they aren't getting their money's worth for taxes. But even if people
are convinced by the arguments, there is the problem of getting them to
give up what they see as in their special interest. Everyone wants to make
sure that he is getting his. Nobody will let go until he's sure the other guy
is, too. And that's the biggest problem.

Playboy: Is there a solution?

Friedman: If there is, it would be in bundling things together. That's how we keep government out of the censorship business. It's not a matter of taking one case at a time and deciding each case on its merits. If we did that, we would have free speech for very few. Someone would be able to get a law passed prohibiting free speech for Seventh-day Adventists. Or vegetarians. Or Black Panthers.

We talked earlier about reducing the tax rates and closing the loopholes. The right wing would be more than willing to give up the loopholes in return for lower rates; and the left wing would probably be more than willing to give up the high rates in return for closing the loopholes. So it looks as if there's a deal to be made. But you can't make a deal through the usual legislative channels, because neither side trusts the other—and both are right. The only way I can see to make such a deal is by a constitutional amendment that says, for example, Congress can impose an income tax as long as the only deductions are for strict occupational expenses and a personal exemption, and as long as the highest tax rate is no more than twice the lowest. Personally, I would prefer a flat rate, but to achieve consensus, it would be better to limit the degree of graduation. That would give both sides some assurance that the deal wouldn't come unstuck.

Playboy: Even if a consensus of right and left could be achieved on a modified version of your flat-rate tax proposal, there are many critics— particularly among the young—of what they feel are your basic assumptions. How would you answer those who claim that capitalism cannot foster a just and orderly society, since it's based on the emotion of greed?

Friedman: What kind of society isn't structured on greed? As a friend of mine says, the one thing you can absolutely depend on every other person to do is to put his interests ahead of yours. Now, his interests may not be greedy in a narrow, selfish sense. Some people's self-interest is to save the world. Some people's self-interest is to do good for others. Florence Nightingale pursued her own self-interest through charitable activities. Rockefeller pursued his self-interest in setting up the Rockefeller Foundation. But for most people, most of the time, self-interest is greed.

So the problem of social organization is how to set up an arrangement under which greed will do the least harm. It seems to me that the great virtue of capitalism is that it's that kind of system. Because under capitalism, the power of any one individual over his fellow man is relatively small. You take the richest capitalist in the world; his power over you and me is trivial compared with the power that a Brezhnev or a Kosygin has in Russia. Or even compared in the United States with the power that an official of the Internal Revenue Service has over you. An official of the IRS can put you in jail. I doubt that there is a person in the United States who couldn't be convicted of technical violation of some aspect of the personal income tax.

One of the great dangers I see in the American situation is that there is a strong temptation in government to use the income tax for other purposes. It's been done. When gangsters couldn't be convicted under the laws they had really violated, they were gotten on income-tax evasion. When John F. Kennedy threatened steel executives in 1962 to get them to drive down their prices, there was the implicit threat that all their taxes would be looked at. Now, that is a much more serious threat—the power an official has in the pursuit of *his* self-interest—than anything Howard Hughes is capable of. We want the kind of world in which greedy people can do the least harm to their fellow men. That's the kind of world in which power is widely dispersed and each of us has as many alternatives as possible.

Playboy: Critics of capitalism feel that too many alternatives cause waste, that we don't need forty-seven models of Chevrolets when one would do.

Friedman: If consumers really preferred one model at a lower price than forty-seven models, G.M. would be foolish not to meet their desires. There are forty-seven models because that is what consumers want. That's what the critics really complain about—that under capitalism, consumers get what they want rather than what the critics think they should have. It's always amused me that the intellectuals who talk loudest about the waste of competition in business are the loudest defenders of the waste of competition in the intellectual world.

Isn't it absolutely wasteful that millions of writers should be deciding what to write on their own—a hundred writers may be writing on the same subject—with no social priorities being imposed on what subjects they write about? Isn't it deplorable that thousands of scientists should each be picking his own subjects for investigation? Shouldn't there be a central planning board that decides which subjects have the highest social priority and assigns those subjects to the researchers most suited to pursue them, to see that there is no duplication?

Suggest this to any of the intellectuals who whine about the waste of competition in the business world and almost all of them will be horrified. Most of them would recognize that it would be terrible. It would be terrible because the essence of the intellectual world is that it's a search for the unknown, an attempt to find new things by a process of trial and error in which you have a great deal of duplication. For every nine people who go off on a bum lead, one person's going to go on a right lead. The same thing is true in the business world.

Playboy: What about the criticism that capitalism leads to material extravagance and aesthetic starvation?

Friedman: The historical fact is precisely the reverse. The greatest opportunity for the expression of nonmaterial motives is in free-enterprise societies. The great triumphs of literature, art, architecture, and science have all been the products of individuals. Are the great examples of architecture the state buildings of Russia or some of the homes Frank Lloyd Wright designed for private people? Did Thomas Alva Edison produce his inventions for a central planning board under a Five-Year Plan or did he produce them under a system of individual incentives?

Only small minorities, whether in a communist society or in a capitalist society, are concerned with nonmaterial ends. Nonmaterial undertakings, therefore, will flourish most in the society where minorities have the greatest opportunities. A free-enterprise society is precisely the kind of society in which a minority can more or less do what it wants. It's free to pursue its own interests, but not in a collectivist society: if it's a perfect democracy, it will be dominated by the majority; if it's a dictatorship, it will be dominated by one minority, but other minorities will not be free to move.

Say I'm in a collectivist society and I want to save an endangered species; I want to save the heron. I have to persuade people in charge of the government to give me money to do it. I have only one place I can go; and with all the bureaucratic red tape that would envelop me, the heron would be dead long before I ever saw a dollar, if I ever did. In a free-enterprise capitalist society, all I have to do is find one crazy millionaire who's willing to put up some dough and, by God, I can save the heron. That's why the variety of minority views expressed in the Western world is enormously broader than in a Soviet society.

Playboy: Yet our minorities right now are criticizing capitalism for many injustices.

Friedman: Of course. Everybody always takes the good things in the world for granted and attributes all the evils of the world to the system. In addition, many of the difficulties they complain about are the result of government action, not of the market.

Playboy: Don't you think blacks have a legitimate complaint when they see that they can't be hired on an equal basis with whites in a job market that's controlled not by the government but by individuals who are freely making the choice to discriminate against them?

Friedman: Of course they have a complaint. But are they better or worse off than they would be in an alternative system? The fact is that blacks are far better off in the U.S. than they are under other systems. Let's get some facts straight. The average income of blacks here is far higher than the average income of *all* the people in the Soviet Union. The official government definition of the poverty line in the U.S. is higher than the average income in the Soviet Union; it's higher than the income received by 90 percent of the people on the world's surface. Now, that doesn't mean blacks aren't subject to injustice; of course they are. Of course there's discrimination. I'm opposed to it; I'd like to see it eliminated. But the point is that—even with discrimination—blacks are far better off under our present system than they would be under alternative kinds of systems, and changing the system isn't going to eliminate people's prejudices.

Let me give you a different example. The Jews—because they were a persecuted people who had the same attitudes toward capitalism in the nineteenth century as many blacks now have toward it in the U.S.— played a disproportionate role in the Communist Party and in achieving the Soviet Revolution. They were represented out of all proportion. Has that been good for the Jews? What country in the world today engages in the most extreme anti-Semitic persecution? The Soviet Union. It's not an accident, because if you have a society with concentrated power, if you have a collectivist society, it's going to be in a position to exercise the preferences and prejudices of its rulers. Moreover, it's going to have an *incentive* to do so, because it's going to need a scapegoat and it will choose some group like the Jews or the blacks to be the scapegoat.

I personally have been very sensitive to this issue because I'm Jewish and I'm very much aware of the history of anti-Semitism. One of the paradoxes I puzzle over is that few people in the world have benefited as much as the Jews from free-enterprise capitalism and competition, yet few other groups have done so much to undermine it intellectually. Let me ask you a question. In what institution in the U.S. are blacks most discriminated against?

Playboy: Schools?

Friedman: Is there any doubt that they're more discriminated against in schooling? Is there any doubt, if you're a parent in a black ghetto, that the thing you will find hardest to acquire is decent schooling for your child? Is it an accident that the schooling is provided by the government? A black in a ghetto who has the money can buy any car he wants. But even if he has the money, he can't get the schooling he wants, or at least he'll have to pay an enormously higher price for it than a white person will. A white person with that income can move into a nice suburb and get the schooling he wants. A black person will have great difficulty doing it.

Let's suppose, on the other hand, that you didn't have government schooling. Let's suppose you had the kind of system that I'm in favor of, which is a system under which the government, instead of providing schooling, would give every parent a voucher for a sum of money equal to what it's now spending per child and the parent could spend that at any school he wanted to. Then you'd have private-enterprise schools developed and blacks could buy much better schooling for their children than they can get under the government.

Under free enterprise, a person who has a prejudice has to pay for that prejudice. Suppose I'm going to go into business producing widgets and that I'm a terrible racist and will hire only whites. You're going into business producing widgets, too, but you don't give a damn about race, so you're going to hire the person who's most productive for the lowest wage. Which of us is going to be able to win out in the competitive race?

Playboy: That depends on the unions.

Friedman: You're departing from competition. One of the major sources of black discrimination has been the unions, but the unions are an anticompetitive element; they're a private monopoly; they're against the rules of free enterprise.

Playboy: You blame the government for discrimination against blacks in the school system because the government controls the schools. But isn't this discrimination really based on residential real-estate patterns that are the result of individual choice?

Friedman: Yes, to some extent it is. But those residential patterns don't necessarily imply segregation of schooling. They don't imply segregation of the kinds of automobiles people have. They don't imply segregation of the kind of movies people go to. If you had a free-enterprise school system, you'd have a much wider variety of schools available to blacks—schools of a higher quality. Moreover, residential segregation itself is partly stimulated by the fact that government provides schooling.

Let me illustrate. You're a well-to-do fellow and you want to send your child to a good school. You don't send him to a private school, because you're already paying taxes for schools and additional money you'd pay for tuition wouldn't be deductible. So, instead, you get together with some of your friends and establish a nice high-income suburb and set up a so-called public school that's really a private school. Now you won't have to pay twice and the extra amount you pay will be in the form of taxes—not tuition—which will be permitted as a deduction in computing your personal income tax. The effect of this will be that your children's education will be partly subsidized by the poor taxpayers in the ghetto. The fact that schooling is generally provided by the state, paid for through taxes that are deductible in computing the federal income tax, promotes a great deal of residential segregation.

The crucial point is this: in a *political* system, 51 percent of the people can control it. That's an overstatement, of course, since no government that's supported by only 51 percent of the people will do the same things that one supported by 90 percent of the people will do. But in a political system, everything tends to be a yes-or-no decision; if 51 percent vote yes, it's yes. A political system finds it very difficult to satisfy the needs of minority groups. It's very hard to set up a political arrangement under which, if 51 percent of the people vote one way and 49 percent vote the other way, the 51 percent will get what they want and the 49 percent will get what they want. Rather, the 49 percent will also get what the 51 percent want.

In a *market* system, if 51 percent of the people vote, say, to buy American cars and 49 percent of the people vote to buy foreign cars and the government lets their votes be effective and doesn't impose tariffs, 51 percent will get American cars and 49 percent will get foreign cars. In a market system, if 40 percent of the people vote that they want to send their children to integrated schools and 60 percent vote that they want to send them to segregated schools, 40 percent will be able to do what they want and 60 percent will be able to do what *they* want. It's precisely because the market is a system of proportional representation that it protects the interests of minorities. It's for this reason that minorities like the blacks, like the Jews, like the Amish, like SDS, ought to be the strongest supporters of free-enterprise capitalism.

Playboy: It's clear by now that you agree with Thomas Jefferson that the government that governs least governs best, that you don't think the federal government should interfere with any private, free-market arrangements whatsoever. But what about such efforts on the municipal level? Some communities, for example, are trying to keep out subdivisions, industry, nuclear power plants, and so on, in order to reduce the impact of commercialism. Do you feel they have this right?

Friedman: Of course. What you want is a world in which individuals have a wide variety of alternatives. You want pluralism, multiplicity of choice. When you get down to small units of government, you have it. If you don't like what one town does and can't change it, you move to another town. You have competition among towns for the provision of services. No reason you shouldn't. On the whole, the formal restrictions on governmental activity should be most severe at the federal level, less so at the state level and least of all at the local level.

Playboy: Then you aren't an anarchist?

Friedman: No. Although I wish the anarchists luck, since that's the way we ought to be moving now. But I believe we need government to enforce the rules of the game. By prosecuting antitrust violations, for instance. We need a government to maintain a system of courts that will uphold contracts and rule on compensation for damages. We need a government to ensure the safety of its citizens—to provide police protection. But government is failing at a lot of these things that it ought to be doing because it's involved in so many things it shouldn't be doing.

What we've really been talking about all along is freedom. Although a number of my proposals would have the immediate effect of improving our economic well-being, that's really a secondary goal to preserving individual freedom. When we began to move toward the welfare state back in the thirties, the justification was that the defects inherent in capitalism jeopardized our economic well-being and therefore reduced freedom. In the ways I've shown, these programs have failed. But it's not enough to object to them simply because they didn't improve—or, in fact made worse—the situations they were designed to correct. We need to resist them on principle. Someone will always come along and say the programs failed because they were underfunded; or because the wrong people were running them. Wage and price controls, for example, are unpopular with a number of people not because they reduce freedom but because they aren't working.

Galbraith said a few years ago that there wasn't anything wrong with New York City that couldn't be fixed by a doubling of the budget. Of course, that's happened and things are worse now than when he made the remark. So one of the things that encourages me just a little is the proven inefficiency of government, regardless of how big it gets. I think people are catching on to it. They sensed that McGovern wanted to ride still further the wave that was started with F.D.R., and they were fed up enough with that trend to vote overwhelmingly against him.

Playboy: So you're hopeful?

Friedman: Not completely. You have to consider the ideological climate. The spirit of the times has gone against freedom and continues to go against it. There are still intellectuals who believe that concentrated power is a force for good as long as it's in the hands of men of good will. I'm waiting for the day when they reject socialism, communism and all other varieties of collectivism; when they realize that a security blanket isn't worth the surrender of our individual freedom even if it *can* be provided by government. There are faint stirrings and hopeful signs. Even some of the intellectuals who were most strongly drawn to the New Deal in the thirties are rethinking their positions, dabbling just a little with free-market principles. They're moving slowly and taking each step as though they were exploring a virgin continent. But it's not dangerous. Some of us have lived here quite comfortably all along.

Chapter One
Nixon Economics

When President Nixon came into office, he faced three major economic problems: inflation, balance of payments deficits, and spiraling federal government expenditures. His announced policy for dealing with *inflation* had three elements: (1) fiscal restraint, (2) monetary restraint, and (3) reliance on private markets to set prices and wages. In fiscal and monetary policy, the administration stressed "gradualism," the importance of slowing down gradually to ease the transition without imposing abrupt shocks on the economy. The announced policy for dealing with the *balance of payments* was to reduce direct controls on foreign investment and lending and to rely on the ending of inflation to expand exports and reduce imports. The announced policy for dealing with *spiraling federal government spending* was to produce fiscal restraint primarily by holding down government spending rather than by raising taxes.

The actual execution of policy falls into two sharply demarcated parts: before August 15, 1971 and after August 15, 1971.

Before that watershed date, there was no change in stated policies, although the actual execution of policy departed from the stated ideal. Fiscal policy was adhered to rather well: federal government spending rose less than 7 percent a year from 1968 to 1971—a sharp reduction from the more than 13 percent a year rise from calendar year 1965 to calendar year 1968. The departure was more significant in market policy. The President engaged in some "jawboning," notably by establishing a productivity commission and by having the Council of Economic Advisers issue "inflation alerts." More important, in the construction industry, the President, after temporarily suspending the Davis-Bacon Act, accepted an arrangement establishing joint management-labor councils to police wage agreements. The departure was greatest of all in monetary policy, where the "independent" Federal Reserve System stepped too sharply on the brakes in 1969 and too sharply on the accelerator in the first seven months of 1971.

I strongly agreed with the stated policies of the President, though I was repeatedly disappointed with their execution, particularly in the monetary area. That disappointment is reflected in many of the columns in Chapter 2 dealing with monetary policy. On the other hand, the columns on budget and price policy that I wrote before August 1971 mostly supported the general direction of policy and defended it against what I considered to be unjust criticism. The last of this series, "Steady as You Go" (July 26, 1971), praised the President for sticking to his policy of gradualism despite the great pressure on him to "do something."

My praise proved premature, as I recorded in "'Steady as You Go' Revisited" (May 14, 1973) which is included in this chapter. On August 15, 1971, under pressure from an international monetary crisis, President Nixon changed course drastically. I heartily approved his actions in closing the gold window—indeed a column titled "A Dollar is a Dollar" on international monetary policy, dated May 15, 1967, recommended precisely the action that the President belatedly took. I equally heartily disapproved of his domestic action in freezing prices and wages, and then subsequently establishing a pay board and a price board. Though these measures were an understandable reaction to strong political pressures, they seemed to me then a major economic mistake and so they have proved. The columns dealing with this unsuccessful experiment are collected together in Chapter 5.

The departure from a free market policy on wages and prices was shortly followed by a departure from fiscal restraint—a development that I saw coming in two columns in Chapter 5, "Why the Freeze is a Mistake" (August 30, 1971), and "Will the Kettle Explode" (October 18, 1971). But in those columns, and others in this chapter, I expected Congress to be the prime actor in departing from fiscal restraint. Congress has more than done its part, but the President had given spending a further major boost: the budget he submitted in early 1972 recommended that federal spending in calendar 1972 as a whole rise more than 13 percent over spending in calendar 1971 and by an even larger percentage in the first half of 1972. The budget called for deficits exceeding any except those incurred during World War Two.

The actual outcome turned out to be very different from the budget forecast. Tax receipts were much higher in the first half of 1972 than anticipated—thanks to a multimillion dollar mistake by Internal Revenue that led to massive overwithholding of taxes. Federal expenditures did not increase as rapidly as anticipated. The result was that the federal deficit for the fiscal year ending June 30, 1972, was the astronomical sum of over $23 billion instead of the superastronomical sum of nearly $40 billion forecast in the budget.

The evaporation of restraint on federal spending during President Nixon's first term is clearly etched in the figures. In calendar 1969 spending was only 4.2 percent higher than in calendar 1968, but then spending went up 7.8 percent from 1969 to 1970, 8.4 percent from 1970 to 1971, and 10.7 percent from 1971 to 1972.

President Nixon's overwhelming re-election in 1972 apparently renewed his determination to revert to his initial policies. He proceeded in early 1973 to recommend a budget which, though extraordinarily large by any absolute standard, was advertised as "tight" and was so characterized by the political opposition as well. In addition, the President "impounded" funds that had been appropriated, which succeeded in at least slowing the growth of spending—to 8.2 percent from 1972 to 1973. I applauded President Nixon's budget message in my column, "The Nixon Budget" (April 2, 1973) found herein, but expressed doubts that his intentions would be translated into practice, discussed some structural reasons for these doubts, and called attention to Governor Reagan's proposal of an amendment to the California State Constitution to limit taxation—a proposal that unfortunately was defeated in the November elections.

In the area of price controls, the President after the elections had moved to return to a free market by introducing Phase III, which removed most price and wage controls—a development I applauded in "Perspective on Controls" (January 29, 1973), reprinted in Chapter 5.

Unfortunately a sudden outburst of price rises in foods (never under controls) plus the growing nightmare of Watergate weakened the President's resolve to return to his initial policies. Once again, he moved in the opposite direction. On the budgetary front, impoundment was eased and the President submitted a very large 1974—75 budget. Spending in calendar 1974 is now scheduled to rise by over 11 percent from calendar 1973, the largest year-to-year rise in the Nixon period, and there is little sign of any subsequent slowdown, though recently, there has been much talk from the White House about the need for holding down federal spending.

On the price control front, the President yielded to political pressure and imposed a new price freeze on June 11, 1973—a development I deplored in the fifth column reprinted here "What the President Should Have Done" (July 16, 1973), as well as in several columns in Chapter 5.

The one bright spot in the recent record has been in foreign financial policy, where the closing of the gold window on August 15, 1971, was followed by a series of developments ending in floating exchange rates and the complete elimination of exchange controls. Most of my columns on these developments are in Chapter 7, but the final column in this chapter, "A Dramatic Experiment" (April 1, 1974), records the contrast between the failure of domestic policy and the success of foreign policy— and also pays tribute to a remarkable man, George Pratt Shultz, successively secretary of labor, director of the Office of Management and Budget, and secretary of the treasury in the Nixon administration, a man of principle and an extraordinarily effective administrator and also not incidentally, an economist.

After the New Economics
[December 9, 1968]

The Nixon Administration will confront major economic problems in three areas: inflation, balance of payments, and the government budget. In each area, there is a stark contrast between John F. Kennedy's inheritance from the Eisenhower Administration and Richard M. Nixon's inheritance from the Kennedy-Johnson Administration. In each area, the New Economics has managed in eight years to turn a comfortable, easy situation into a near-crisis, to squander assets and multiply liabilities.

Inflation
Kennedy: Consumer prices rose at the average rate of 1.4 percent per year from 1952 to 1960. More important, the price rise had been slowing down. A burst of inflationary pressure in 1956 and 1957 was

surmounted and replaced by essential price stability. As a result, widespread fears of inflation were converted into expectations of price stability.

Nixon: The consumer-price index is currently rising at a rate of 5 percent per year. The creeping inflation that started in 1964 has turned into a trot. Expectations of substantial further inflation are nearly universal.

The New Economists argue that Eisenhower bought price stability at the cost of heavy unemployment. Yet unemployment during the Eisenhower years was only fractionally higher than during the Kennedy-Johnson years: 4.87 percent vs. 4.85 percent. The time pattern was different: unemployment was higher at the end of the Eisenhower years than at the beginning, when the Korean War boom was in full blast; unemployment was higher at the beginning of the Kennedy-Johnson years than at the end when the Vietnam war is in full blast.

Balance of payments

Kennedy: The balance of payments deteriorated somewhat in the final three years of the Eisenhower Administration. The gold stock declined roughly $5 billion and there was a minor run on gold in 1960. *But,* the gold stock was still a healthy $18 billion, sales of goods and services abroad exceeded purchases by $4 billion, this trade surplus was growing rapidly, and, most important, there were no controls on exchange transactions, no concealed devaluation, no financial gimmicks to make the figures look better.

Nixon: Eight successive years of substantial deficits in the balance of payments have reduced the gold stock from $18 billion to less than $11 billion. An "interest equalization tax" on purchases of foreign securities was levied in 1964 as a "temporary" measure—a concealed devaluation of the capital dollar that is still with us.[1] Direct controls were imposed on foreign lending by commercial banks and on foreign investment by businesses—first on a "voluntary," then on a compulsory basis. Ingenuity has run wild in creating financial gimmicks to hide the true situation—beginning with the so-called Roosa bonds (which some of us dubbed subrosa bills). And withal, the surplus on trade account has essentially disappeared for the first time in many years. The recent improvement in published figures simply reflects a shift of capital

[1] [Finally removed in 1974. See final column in this chapter.]

funds in reaction to the disturbances in France and the invasion of Czechoslovakia.

The New Economists leave Mr. Nixon scant reserves; even worse, they leave him a mess of controls and a set of cosmetic measures that must be eliminated before he can even guess the real size of the problem.

The government budget

Kennedy: In 1960, the federal government spent $94.7 billion and took in $98.3 billion—a cash surplus of $3.6 billion. Expenditures were 32 percent higher than in the final year of the Truman Administration, receipts 38 percent higher.

Nixon: In the first six months of 1968, the Johnson Administration spent almost as much as the Eisenhower Administration in all twelve months of 1960: $92.1 billion compared with $94.7 billion; but took in much less, $86.4 billion compared with $98.3 billion. Despite the 10 percent surtax and the reduction in expenditures legislated by Congress, the budget continues in deficit, and spending continues to grow.

And this is not all. Many programs have been started on a small scale but call for large increases in expenditures in later years. It will be a major achievement just to keep spending from growing at a rapid pace.

Many a New Economist may well have secretly sighed in relief when the election results were in. What a mess to have to straighten out! What a legacy to leave the opposition!

Last Readings on the Old Game Plan
[September 27, 1971]

By now, most sophisticated observers of the economic scene recognize that economic activity today reflects monetary and fiscal actions of many months ago, and that today's actions will have their major effects many months from now. Accordingly, the course of the economy over at least the next six months depends more on the old game plan for restoring prosperity without inflation than on the new one unveiled by the President on August 15.

However this fact will not keep the public at large from attributing whatever occurs during the coming months to the new game plan. And they will be encouraged to do so by the news media, with their almost hysterical emphasis on the immediate, their short-time perspective, and their craving for the dramatic.

Before this process goes very far—it began minutes after Mr. Nixon finished speaking—it may be worth recording what we now know about the state of the economy before Mr. Nixon spoke, as the last unambiguous evidence on the old game plan. This evidence belies the doom-and-gloom prophecies that did so much to force Mr. Nixon's hand.

Inflation

Was it true that "no" or "negligible" progress was being made against inflation?

In July 1971, the consumer price index rose at the rate of 2.4 percent per year—lower than in all but three months in the past three years, and two of those months were also in 1971. Of course, one month may be misleading, so here are the annual rates of price increase during the first seven months of the past five years:

1971   3.8 percent
1970   5.7 percent
1969   6.1 percent
1968   4.8 percent
1967   2.6 percent

One must go back to 1967 for a slower rate of price increase.

The more comprehensive index used to deflate the GNP tells the same story. For the second quarter of 1971, it records prices rising 4.1 percent per year, the lowest rate for any quarter in nearly three years.

Output

The GNP estimates for the second quarter of 1971 show output growing at 4 percent per year—still too slowly to absorb unused resources rapidly but a clear improvement over the 2 percent average rate for the final quarter of 1970 and the first quarter of 1971 (it is best to combine these two quarters to avoid the distorting effects of the GM strike). Except for the post-GM-strike quarter, this is the highest rate in almost three years.

Other indicators confirm the impression that the economy was accelerating from a recession to a vigorous expansion. In the first seven months of this year, industrial production rose at the annual rate of more than 2 percent, after declining at the rate of 5 percent during the prior fifteen months. Housing, always an early starter, has been booming. In the first seven months of this year, housing starts were almost 50 percent higher than in the same months of 1970.

Consumer spending
There has been much wailing and gnashing of the teeth about the supposedly reluctant consumer, who was allegedly insisting on stashing away his income instead of spending it—not a bad thing, incidentally, particularly for interest rates. Yet in the second quarter of 1971, total consumer expenditures rose at a rate of more than 10 percent per year. Retail sales have been even more bouyant. In the first eight months of this year, they rose at the rate of more than 14 percent per year. Apparently, there is no satisfying some people.

Unemployment
Unemployment is always slow to decline in a recovery and highly erratic from month to month. Yet even so, unemployment, which reached a peak of 6.2 percent in December 1970, and again in May 1971, was 5.8 percent in July and 6.1 in August (the unemployment survey was completed prior to the President's talk).

Putting it all together
The evidence is entirely consistent with my forecast in this space several months ago of "a vigorous expansion with or without further fiscal measures. . . . . [T]he real danger is an expansion so rapid that it will reignite inflation" (*Newsweek*, July 5).

   Mr. Nixon's abandonment of the old game plan was forced by the international monetary crisis and by the widespread though mistaken belief that the economy was in serious trouble. It was not called for by the state of the economy. The old game plan was working. It will continue to produce a vigorous expansion despite the dust being thrown into the wheels of the economy by the freeze.

The Nixon Budget
[April 2, 1973]

The President deserves credit for tackling head-on in his Budget Message some federal programs that have become sacred cows—such as agricultural subsidies, urban renewal and other so-called poverty programs. These programs have failed dismally—as even some of their original sponsors have admitted (see Charles Schultze, et al., "Setting National Priorities"). The intentions may have been excellent, but the effects have been waste, corruption, and indiscriminate subsidies, with the poor as usual getting the short end of the stick. I honor the President's courage and good sense in proposing to bury these mistakes instead of again papering them over with greenbacks.

The virulent criticism of Mr. Nixon's proposed cuts by some liberal commentators and cartoonists does them little credit. If these critics believe what they say—that the cuts are an attack on the poor—they demonstrate a level of ignorance that disqualifies them for their jobs. If they do not believe what they say, they demonstrate a lack of integrity that is even more shocking.

The much-publicized cuts in specific programs aside, the budget total of $269 billion proposed by the President for 1973—74 is very far from a "tight" or "austere" budget. Consider: $269 billion divided by 210 million residents of the U.S. = $1,280, for each man, woman and child, or more than $5,000 for that family of four so beloved by statisticians and policy-makers. A starvation budget?

—$269 billion divided by an estimated national income of about $1,050 billion in fiscal 1974 = 25.6 percent. And this in addition to more than 15 percent that will be spent by state and local governments. Are you getting your money's worth for the more than 40 cents out of every dollar of your income that you are paying for government services?

—Even these figures understate the real budget. The $269 billion does not include such items as the deficit of the so-called independent Postal Service or borrowings on account of other government corporations.

—True, you may say, but the budget is tight compared with the past. Not so. The $269 billion is $19 billion or 8 percent higher than expenditures in fiscal 1973—a rate of increase roughly equal to the expected rate of increase in national income.

—But are not the cartoonists right that the social services are being starved to fatten the military? Not at all. Only 35 percent of the $269 billion is for national defense plus veterans' benefits—a lower percentage than in the 1972 budget and a far cry from the 56 percent in the 1960 budget. By contrast, 42 percent is for education, health, social security and welfare—a higher percentage than in the 1972 budget and nearly twice the percentage in the 1960 budget (table).

WHERE THE DOLLARS GO

Fiscal Year	Defense and Veterans	Education, Health, Social Security and Welfare	Other
	Percent of Federal Spending		
1960	55.7	21.7	22.6
1965	46.7	25.1	28.2
1970	45.2	32.6	22.2
1972	38.4	39.5	22.1
1974*	34.6	42.3	23.1

*Proposed

And all this is for the budget *proposed* by the President, not the budget that will finally emerge from the legislative process. It will be a miracle if actual spending is not substantially higher—no matter how vigorous and effective a political campaign the President mounts.

Does the rising level of federal spending mean that Congress is simply reflecting the public's wishes, that the public at large believes that it is getting its money's worth for government spending and is willing to tax itself still more to finance still higher spending? I do not believe so. I believe rather that the inability of present political institutions to check government spending reflects a defect of those political institutions in effecting the public will. The key problem is that each spending program is considered separately. Each program affects a small special-interest group substantially, the public at large trivially. The voice of the special interest is a shout, the voice of the general public is a whisper. That is why every attempt to hold down total spending by controlling individual programs has failed—defeated by a coalition of special interests. The only hope of making the public interest prevail is to handle the budget as a whole rather than piecemeal.

President Nixon has been trying to move in that direction by proposing a legislative ceiling on total spending. But I fear that this approach is doomed to failure. To ask Congress to set an effective limit on its own powers is like asking the Pope to disseminate birth-control information.

Gov. Ronald Reagan has suggested a more promising approach for California: an amendment to the state constitution setting an upper limit on the amount of taxes that the state could collect, the limit being expressed as a percentage of the total personal income of residents of California. The percentage would start at its current level of 8.75 percent and decline gradually to 7.25 percent at the end of fifteen years. The proposed amendment provides for emergencies, both by the accumulation of an emergency fund and by permitting the limit to be breached by a two-thirds vote of the legislature, subject to confirmation by a popular referendum at the next statewide election.

Reasonable men may disagree with the details of the amendment, but surely the general principle is sound. By expressing the limit as a *percentage* of income, rather than as an absolute amount, allowance is made automatically for inflation, and real growth. By setting a limit, the legislature is made subject to the same kind of budget restraint that you and I are subject to. It is required to consider the best way to spend a given sum and cannot simply yield to the vocal special interests by upping the burden on the all-but-silent taxpayer.

Under California's constitution, the proposed amendment can be submitted to a public referendum through an initiative process without approval of the legislature. If the public approves, and the amendment succeeds in holding down state spending, California will have set a standard to which other states and perhaps even Washington—may repair. It will also have demonstrated once again the virtues of a truly federal system, with states that are more than administrative subdivisions of an all-encompassing national government.

"Steady as You Go" Revisited
[May 14, 1973]

In a masterpiece of bad timing, I chose the *Newsweek* issue of July 26, 1971, to pen a tribute to President Nixon's "vision and courage" in following an economic policy of (1) steady and moderate fiscal restraint, (2) steady and moderate monetary restraint and (3) the avoidance of price and wage controls—a policy that George Shultz had earlier termed "steady as you go."

Just three weeks later, on Aug. 15, 1971, the President imposed a wage-price freeze. In addition, he encouraged a highly expansionary fiscal policy, and the Federal Reserve moved in early 1972 to a highly expansionary monetary policy. Thus, within six months of my column, all three elements had been abandoned.

If inflation was so serious a problem then that it led the President to abandon "steady as you go," what is it now? In June and July 1971, consumer prices rose at the annual rate of 3 percent, wholesale prices, of 6.5 percent; in February and March 1973, consumer prices rose at the annual rate of 10 percent, wholesale prices, of 13.5 percent. One has to go back to the Korean War inflation to find comparable rates of price rise. This "experiment" in price control has ended as have all others—in an inflationary explosion.

What now? Why not a return to "steady as you go"? Can there be much doubt that the economy today would be vastly healthier, that inflation today would be a far less serious problem if the President had truly had the "vision and courage" in 1971 to stick to "steady as you go"? If he had met the international monetary crisis he faced in August 1971 simply by closing the gold window and letting the dollar float, without the window dressing provided by a drastic change in domestic economic policy?[1]

Those are "iffy" questions, but so are all really important questions of interpretation. The past can be a guide to the future only if we use it to judge what might have been, had different policies been followed.

In the fiscal area, "steady as you go" would have meant lower federal spending and lower deficits; in the monetary area, a lower rate of monetary growth. Both would have contributed to avoiding the "boom" now under way. This "boom," which is directly responsible for the sharp acceleration of inflation, cannot be sustained and will almost certainly be followed by a recession. In the price and wage area, "steady as you go" would have avoided the turmoil and disruption of

[1] To show this is not just hindsight, let me quote my column of Oct. 18, 1971. "The most serious potential danger of the new economic policy is that, under cover of price controls, inflationary pressure will accumulate, the controls will collapse, inflation will burst out anew, perhaps sometime in 1973, and the reaction to the inflation will produce a severe recession."

the freeze, phase one and phase two; and the accompanying distortions in lumber, hides, and other areas. It would have saved the millions of highly skilled man-hours wasted in issuing regulations, conforming with them and evading them.

Most important of all, "steady as you go" would have avoided miseducating the public about the cause and cure of inflation. The sophisticated economist may recognize that this episode is of a piece with all earlier episodes: an initial appearance of success as controls repress inflationary symptoms; growing difficulties as distortions accumulate; a final explosion when controls collapse or are terminated. But the man in the street interprets the price explosion as a consequence of easing the controls, not of the controls themselves. He is confirmed in his naive belief that higher prices of the things he sells is a just reward for his efforts while higher prices of the things he buys is the work of evil profiteers exploiting the hapless buyer. He learns that the way to stop inflation is for the government to fix prices and wages. This miseducation will return to haunt us.

The President's budget proposals represent a return to "steady as you go" policies in the fiscal area. The recent slow rate of monetary growth represents a return to "steady as you go" policies in the monetary area—albeit as yet a highly tentative and undependable return. To complete the trinity, we need, not ceiling prices on meat, not wider and more sweeping controls, but a wholesale abandonment of price and wage controls in all their nefarious forms. That cannot erase the damage already done, but at least it would end further erosion of our economic system. Unfortunately, Mr. Nixon seems to be moving in the opposite direction, sinking still deeper into the quicksand of controls.

What the President Should Have Done
[July 16, 1973]

As a severe critic of the new price freeze, I have repeatedly been asked, "What should the President have done instead?" Herewith is an abbreviated draft of the talk that I wish he had given instead of the one that he did give on June 13. (The quoted passages are from his actual talk.)

"In August 1971, I announced the New Economic Policy," in which, against my better judgment, I imposed a 90-day freeze on prices and wages to be followed by more flexible controls.

Ever since my Inauguration, I had been trying to avoid such controls. Again and again, I had warned the American people that controls threaten our freedom and our prosperity. But when inflation proved un-expectedly stubborn, a consensus developed among legislators in both parties, among businessmen, and among citizens at large, in favor of con-trols. Reluctantly, I yielded to this consensus.

Twenty-two months later, it is clear that controls have been an utter failure. Prices are now rising more than twice as fast as in early 1971. We can now see that controls only concealed inflation; they did not elim-inate inflation. As soon as phase two was eased, controlled prices bounded forward, joining the rapidly rising prices of uncontrolled foods.

What should we do now? One thing we are not going to do: "put the American economy in a strait jacket. We are not going to follow the ad-vice of those who have proposed actions that would lead eventually to a permanent system of price and wage controls. Such actions would bring good headlines tomorrow and bad headaches six months from now for every American family."

We must tackle the basic causes of inflation: ever-rising government spending financed by the creation of money. These are the flames that have caused the economic pot to boil. We must turn them down, not sim-ply put a heavier brick on top of the pot.

Accordingly, I am today asking Congress to enact an emergency across-the-board reduction of 5 percent in every item of government spending that is not mandated by contractual arrangements already en-tered into. I am today requesting the independent Federal Reserve System to hold the growth in the quantity of money to not more than 5 percent a year for the next two years. I am today abolishing all controls over prices, wages, interest rates, dividends, and rents that were imposed under phase three and its predecessors.

These measures will simultaneously turn down the heat and remove the brick from the pot. They will set free the unrivaled energies of our citizens cooperating through a free market.

Once inflation has gotten the start it has here, there is simply no way to stop it without some hardship, without at least a temporary slowdown in the economy while prices and wages are adapting to the new realities.

To make certain that the burden does not fall on those least able to bear it, I am today asking Secretaries Weinberger and Brennan to survey our unemployment-insurance and welfare programs to assure that no family suffers acute distress because of the necessary economic adjustment. The adjustment will be far less painful if we take these measures today than if we let the inflationary virus grow by what it feeds on, or to seek to suppress it by more rigid controls.

"Let there be no mistake: if our economy is to remain dynamic, we must never slip into the temptation of imagining that in the long run controls can substitute for a free economy or permit us to escape the need for discipline in fiscal and monetary policy. We must not let controls become a narcotic—and we must not become addicted. . . .

"Today, in America, we have a magnificent opportunity. We hold the future—our future—in our own hands. By standing together, by working together, by joining in bold yet sensible policies to meet our temporary problems without sacrificing our lasting strength, we can achieve what America has not had since President Eisenhower was in this office: full prosperity without war and without inflation. This is a great goal, and a goal that together we can reach."

This hypothetical talk reflects President Nixon's basic principles far better than the talk he did give. More tragically, it also responds far better to the nation's true need.

We shall come to this policy in the end, but only after much needless travail, only after the narcotic of controls has permanently weakened the foundations of this great nation.

A Dramatic Experiment
[April 1, 1974]

The daily news stories on gyrations in the price of gold invariably link the price of gold to the price of the dollar in terms of other currencies. This reflects a cultural lag. Gold today has no special relation to the dollar. It is simply a highly speculative commodity like soybeans. The use of gold for many centuries as money has established attitudes that will make a comparison of gold to soybeans appear far-fetched. However, as the cultural lag disappears, and after the price of gold takes a tumble or two, as it soon will from either its present price or an even higher interim price, the changed role of gold will become much more widely recognized.

The link between the dollar and gold was cut on Aug. 15, 1971, when President Nixon ended the commitment of the U.S. to convert dollars held by foreign governments into gold at a fixed price. He thereby paved the way for ending government control not only over the price of gold but also over a far more important set of prices, namely, exchange rates.

On that same fateful day of Aug. 15, 1971, President Nixon froze prices at home—moving sharply away from a free market at home at the same time that he moved toward a free market abroad. No scientist designing a test of free markets could have produced a more dramatic experiment.

The results have been crystal-clear. At home, the successive price freezes and controls have fostered rather than countered inflation, have produced widespread shortages and distortions and have created a vast governmental bureaucracy. By now, just about everyone recognizes that the whole effort has been a fiasco.

Price controls have been front-page news. In sharp contrast, it has hardly been noticed that the free market abroad has worked like a charm, confounding all those "realistic" bankers who predicted unstable markets and recurrent chaos, and behaving just the way that starry-eyed academic theorists had said it would.

There is a Sherlock Holmes story in which the clue is the dog that did not bark. The key evidence of the success of floating exchange rates is the crisis that did not happen. Had the pre-1971 Bretton Woods system of exchange rates still been in existence when the Arab-Israeli war broke out, followed by the oil embargo, a major financial crisis would have erupted—as had occurred repeatedly under the earlier system. This time, the massive flows of "hot money" would have been out of the mark, the franc, the yen and the pound and into the dollar. Central banks would have "lost" or "gained" billions in reserves overnight. Foreign-exchange markets would have been closed while central bankers hastened to some pleasant locale for a crisis meeting to "solve" the problem. None of this occurred. Instead, the price of the dollar in terms of other currencies rose some 5 to 10 percent, subsequently declined again, and the world continued about its business.

This success enabled President Nixon to end recently the foreign exchange controls that had been imposed by Presidents Kennedy and Johnson in a vain attempt to ameliorate balance-of-payment problems produced by the government price-fixing of exchange rates.

Outgoing Secretary of the Treasury George Shultz deserves much of the credit for so rare and so happy an event as the elimination of governmental controls. He favored the initial closing of the gold window, resisted repeated pressures from the Federal Reserve and from foreign central banks for the United States to intervene in exchange markets and pressed for the prompt end of the exchange controls. He has played the major role in establishing a workable international economic order.

The same principles that led George Shultz to press for freedom abroad made him a consistent critic of controls at home. As he said recently in an interview published in the *Chicago Tribune*, "I have never been an advocate of wage and price controls. I have always felt they would wind up causing us more grief than good. Wage and price controls, however, are in a sense like the Vietnam war; it is very easy to march in and it's very hard to march back out again."

We have paid a heavy price for a dramatic experiment. But have we learned from it? The spate of congressional proposals to roll back the price of oil, to require gasoline rationing and so on and on, suggest that we have not. How many such experiments do we need—or can we stand?

Chapter Two
Monetary Policy

My major professional interest for many years has been the role of money in the economy. This fact has led me to write more on money, including international monetary arrangements (Chapter 7), than on any other topic. But it has also made it more difficult for me to write on a level that is accessible to the general reader—or at least so I infer from the many letters I have received complaining that these columns are too technical. I have tried to mend my ways, but with imperfect success. Perhaps the repetition of some of the same ideas in slightly different form will make the set of columns more accessible than each one separately.

The reader who is not an expert in the field of money may find it helpful to start with the column, "The Case for a Monetary Rule" (February 7, 1972) since that states the basic viewpoint that underlies the discussion of specific episodes in the separate columns.

There is no other area in economics in which professional and lay opinions have changed so greatly in recent years. As of the end of World War Two, the revolution in economic thought produced by John Maynard Keynes's *General Theory of Employment, Interest, and Money* led most of the economic profession to dismiss the quantity theory of money—which had held undisputed sway until the 1930s—as an outmoded superstition having about as much relation to "correct" economics as astrology has to astronomy. The Keynesian revolution replaced the emphasis on money with emphasis on investment and government spending. Fiscal policy was the road to high and stable employment.

Experience and scholarly work have produced drastic changes in these views in the past quarter century. The enormous confidence placed in fiscal policy as a precision instrument for controlling the economy was shaken by the political and technical difficulties encountered in trying to use it for that purpose. The confidence was temporarily restored when the 1964 tax cut, sold as a device to stimulate the economy, was followed by economic expansion. But it was then shaken again when the expansion bred inflation and especially when the tax increase of 1968 failed to stem the inflation.

On the monetary front, "cheap money" policies—i.e., low interest rate policies—were adopted in country after country in response to Keynesian theories. In every country, they had to be given up when inflation rather than the widely heralded postwar depression proved to be the order of the day. The result was a revival of interest in monetary policy and the role of money.

In the scholarly world, the most important event was the reinterpretation of the Great Depression. The initial rejection of the quantity theory and acceptance of Keynesian ideas was strongly fostered by the belief that monetary policy had been tried as a means of stemming the Great Depression and had failed. When Anna Schwartz and I came to examine this episode (in our book *A Monetary History of the United States, 1867–1960*), we found that this conventional view was almost precisely the reverse of the truth, that the Great Depression was a tragic testament to the potency of bad monetary policy. From 1929 to 1933, the quantity of money in the United States *declined* by no less than one-third. More important, the Fed at all times had the power to prevent that decline. The policies required to do so were neither novel nor daring. They were of a kind explicitly contemplated by the founders of the system to meet precisely the kind of banking crisis that developed in late 1930 and persisted thereafter. Had the decline in the quantity of money been prevented, it is almost certain that the Depression, if it had occurred at all, would have been much milder and briefer.

These findings were buttressed by extensive statistical analyses of the relationship between the quantity of money and other variables, and by statistical comparisons between the performance of the quantity theory and the Keynesian theory in predicting movements in income. A professional controversy developed that filled the pages of the journals—and also changed many opinions.

The final clincher was a series of almost controlled experiments that happened to develop in the late 1960s and that are summarized in the column, "Which Crystal Ball?" (July 5, 1971). These pitted monetary effects against fiscal effects. In each case, monetary effects proved more potent than fiscal effects.

The result is that the area of dispute in the profession has shifted. To begin with, those of us who maintained that the quantity of money mattered at all were a beleaguered minority, viewed with almost amused tolerance by the more advanced members of the profession. Today, this issue has disappeared. Everyone agrees that the quantity of money affects the flow of spending, income, and prices. The issue is now whether the fiscal influences stressed in Keynesian analysis have a major effect independent of what is happening to the quantity of money or exert their influence primarily by affecting the quantity of money.

As this way of putting it makes clear, Chapter 3 on Fiscal Policy is in many ways a mirror image of this chapter on Monetary Policy. They complement and reinforce one another.

The change in the conduct of monetary policy has, I am sorry to say, been less drastic than in professional ideas about the role of money in the economy. Yet even here there has been great change. The views about policy that I express in these columns were regarded as "crackpot" by central bankers and commercial bankers a decade ago. Bankers knew that credit and interest rates mattered, not the quantity of money.

They are largely still of that view, but they have begun to pay far more attention to what happens to the quantity of money. The key actions in the United States were the decision by the Fed in January 1970 to give "monetary aggregates" (quantity of money) pride of place in preference to "credit market conditions" (interest rates); and in January and February 1972, to change the technique of monetary management by adopting bank reserves as an intermediate policy target. These actions are in the direction that I have consistently recommended in the columns reprinted here: of recognizing that the proper function of the Fed is to control the quantity of money and that it should not permit itself to be diverted by what happens to interest rates.

I had high hopes at the time that the better understanding reflected in these actions of the Fed would be converted into better performance. In "The Fed on the Spot" (October 16, 1972), I pointed out the crucial role of the Fed in avoiding inflation, and sketched the policy actions required.

Unfortunately, my hopes were disappointed as I pointed out in "The Inflationary Fed" (August 27, 1973) reprinted here, a deliberate reprise of a title used four years earlier.

As I write this, the Fed is now once again on the spot. Inflation is raging. Monetary growth has been high. And once again, the Fed, through its Chairman and other officials, has expressed the right intentions: to slow down monetary growth. The column in Chapter Four. "Perspective on Inflation" (June 24, 1974), underlines the urgency that, this time, its actions conform to its intentions.

The question that inevitably arises about this sorry record is "why"? If, as I argue in the second "The Inflationary Fed" column, misunderstanding is no longer the explanation, what is? Those who govern the Fed are able, distinguished men who are sincerely concerned about the public interest. They have no desire to be the architects of inflation. On the contrary, their every impulse is precisely the opposite. They have no personal axes to grind, no political careers to further. The easy answer is "political pressure." In the simple version of this answer so often expressed—namely, that under direct pressure from the White House, the Fed adopts policies designed to affect elections—I am persuaded that it is wholly wrong. The fourteen-year terms of the members of the board do give them a very large degree of independence from the White House. The board is fully aware of the charges that will be made against it. They are determined to lean over backwards in this respect. Moreover, the mistakes of policy have been the same, whether the board's membership was predominantly of the President's political party or of the opposition party.

But in a more subtle and sophisticated fashion, "political pressure" may well be the answer. In the first place, located in Washington, the board is immersed in and subject to the Washington political atmosphere, which, in particular, means its short-term perspective. The same forces which in the past few decades have produced a much stronger political reaction in Congress to threats of unemployment than to threats of inflation have affected the board. These effects have been reinforced by the important role of Congressman Patman as an alternate chairman of the Joint Economic Committee and as chairman of the House Banking and Currency Committee. A populist of longstanding, Congressman Patman is a firm believer in low interest rates under any and all circumstances, a long-time proponent of the view that the banks artificially raise interest rates, and are aided and abetted in that nefarious action by the Federal Reserve System. He, and other legislators of like mind, continually threaten to introduce measures that will give Congress greater control over the Fed. The Fed in effect, though not explicitly or consciously, refrains from exercising its independence for fear that it will be taken away. This subtle congressional pressure is far more important, in my view, than explicit presidential pressure.

In the second place, the fusion in the Federal Reserve of regulatory authority over banks (control of "credit") with control over the quantity of money means that its major contacts are with bankers. Every banker is against inflation. But he is also for "easy" credit. His general interest is invariably dominated by his particular interest. A reduction in the rate of monetary growth does tend initially to "tighten" credit in the sense of raising interest rates, even though, as I point out repeatedly in these columns, it subsequently has the opposite effect. But the initial effect sends bankers in droves to Washington asking relief from the board.

In short, there is no concentrated, organized interest group pressing for monetary restraint. There is always strong pressure for monetary expansion. A legislative rule for monetary growth or a gold reserve or similar requirement would provide an offset to such pressure. But there is no offset if, to quote a recent reiteration of ancient clichés by Alfred Hayes, president of the Federal Reserve Bank of New York, "The central banker must still use a very large portion of judgment in reaching policy conclusions. He must always take account of a wide variety of factors, including the business outlook, price and wage prospects, the international scene, Treasury financing problems, developments in measures of money and credit and in interest rates, etc. . . . There is no scientific way to determine exactly what percentage rate of growth in one or several money aggregates will best contribute to a given economic goal." The result has been that the Federal Reserve has repeatedly given in to the political pressure for inflation.

I do not offer this as a final and full answer to the mystery of the contrast between the Fed's announced intentions and its performance. Since I have been wrong before in my explanation of why that difference arose, I cannot have full confidence in my present explanation. I am persuaded that the issue is an extremely important one and that we need more understanding and investigation of it.

Inflationary Recession
[October 17, 1966]

Our record economic expansion will probably end sometime in the next year. If it does, prices will continue to rise while unemployment mounts.

There will be an inflationary recession.[1] Many will regard this prediction as a contradiction in terms, since it is widely believed that rising prices always go with expansion and falling prices with recession. Usually they do, but not always. In the great boom of the 1920s, for example, prices of goods and services held stable or fell; in the recession of 1957 and 1958, prices rose.

Since 1961, when the current expansion began, consumer prices have been rising, slowly at first, then more rapidly. Since January, they have been rising at a rate of more than 4 percent per year.

This price rise is a result mainly of rapid growth in the quantity of money—the number of dollars of coin, currency and deposits in commercial banks (demand and time) held by the public. This quantity grew 7.5 percent per year from 1961 to 1965; total output, 5 percent per year.

Though most money consists of deposits of commercial banks, these banks must hold reserves in currency or deposits at Federal Reserve banks. The Fed can therefore control the quantity of money by such measures as buying and selling government securities. The quantity of money rose as rapidly as it did because the Fed chose to let it do so.

At first, monetary growth stimulated production but had little effect on prices. There was much slack in the economy and many prices, particularly wages, had been set in advance in the anticipation that prices would be stable—an anticipation that was fostered by the low level of economic activity from 1958 to 1961.

As rapid monetary growth continued, the pressure of demand raised prices as well as production. Two factors accelerated the price rise. First, people came to expect rising prices and this expectation was embodied in higher wage and price contracts. Second, the Federal Reserve let the quantity of money grow still faster—at the rate of nearly 9 percent a year from 1965 to April 1966.

At this stage, rising prices stimulated economic activity because they were rising faster than people had anticipated. Hence, selling prices rose more rapidly than costs, which are typically set by advance contracts, so profits rose even faster.

The only way to make an expansion of this kind last is to continue to accelerate monetary growth. However, that would produce still more

[1] [There was a sharp slowdown in economic activity in the first half of 1967 that came to be designated a "mini-recession" because it was brief and mild. Prices did continue to rise during the mini-recession, though the rate of rise slowed appreciably. Since this column was published, the term "stagflation" has been coined to describe the phenomenon that I called "inflationary recession," and that has since recurred in the U.S. in 1967, 1970, and 1973–74.]

rapid inflation. To avoid this consequence, the Federal Reserve has already sharply reduced monetary growth—indeed, too sharply—to a rate of about 3 percent a year since April.

The tapering off of monetary growth, like the initial monetary expansion, will at first affect production more than prices. Prices and wages, now set in the light of anticipations of inflation, will continue to rise. Inflation has a momentum of its own; it cannot be turned off like a water tap. With lower monetary growth, total spending will not be sufficient to support these higher prices at full employment. This will check the rise in prices somewhat and produce some unemployment. Prices will rise less than anticipated, thus discouraging production and employment.

The inflationary recession will present a dilemma to the Federal Reserve, the Treasury, and the President. Rising prices will tempt them to step hard on the brake by slowing down monetary growth, raising taxes, and reducing government spending. Rising unemployment will tempt them to step hard on the accelerator by speeding up monetary growth, cutting taxes, and increasing spending.[2]

Both polices would be wrong. The right policy—not alone for this episode but as a general rule—is to *let the quantity of money increase at a rate that can be maintained indefinitely without inflation* (about 5 percent per year) and to keep taxes and spending at levels that will *balance the budget at high employment*.

If this is done, the public will gradually adjust to the new policy. People will stop expecting perpetual inflation. It is probably too late to avoid a mild recession, but this policy will at least prepare the basis for a subsequent noninflationary expansion.

Current Monetary Policy
[October 30, 1967]

Last January (*Newsweek*, Jan. 9), I criticized the Federal Reserve Board for producing the sharpest turnaround in monetary growth since the end of the war—the sharp deceleration in growth beginning in April 1966 that is recorded in the accompanying chart. "Slower monetary growth was badly needed in order to stem inflation," I wrote, "but a good thing was carried too far."

---

2 [In the event, the rising unemployment proved more potent. The Fed did step sharply on the accelerator.]

The same month, the Fed reversed its policy. A decline in M_1, the total usually designated "the money supply" by the Fed, was succeeded by an even more rapid rate of growth than in 1965. Slow growth in M_2, a broader total including time deposits at commercial banks, was succeeded by one of the fastest rates of growth on record. The turnaround in January was even sharper than in the prior April, setting a new postwar record.

In my earlier column I wrote, "It is almost surely too late to prevent a recession—that damage has already been done. It is not too late to prevent the recession from turning into a severe downturn. To that end, the Fed should at once act to increase the quantity of money at a rate of about 5 percent per year for M_2. If the Fed adopted and persisted in such a policy, it could moderate the coming recession without paving the way for a new burst of inflation."

There is much dispute about whether we have in fact experienced the recession that I saw looming, but the dispute is wholly semantic. Total output, which had been rising vigorously, showed no gain at all in the first quarter of 1967 and only a mild gain the second quarter; industrial production fell absolutely; and so did civilian employment (from January 1967 to May 1967). The percentage of the labor force reported as unemployed rose slightly, despite an almost unprecedented recorded exodus from the labor force. A slowdown in economic activity clearly occurred. But many economic analysts regard it as too mild and too brief to justify calling it a full-fledged recession.

The slowdown was mild and brief because the Fed did turn around. Unfortunately, the Fed once again carried a good thing too far. Instead of increasing M_2 at 5 percent per year, it increased it at two-and-a-half times that rate. The result was to moderate the recession (or slowdown, if you prefer), but also to pave the way for a new burst of inflation.

This monetary expansion, not the state of the federal budget, deplorable as that is on other grounds, has produced the widening signs of inflationary pressure. Just as it took some time—from April 1966 to December 1966—for monetary tightness to slow down the economy, so also it took some time—from January 1967 to June or July 1967—for monetary ease to stimulate the economy. That is why we are only now seeing the effects, and still only the early effects, of the Fed's overreaction in January.

The Fed is naturally reluctant to accept responsibility for inflation.

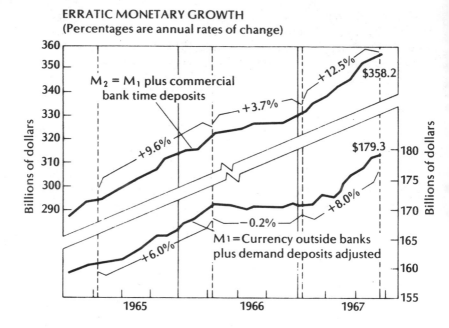

ERRATIC MONETARY GROWTH
(Percentages are annual rates of change)

SOURCE: *Federal Reserve Bulletin*

Consequently it blames federal spending and says that only higher taxes will stop inflation. But that is simply passing the buck.

If the Fed lets the quantity of money continue to increase at the pace of recent months—8 percent per year for M_1 and 12.5 percent for M_2—further acceleration of inflation is a near certainty, whether taxes are increased or not and whether federal spending is reduced or not.

What happens to taxes is important. It may affect the level of government spending. It may affect the rate of interest that accompanies whatever monetary policy is followed. But it is not decisive for the course of prices.

The Fed's behavior in this episode is part of a general pattern. Throughout the postwar period—and for much of its earlier life as well—the Fed has tended first to delay action and then, when it did act, to go too far. Too late and too much has been the general rule. The reasons for this pattern are complex—partly the economic analysis accepted by the Fed, partly its administrative convenience, partly the political environment in which it operates. But the results are simple. Instead of offsetting other forces making for economic instability, the Fed has itself been a major source of instability.

It is almost surely too late to prevent an appreciable price rise—that damage has already been done. It is not too late to prevent the price rise from turning into a severe inflation. To that end, the Fed should at once act to limit the increase in the quantity of money to a rate of about 5 percent per year for M_2. If the Fed adopted and persisted in such a policy, it could moderate the coming inflation without paving the way for a new recession.

Any resemblance between this prescription and the one in my January column is not purely coincidental.

Money and Inflation
[May 26, 1969]

Money tightens. Prices soar. So go the headlines. Since December, the rate of monetary growth has been reduced sharply. Yet, the cost of living rose from February to March at the incredible rate of 9.6 percent per year.

Does this mean that monetary policy is impotent to stem inflation? Or, that the Fed has not tightened enough? No.

The explanation is different. A monetary slowdown affects prices only after a considerable delay. Prices today are still being pushed up by the rapid monetary growth of 1968. Such a pattern is entirely consistent with experience. It was fully anticipated by those of us who have long urged monetary restraint to stem inflation.

As I wrote some months ago (*Newsweek*, Jan. 20), "The inflation produced by the Fed cannot be stopped overnight. Monetary growth today has little effect on today's income and prices. Its major effects are on income and prices three or six or more months from now. The rapid monetary expansion of the past six months assures continued inflation for some months to come.

"But the Fed can and should start at once to slow down monetary growth. That is the only way to slow down inflation six months from now."

Just about the time that column was written, the Fed changed its policy. But six months have not yet elapsed, so there is as yet no reason to expect any significant change in the pace of inflation.

It would be a major blunder for the Fed to step still harder on the monetary brakes. That would risk turning orderly restraint into a severe economic contraction. If anything, the Fed has already gone too far.

These conclusions are derived from the examination of the monetary experience in many countries for many decades—in the U.S., for more than a century.

Evidence for the past decade for the United States is summarized in the accompanying table, which gives the annual rate of growth for two monetary totals, for industrial production, which is a sensitive index of changes in economic activity, and for consumer prices.

The time periods for money are defined by dates when monetary growth changed its pace significantly, either speeding up or slowing down. The periods for income and prices begin six months later than the corresponding periods for money, to allow for the time that it takes for a changed rate of monetary growth to exert its influence. Of course, this time delay is itself variable: sometimes three months, sometimes nine months, sometimes longer. Six months is about the *average* delay.

To facilitate reading the table, the periods of slow monetary growth are in bold face. With one exception, they alternate with periods of rapid growth. The exception is the shift in April 1965 from an already high rate of growth to a still higher one. That shift ushered in the inflation that has been plaguing us ever since.

There clearly is a close relation between monetary growth and the behavior of output and prices. Every period of slower monetary growth is followed by slower growth in industrial production. Every period of more rapid monetary growth is followed by more rapid growth in production. For prices, there is one exception—the 1959 – 60 slowdown. However, even that exception simply reflects the fact that the speed-up in monetary growth that started in June 1960 took rather longer than usual to have an impact on price change: the rate of price change is less from November 1959 to May 1961 than either before or after.

Until 1965, the price rise was modest—at most 1.5 percent per year. And even these numbers may overstate the true rise in prices because they probably do not allow sufficiently for improvements in quality.

By 1965 we were rapidly approaching full utilization of our resources.

Rate of change (percent per year)

Period for Money	Money* M₁	Money* M₂	Industrial Production	Consumer Prices	Period for Production and Prices
Jan. '58 to May '59	4.3	6.2	7.4	1.0	July '58 to Nov. '59
May '59 to June '60	**—2.0**	**1.0**	**0.2**	**1.3**	**Nov. '59 to Dec. '60**
June '60 to Mar. '62	2.4	6.1	8.6	1.2	Dec. '60 to Sept. '62
Mar. '62 to Sept. '62	**—0.3**	**3.8**	**3.6**	**0.2**	**Sept. '62 to Mar. '63**
Sept. '62 to Apr. '65	3.8	7.1	7.1	1.5	Mar. '63 to Oct. '65
Apr. '65 to Apr. '66	6.0	8.9	9.6	3.7	Oct. '65 to Oct. '66
Apr. '66 to Jan. '67	**0.0**	**4.4**	**—2.6**	**2.4**	**Oct. '66 to July '67**
Jan. '67 to Dec. '68	6.8	9.4	5.3	4.6	July '67 to Mar. '69
Dec. '68 to Apr. '69	**4.3**	**4.0**			

*M₁ = Currency plus adjusted demand deposits. M₂ = M₁ plus time deposits in commercial banks other than large Certificates of Deposits. CD's are excluded partly to make the data more homogeneous over the whole period (CD's where negligible before 1961) and partly because their amount is so sensitive to Regulation Q ceilings on interest rates.

The further acceleration of monetary growth that occurred in that year therefore had its impact mainly on prices, which, six months later, started rising at a rate of nearly 4 percent per year.

The crunch of 1966 produced a tapering off of the price rise. However, the Fed, having overdone the crunch, also overdid the subsequent expansion. As a result, inflation resumed at a still more rapid pace.

The final line records the most recent change in monetary policy. There are no entries for production and prices because six months have not yet elapsed since the change in monetary growth.

Fortunately, the change in monetary growth has been more moderate than in 1966, so it is less likely to produce an overreaction later. Even so, the change is probably somewhat too severe to produce the kind of gradual unwinding of our inflationary binge that will do the least harm. A long-term rate of growth of about 5 percent per year in M₂ would be consistent with roughly stable prices—this is roughly the average rate of rise in M₂ from 1958 to 1965. It seems most unwise to hold monetary growth below that level for any extended period.

If the Fed continues its present policy of modest growth in the money stock, we should start seeing results in the near future. By summer or early fall, the rise in income should start slackening. The effect will first be on output. However, by fall at the latest, the pace of price rise should start coming down.

Patience, perseverance, and moderation—those are the requisites of sensible monetary policy at the present juncture.

Money—Tight or Easy?
[March 1, 1971]

The increasing importance assigned to monetary policy in recent years has brought to the fore the problem of how to assess what the stance of monetary policy is—let alone what it should be.

Recent experience highlights the problem:

—Short-term interest rates have declined sharply since August—the rate on three-month Treasury bills, for example, has fallen from 6.5 percent to less than 4 percent. By this measure, money has "eased" substantially in recent months.

—The money supply defined as currency plus demand deposits (M_1) has grown since August at a rate of 3.5 percent a year, less than half as fast as from February 1970 to August 1970 (table). By this measure, money has "tightened" substantially in recent months.

—The money supply defined to include also time deposits of commercial banks other than large negotiable certificates of deposit (M_2) has grown since August at a rate of more than 10 percent per year—a higher rate than from February 1970 to August 1970, and, indeed, a higher rate than preceded the acceleration of inflation. By this measure, money has been easy since February 1970 and has eased still further since August.

Which measure is the relevant one?

Interest Rates Versus Monetary Aggregates: Interest rates are the price of "credit" not of "money." Interest rates may be low because the Fed has been increasing the quantity of money and thereby indirectly the quantity of credit or because the demand for credit is low. For example, short-term interest rates fell in the U.S. from 1929 to 1933, yet the quantity of money *declined* by one-third. Similarly, interest rates may rise sharply as they did in 1967 and 1968, even though the quantity of money is rising rapidly.

Clearly, interest rates are an exceedingly unreliable measure of the stance of monetary policy.

M_1 *Versus* M_2: Wide divergence between the growth rates of M_1 and M_2 is a new phenomenon, reflecting the effect of Regulation Q, which specifies the maximum rates of interest that commercial banks may pay on deposits (zero on demand deposits, and specified higher rates on various categories of time deposits). True, legal maxima have been in force ever since the mid-1930s. However, most of the time the legal maxima were higher than market rates, and hence were largely irrelevant. The rapid rise in market interest rates in 1968 and 1969, and the reluctance of the Fed to raise the legal maxima, changed the situation drastically.

As market rates rose above the maxima, time deposits became less attractive than market instruments. Holders of such deposits tried to shift into Treasury bills, commercial paper, and the like. But this involved a loss of liquidity, so part of the shift out of time deposits took the form of an increased demand for demand deposits. As a result, during 1969, M_1 rose more rapidly than M_2. Money was tighter than indicated by M_1, less tight than indicated by M_2.

As interest rates declined in 1970, especially after August, the process was reversed. M_2 rose more rapidly than M_1. Money was "easier" than indicated by M_1 but "tighter" than indicated by M_2.

So long as Regulation Q operates in this intermittent fashion, it will distort the behavior of these aggregates. There is every reason on other grounds to get rid of Regulation Q. It involves compulsory government price fixing of precisely the kind that President Nixon and Federal Reserve Board chairman Arthur Burns have repeatedly objected to in other connections. Abolition of Regulation Q would make *either* M_1 or M_2 a satisfactory measure of the ease or tightness of money and *both* would tell the same story.

Until this occurs, the observer of monetary policy must monitor both M_1 and M_2 and allow as best he can for the distorting effect of Regulation Q. On this basis, money cannot be said to have become either appreciably tighter or appreciably easier since August. Monetary policy has been highly expansive ever since February 1970—not as expansive as it

Monetary Growth Rates

Period	Rate of Change (Percent per year)	
	M1	M2
January 1967 to January 1969	7.6	9.8
January 1969 to July 1969	5.1	3.9
July 1969 to February 1970	1.2	0.1
February 1970 to August 1970	7.3	9.8
August 1970 to January 1971	3.5	10.4

M1 = Currency plus adjusted demand deposits

M2 = M1 plus time deposits in commercial banks other than large negotiable certificates of deposit

Source: Federal Reserve Bank of St. Louis

was in 1967 and 1968 yet more expansive than can long be maintained without reigniting inflation.

In late 1969, and again in late 1970, the Fed revised its prior estimates of the monetary aggregates, raising them substantially both times. For example, the unrevised figure for M_1 in October 1970 was $206 billion, the revised figure $213—a difference of 3.4 percent. The unrevised figures showed M_1 growing at the annual rate of 5.1 percent from February 1970 to October 1970; the revised figures, at the rate of 6.3 percent! Money was in fact appreciably easier than the Fed intended it to be.

Statistical errors of this magnitude are, to put it bluntly, inexcusable. Imagine what would happen in a well-run private enterprise if the chief accountant reported that for many months he had been underestimating total costs substantially. Heads would roll. So should they at the Fed.

The explanation of the major errors of the past two years is highly technical and cannot be spelled out here. I can only report my judgment that the errors would not have been anything like so large, and might not have occurred at all, if, years ago, the Fed had devoted to improving its measures of the money supply anything like the attention and research effort it has lavished on its index of industrial production, let alone on its surveys of liquid assets.

The Fed neglected monetary statistics for years because it took interest rates rather than monetary aggregates as its criterion of policy. It has corrected the mistake in policy. But it has not corrected the mistake in statistics. As a result, its present estimates of monetary aggregates are still defective.

By removing Regulation Q and improving its monetary statistics, the Fed could assure itself far more reliable measures of its actual policy than it now has. By modernizing its operating procedures in New York, it could make its actual policy conform more closely to its intended policy—but that is grist for another column.

Which Crystal Ball?
[July 5, 1971]

Another test is developing between two competing economic theories—the Keynesian theory that stresses the effect of taxes and government spending on the course of the economy, and the modern quantity theory that stresses the effect of changes in the quantity of money.

Keynesian economists, most notably the New Economists of the Kennedy-Johnson Administration, are forecasting that the current recovery will remain weak unless taxes are reduced promptly and government spending increased sharply. Further, they forecast that such a stimulus would affect mainly output rather than prices.

The monetarists—a smaller though growing group—are forecasting a vigorous expansion with or without further fiscal measures. We believe that the real danger is an expansion so rapid that it will reignite inflation.[1]

The federal budget is now running a deficit of more than $20 billion a year. However, this deficit reflects mainly the recession. The so-called full-employment budget—what expenditures and receipts would be if the economy were operating at full capacity—is in rough balance. The New Economists believe that a large full-employment deficit, which means an even larger actual deficit, is needed for a vigorous expansion.

The quantity of money grew from February 1970 to January 1971 at the annual rate of 5.5 percent for M_1 (currency plus demand deposits), 10.1 percent for M_2 (currency plus all commercial bank deposits other

[1][The new economic policy introduced by Mr. Nixon on August 15, 1971, changed the ground rules drastically. That development temporarily slowed the expansion and was accompanied by a sharp slowdown in monetary growth. Then in 1972, a vigorous expansion did get underway and in 1973 inflation sharply accelerated.]

than large CD's). Since January, there has been a veritable monetary explostion—to 13.6 percent for M_1, 18.3 percent for M_2. Monetary acceleration in February 1970 was followed by an end to the recession nine months later—about the usual delay. The recent monetary explosion will start showing up later this year. That is why monetarists forecast a vigorous recovery.

This is the fourth such test in the past five years:

—In 1966, the Fed sharply slowed monetary growth, while fiscal policy was expansive. The New Economists forecast continued expansion in 1967; the monetarists, a slowdown or recession. A "mini-recession" did occur in the first half of 1967.

—In mid-1968, a temporary 10 percent surtax was enacted to stem inflation. The Fed, fearful of overkill, proceeded to expand money rapidly. The New Economists forecast a slowdown in the first half of 1969 and a recovery in the second half. The monetarists correctly forecast continued boom into 1969. Then, when monetary expansion finally slowed in early 1969, they forecast the end of the boom by late 1969. Inflation reached its peak at the end of 1969 or early 1970.

—In late 1969, the New Economists forecast continued expansion. Ebullient Pierre Rinfret—a New Economist in approach though a sometime Nixon adviser—proclaimed confidently, "There ain't gonna be no recession." The monetarists, impressed by mild retardation in monetary growth in the first half of 1969 and severe retardation in the second half of 1969, correctly forecast a recession in 1970.

Score so far: New Economists, 0; monetarists, 3.[2] The next six to nine months will provide another tally.

I hasten to add that this evidence alone justifies little confidence in the monetarist views. Three swallows do not make a spring. Moreover, proponents of neither view claim anything like infallible ability to predict. All recognize that forces other than fiscal and monetary policy have an important influence on the course of events.

However, this is far from all the evidence. Scholarly work on the relation between changes in the quantity of money and in economic activity covers more than a century of U.S. experience, as well as experience in many other countries. My own confidence in the importance of the quan-

2 [For my own forecasts, see my *Newsweek* columns, "Inflationary Recession," Oct. 17, 1966; "Taxes: The Hard Sell," May 13, 1968; "The Inflationary Fed," Jan. 20, 1969; "Economic Perspective," Dec. 22, 1969.]

tity of money rests primarily on this evidence, not on the recent episodes. However, these episodes are newsworthy and dramatic. As a result, they have probably done more to promote acceptance of the monetarist view by the public at large than more basic scholarly work.

The fiscal and monetary authorities have made an important scientific contribution by their erratic policies. They have provided four successive experiments for our edification. But scientific knowledge has been bought at heavy cost—a mini-recession, an inflationary spiral, a real recession and now, the danger of renewed inflation. As a scientific observer, I am grateful. As a citizen, I am indignant. Why must the Federal Reserve swing so erratically from side to side? We urgently need a steady course.

Irresponsible Monetary Policy
[January 10, 1972]

Monetary growth was more erratic in 1971 than in any year for the past two decades and more. From January to July, M_1 (currency plus demand deposits) rose at a rate of nearly 12 percent per year, M_2 (currency plus demand deposits plus commercial-bank time deposits other than CD's) at a rate of nearly 15 percent per year. These are truly explosive rates. Then the Federal Reserve Board slammed on the brakes. From July through the latest four weeks for which data are available as I write this (four weeks ending December 15, 1971), M_1 was essentially unchanged, and M_2 rose at the annual rate of 5 percent.

True, the *average* rate for the year as a whole, though on the high side, is not too bad, but that is like assuring the nonswimmer that he can safely walk across a river because its *average* depth is only four feet.

Why should we be concerned about these gyrations in monetary growth? Because they exert an important influence on the future course of the economy. Erratic monetary growth almost always produces erratic economic growth. The monetary explosion is only now beginning to show up in the pace of economic recovery—several months behind schedule because of the chilling effect of the new economic policy on business activity. The monetary freeze has not yet had a significant impact (except perhaps in the stock market) but, unless we are extremely lucky, it will produce a decidedly slower pace of economic recovery in the first half of 1972 than is now envisioned by the much publicized and highly optimistic "consensus" forecast.

The chart illustrates the kind of evidence that underlies these statements. For each month of the past five years, the solid line shows the rate of growth over the preceding six months of personal income (that is, the total received income of all the persons in the U.S.). A six-month period is used to average out the highly erratic month-to-month changes. The dashed line shows the corresponding rate of growth of M_2 nine months earlier, adjusted in scale to correspond to personal income—which is why it is designated "predicted." (The adjustment is based on a correlation computed for the period 1954 to 1970.)

Clearly, the actual rate of change of personal income mirrors with remarkable fidelity the rate of change of M_2 nine months earlier.

There are only four significant discrepancies, which I have numbered on the chart. Each has a readily identified special explanation.

1. The upward spike in early 1970 reflects a retroactive federal pay increase that was statistically reported in two months.

2. The downward spike in late 1970 is the result of the General Motors strike.

3. The upward spike and subsequent downward spike in mid-1971 are the result of stockpiling for the steel strike that never occurred and the subsequent running down of stockpiles.

4. The downward movement in September, October, and November 1971 is the result of the new economic policy. By spreading uncertainty and confusion domestically and internationally, the new policy nipped a healthy recovery in the bud, at least temporarily. The outcome has been the opposite of the intention.

The November figure is the latest available for personal income. But we can follow the path presaged by earlier monetary growth for a further nine months. It rises sharply to a peak in early February—reflecting the monetary explosion—then declines sharply to August—reflecting the monetary freeze.

The tough question is how the discrepancy introduced by the new economic policy will work itself out. Will personal income return to the predicted path before the monetary freeze starts taking effect? Will dissipation of uncertainty by the actual operation of phase two and by the international monetary agreement counter some of the effects of the mon-

MONEY IN THE POCKET

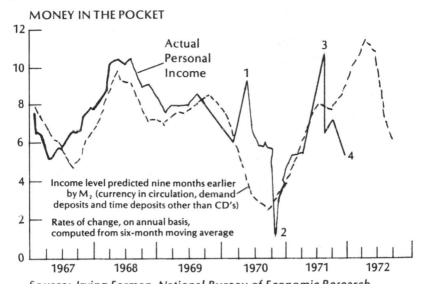

Source: *Irving Forman, National Bureau of Economic Research*

etary freeze just as the creation of the uncertainty countered some of the effects of the monetary explosion? We shall be very fortunate indeed if this occurs.[1] But the Fed will be pushing our luck beyond reason if it continues the monetary freeze. That can be counted on to kill and not merely slow down the economic revival under way.

Responsible policy calls for staying in the middle of the road, not lurching from side to side. And the Fed can produce a steady rate of monetary growth if it only overcomes the infatuation with interest rates that has sapped its will.

[1] [As the updated chart which follows shows, the answer was intermediate between the two outcomes offered as possibilities but closer to the first.]

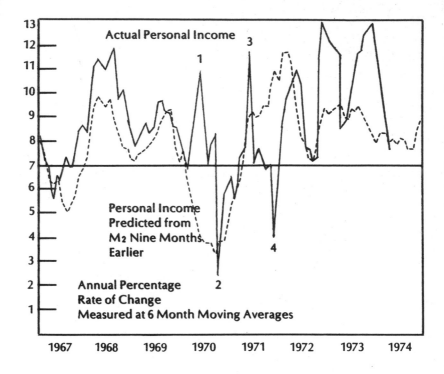

Updating of Chart
The chart in the prior column proved such a useful, simple measure of
the influence of monetary change alone—and discrepancies between the
actual and predicted rate of change of personal income such a useful

measure of the net effect of non-monetary forces—that I have kept it up to date. The updated version that follows uses the same formula as the published chart for predicting personal income change from earlier monetary growth. It includes data for about two and a half additional years. In addition, there are slight differences for the overlapping period because I have taken the opportunity to use the most recently revised data.

The predicted curve clearly continues to trace the main sweep of the actual curve, but there have been two major upward bulges, one after the 1972 presidential election, the other, at the time of the late 1973 oil crisis. Taken together, these bulges just about offset the downward bulge in late 1971 and early 1972, so that the relation between money and income is about back in line with the longer-term relation.

The Case for a Monetary Rule
[February 7, 1972]

I and most other monetarists have long favored a policy of a steady and moderate rate of growth of the quantity of money. We have strongly opposed the Fed's trying to fine-tune the economy.

Recent policy conformed to our prescription only in 1970.

Critics ask why we are so modest. Why not use the powerful instrument of monetary policy to offset other forces pushing the economy toward inflation or recession? Why tie the hands of the Fed? Why not trust their discretion in adapting to changing circumstances?

We favor the rule of steady monetary growth for several reasons.

1. *The Past Performance of the Fed:* Throughout its history, the Fed has proclaimed that it was using its powers to promote economic stability. But the record does not support the claim. On the contrary, the Fed has been a major source of instability.

The Fed was responsible for converting what would have been a serious recession after 1929 into a major catastrophe by permitting the quantity of money to decline by one-third from 1929 to 1933, even though it had ample power to prevent the decline.

In recent years, the Fed set off the accelerating inflation that Mr. Nixon inherited by expanding the money supply too rapidly in 1967 and 1968, then stepped too hard on the brake in 1969, and too hard on the accelerator in the first seven months of 1971. Federal Reserve officials have often admitted their errors after the fact—as Chairman Arthur Burns did in July 1971, in testimony before the Joint Economic Committee—and have promised better performance in the future. But then the same forces have produced a repetition of the same errors.

We conclude that the urgent need is to prevent the Fed from being a source of economic disturbance.

2. *The Limitations of our Knowledge:* Economic research has established two propositions: (1) there is a close, regular, and predictable relation between the quantity of money, national income, and prices over any considerable period of years; (2) the same relation is much looser from month to month, quarter to quarter, or even year to year. In particular, monetary changes take time to affect the economy, and the time delay is itself highly variable.

The first proposition means that a steady price level over the long pull requires that the quantity of money grow at a fairly steady rate roughly equal to the average rate of growth of output.

The second proposition means that any attempt to use monetary policy for fine-tuning is likely simply to introduce additional instability. And this is indeed what has happened.

3. *The Promotion of Confidence:* An announced, and adhered to, policy of steady monetary growth would provide the business community with a firm basis for confidence in monetary stability that no discretionary policy could provide even if it happened to produce roughly steady monetary growth.

4. *Neutralization of the Fed:* An independent Fed may at times be too insulated from political pressures—as it was in the early thirties—and yet at other times unduly affected by political pressures. If we really knew enough to use monetary policy for fine-tuning, we would probably experience a four-year cycle, with unemployment reaching its trough in years divisible by four and inflation reaching its peak in the succeeding year.

A monetary rule would insulate monetary policy both from the arbitrary power of a small group of men not subject to control by the electorate and from the short-run pressures of partisan politics.

Is the rule that we have proposed technically feasible? Can the Fed control the quantity of money? No serious student of money—whatever his policy views—denies that the Fed can, if it wishes, control the quantity of money. It cannot, of course, achieve a precise rate of growth from day to day or week to week. But it can come very close from month to month and quarter to quarter.

As I wrote five years ago, if the monetary rule were followed, "other forces would still affect the economy, require change and adjustment, and distort the even tenor of our ways. But steady monetary growth would provide a monetary climate favorable to the effective operation of those basic forces of enterprise, ingenuity, invention, hard work and thrift that are the true springs of economic growth. That is the most that we can ask from monetary policy at our present stage of knowledge. But that much—and it is a great deal—is clearly within our reach."

The Fed on the Spot
[October 16, 1972]

Most experts on the economy agree that (1) inflation has tapered off substantially in the past two years; (2) economic expansion is likely to continue through 1973 and may well accelerate in coming months; (3) further expansion threatens a new burst of inflationary demand; (4) increasing federal deficits add to that danger; (5) existing price and wage controls cannot contain a rapid rise in demand.

It follows that if acceleration of inflation is to be prevented, the Federal Reserve System will have to do the job.

This conclusion is valid for economists who stress fiscal policy and economists who stress monetary policy; for economists who favor price and wage controls and economists who oppose them. Whatever the influence of fiscal policy, it will operate in the coming year to stimulate rather than to check inflation. Whatever the influence of price and wage controls, that influence has already been exerted. Hence there remains only monetary policy to check inflation.

How has monetary policy been performing? What are the prospects that it will surmount the challenge?

The Fed deserves great credit for two major changes:

1. Substitution in January 1970 of monetary growth for interest rates as the primary *target* of policy.

2. Substitution in early 1972 of reserve growth for "credit conditions" as the primary *instrument* of policy.

In my opinion, these are the most important changes in Federal Reserve procedures in the past four decades. The first change means that, at long last, the Fed is aiming for the right target; the second, that it has taken the first step toward adapting its operating procedures to its new target.

Under the new procedures, the Fed has been aiming at something like a 6 percent per year rate of growth in the quantity of money, defined as currency plus demand deposits (M_1). The actual rate was more than 10 percent for the first seven months of 1971, less than 1 percent for the rest of 1971, more than 8 percent so far this year.

Such wide fluctuations in monetary growth are undesirable. They contribute to economic instability, serve no useful function, and should be eliminated. In addition, they make it difficult to judge the performance of the Fed. Critics point to growth rates since December 1971 of more than 8 percent in M_1, and 11 percent in M_2 (M_1 plus commercial-bank time deposits other than large CD's) as evidence that the Fed has been feeding the fires of inflation. Chairman Arthur Burns counters by pointing to growth rates from August 1971 to August 1972 of 5.5 percent in M_1 and 9.6 percent in M_2.

Both comparisons are biased—the first, by starting from an unduly low point, the second, from an unduly high point. For the whole period since January 1970—when the new target was adopted and Burns became chairman—M_1 has grown at just over 6 percent per year and M_2 at just over 10 percent and there has been no trend toward higher or lower rates.

These long-period growth rates are high by historical standards and are higher than I myself favored but, *for this period,* they have not been dangerously high.

The verdict on performance is thus: excellent with respect to average monetary growth; poor with respect to stability of monetary growth.

So far this year, the Fed has operated in a favorable environment. Despite economic expansion, long-term interest rates have been steady or declining and short-term interest rates have risen only recently and moderately. As economic expansion continues, short- and long-term interest rates are likely to rise appreciably. This will put the Fed to a real test. Will it revert to its bad old habits of trying to hold down interest rates or will it stick to its new determination to control monetary aggregates and leave interest rates to the market?

A second danger is more subtle and for that reason more disturbing.

Although the average rates of monetary growth since January 1970 have been consistent with a tapering off of inflation, they are too high to be consistent with a continuation of the present 2 to 3 percent rate of inflation.

Before explaining the basis for this judgment, perhaps I can make it plausible by an analogy. To accelerate your car from thirty to fifty miles an hour takes more gas than to keep it going at fifty miles an hour; when you get to that speed you can let up on the gas pedal a bit. Similarly, it takes a larger inflow of money to go from a low level of employment at 6 percent inflation to a high level at 3 percent inflation than to keep an economy going at a high level of employment and steady 3 percent inflation.

Three factors explain why continuation of present rates of monetary growth would mean a higher rate of inflation: (1) Absorption of unused resources after the end of the 1970 recession required and permitted output to grow more rapidly than it can over the long pull. The matching monetary growth produced no inflationary pressure. As we approach fuller employment of resources, output will grow more slowly. (2) The tapering off of inflation made it less expensive to hold money. It now costs you only 2 or 3 cents in purchasing power instead of 6 or 7 cents to hold a dollar bill for a year. As a result, people wanted to hold more cash relative to their income, offsetting some of the monetary growth. Once inflation stops declining, this offset will disappear. (3) The wage and price freeze and subsequent controls introduced additional uncertainty into the economy, which also raised the demand for cash balances. I estimate that this effect offset roughly 2 percentage points of the monetary growth over the past year. Elimination of controls might reverse this process. More important, a final end to our Vietnam involvement will undoubtedly reduce uncertainty and thereby reduce the demand for cash balances.

One striking lesson from past inflations in the U.S. and in other countries is how often success in curbing inflation has proved temporary because of the failure of the monetary authorities to allow for points one and two of the preceding paragraph.

Will the Fed be more successful? Will it have the courage and the willpower to withstand the pressures to manipulate interest rates and to finance the Federal deficit by creating money? Will it have the wisdom to recognize that keeping inflation at 2 or 3 percent a year, let alone reducing it to zero, requires that it reduce the rate of growth of M_2 from more than 10 percent a year to roughly 6 or 7 percent? [1]

The rate of inflation over the next five years will be determined largely by the answers to these questions.

The Inflationary Fed
[August 27, 1973]

"Seldom has promise diverged so widely from performance as it has in recent monetary policy. . . .

"Listen to the words that emanate from the Federal Reserve System and you will conclude that the Fed is a bastion of defense against inflation. . . .

"Look at the Fed's actions, and you will reach precisely the opposite conclusion. . . .

"The plain fact is that inflation is made in Washington, in that stately and impressive Grecian temple . . . that houses the Board of Governors of the Federal Reserve System."

Tragically, these words are no less relevant today than when they first appeared in this space in 1969.

I then attributed the divergence of promise from performance to misunderstanding. The men who run the Fed, I wrote, have "taken the behavior of interest rates rather than the quantity of money as their guide—and this mistake has led them far astray from their intended path."

That explanation is not valid today. In January 1970, the Fed gave primacy in its policy directive to "monetary aggregates" rather than interest rates. In February 1971, Chairman Burns testified to Congress: "We know . . . that while a high rate of growth of narrowly defined money may well be appropriate for brief periods, rates of increase above the 5 or 6 percent range—if continued for a long period of time—have typically intensified inflationary pressures." He went on to "reaffirm the assurance that I gave this committee and the nation a year ago—namely that the Federal Reserve will not become the architect of a new wave of inflation."

[1] [In the event, the answer was NO. The monetary growth continued at roughly 10 percent for M_2, and inflation accelerated.]

The rates of monetary growth specified by chairman Burns are too high. Yet, even so, actual monetary growth has been substantially higher.

The standards: In not a single one of the 216 months from January 1948 to January 1966 did the year-to-year growth in the narrowly defined money supply (M_1) exceed 6 percent. These eighteen years included the Korean inflation, yet M_1 rose at the average rate of only 2.4 percent per year; consumer prices, of 1.7 percent; wholesale prices, of 1.2 percent.

The two years 1966 and 1967 set the stage for the subsequent burst of inflation. Yet the year-to-year growth in M_1 exceeded 6 percent in only four out of 24 months. M_1 rose at the average rate of 4.3 percent; consumer prices, of 3.4 percent; wholesale prices, of 1.3 percent.

The evidence therefore supports a "3 or 4 percent range" rather better than Burns's "5 or 6 percent range."

Performance: In the three and a half years since January 1970, the year-to-year growth in M_1 has exceeded 6 percent in 25 out of 42 months, and has averaged 6.7 percent. *Moreover, monetary growth has been speeding up, averaging 7.3 percent since January 1971, 7.8 percent since January 1972.* Consumer prices rose at an average rate of 4.6 percent, wholesale prices, of 6.7 percent.

Over short periods, many factors other than monetary growth affect the rate of inflation. But, as Chairman Burns implied, over long periods, monetary growth is dominant.

It takes several years for monetary growth to exert its full influence on prices. As a result, we have so far experienced only the early effects of the nearly 8 percent rate of growth of the past year and a half. *That rate of monetary growth, probably even now, and certainly if long continued, implies that inflation in consumer prices will reach something like 7 percent per year after full adjustment.* [1]

When the Fed changed its directive in January 1970, those of us who had long been urging such a change confidently expected steady monetary growth at a noninflationary rate—especially after Chairman Burns stated in a May 1970 talk, "In recent years, growth rates of major monetary aggregates have been permitted to vary over an extremely wide range. . . . There has been much loose talk of 'fine tuning' when the state of knowledge permits us to predict only within a fairly broad level the course of economic development and the results of policy actions."

[1] See my "How Much Monetary Growth?," Morgan Guaranty Survey, February 1973.

Our hopes have been shattered. Monetary growth has been both higher and more variable in the past three and a half years than in any other postwar period of equal length.

What now explains the divergence between the Fed's promises and its performance? Why does the Fed remain an engine of inflation? I confess that I am baffled.

Is Money Too Tight?
[September 23, 1974]

Almost every news report on the September 5 presummit meeting of twenty-eight economists with President Ford featured the statement, "A majority of the economists favored some easing of monetary policy."

As one of the minority, I can ruefully testify that the report was correct—but it was misleading. First, almost without exception, the economists favored "monetary restraint." Second, with one exception, none of the economists who favored "less restraint" specified what he meant by "tight" or "easy" money or assigned a numerical value to either present monetary policy or his preferred alternative. Most were simply expressing the dismay we all feel at high interest rates and the hope we all share that interest rates will come down.

A major source of bad monetary policy has been and remains the confusion between two meanings of "tight" or "easy." One meaning associates "tight" money with high interest rates and "easy" money with low interest rates. The other meaning associates "tight" money with slow growth in the quantity of money and "easy" money with rapid growth. There is no doubt that interest rates have been at record highs for some time, and hence in the first sense money has been extremely tight. But until a few months ago at best, these high interest rates have been accompanied by extremely high rates of monetary growth, so that in the second sense money has been extremely easy.

By now, even the monetary authorities have recognized that it is highly misleading to take interest rates as a criterion of monetary policy —that confuses "credit" with "money." Rapid monetary growth ("easy" money in the second sense) initially does tend to reduce interest rates ("easy" money in the first sense). But after a few months, as the rapid monetary growth raises incomes and the demand for loans—and promotes inflation—the effect is to raise interest rates ("tight" money in the first sense). That is why, historically, interest rates have been high when monetary growth is rapid and low when monetary growth has been slow. Moreover, as the markets have come to understand this relation, the initial phase when the two senses coincide has become shorter and shorter.

The Fed controls the quantity of money, not interest rates, and the right way to judge whether monetary policy is tight or easy is to look at the rate of monetary growth.

If we do so, the fact is that there was no appreciable tightening of monetary policy until two or three months ago; the apparent tightening since has been modest, and may prove in retrospect transitory.

From early 1971 to mid-1974, the monetary aggregates grew at a roughly constant rate, with erratic deviations about a trend of a 6.7 percent annual rate for M_1 (currency plus adjusted demand deposits) and a 9.6 percent rate for M_2 (M_1 plus time deposits at commercial banks other than large CD's). These are extremely high rates—higher than for any other equally long period since World War Two, which goes far to explain why inflation has also been higher.

As of June of this year, M_1 was *above* a trend calculated from the data for March 1971 to March 1974. It has since moved a trifle below, but currently is less than one-half of 1 percent below the trend. The story is similar for M_2. It was on its trend in April and is now less than 1 percent below it. Equally large deviations have occurred several times during the past three years, which is why the data to date, while consistent with some tightening of monetary policy, do not demonstrate that any real change has yet occurred.

In terms of the more usual presentation, M_1 has recently been growing at a rate of 4 to 5 percent compared to the 6.7 percent average rate of growth of the past three years; M_2 at 7 to 8 percent compared to 9.6 percent. These are certainly modest reductions in monetary growth.

We must move gradually to conquer inflation. It would be a mistake to jam on the brakes so hard as to catapult us through the windshield. But it would be no less a mistake to let gradualism mean inaction. Recent rates of monetary growth are not too low. If anything they are still too high to bring inflation to an end in a reasonable period of time. It will be a tragedy if the confusion between "interest rates" and "monetary growth" once again leads the Fed to falter in its task. Faint hearts ne'er won fair price stability.

Chapter Three
Fiscal Policy and Taxation

The columns in this chapter stress three main themes: (1) the limitations of fiscal policy as a means of countering inflation or recession; (2) the relation between taxes and the scope of government; and (3) the defects of the individual income tax.

The first theme, as noted in the introduction to Chapter 2, is the mirror image of the emphasis in that chapter on the importance of monetary policy. As I say in the first column in this chapter, questioning whether higher taxes would necessarily be contractionary was, in the light of the economic orthodoxy of the day, "like questioning whether two plus two equals four." The failure of the 1968 surtax to stem inflation shook that orthodoxy, so the situation today is somewhat less extreme. Yet the stress in late 1971 and early 1972 on "expansive fiscal policy" (i.e., big deficits—and in 1974 on tax cuts—to stimulate the economy) both by the administration and its leading Democratic opponents, reveals that the belief in the potency of fiscal policy is still alive and well. It is kept alive primarily, I believe, by two factors stressed in these columns: first, the tendency to look only at the direct effects of government spending and taxes and to neglect the indirect effects; second, the failure to keep fiscal effects separate from monetary effects. Insofar as government deficits are financed via the printing press (whether literally in the form of currency or figuratively in the form of Federal Reserve creation of deposits to purchase government securities), the resulting monetary growth will stimulate spending, and it is easy to attribute this effect to the deficits per se rather than to the method of financing them.

My view seems to be supported by the bulk of the empirical evidence on this question. Yet I should warn the reader that even more than on the issue of monetary policy, that view is a minority view in the economic profession.

The second theme—the relation between taxes and the scope of government—reflects a political judgment rather than an economic judgment. As a matter of technical economics, the decision about how much to spend and the decision about how to finance the spending can be regarded as largely independent if related decisions. As a political matter, I believe that in the long run the level of taxes comes closer to determining the level of spending than the other way around. Occasionally, as in World War Two, a special emergency that produces a willingness to raise taxes and spending is the moving force. But once the new level of taxes is in place, it tends to become permanent or nearly so, and thereafter spending is determined in large part by how much the revenue structure will raise.

Explicit increases in tax rates are one source of increased revenue and spending. But in the postwar period an even more important source has been the automatic and unlegislated increase in the burden of taxes as a result of economic growth and inflation. Both tend to raise not only the amount of tax revenue but, even more important, the *fraction* of total income going to the tax collector. They have this effect by pushing individuals into higher tax brackets of our graduated income tax.

In this way, the second theme is related both to the first (how to control inflation) and to the third (the defects of the individual income tax). My own favorite device for reforming the tax is to substitute a flat rate tax on income above personal exemptions for the present graduated rates and at the same time to eliminate all deductions other than strictly defined business and occupational expenses. In addition, I would provide for inflation-proofing of taxes.

Because there has been so much recent interest in indexation, the columns on that subject have been brought together in Chapter 6, but several of those could as well have been included in this chapter.

The final column of this chapter, written during the 1972 presidential campaign, expresses a rather pessimistic view of the likelihood that the growth of government will be halted. Unfortunately, as the introduction to Chapter 1 indicates, developments since that column was written reinforce rather than mitigate that pessimism.

Higher Taxes? No
[January 23, 1967]

Like many other economists, I oppose the increase in taxes recommended by President Johnson—but for different reasons than most.

I oppose a tax increase because I believe that the federal government is already absorbing too much of the community's resources. We need lower taxes, not higher taxes.

My fellow economists will tell me that I am confusing taxes and spending. Government *spending* measures the absorption of resources. The level of *taxes* determines "only" how much of the spending is financed by taxes and how much by borrowing.

This is true as an accounting matter—but not politically. The postwar period has demonstrated time and again that Congress will spend whatever the tax system will raise—plus a little more. Raise taxes and the main effect is likely to be higher spending. The President has asked for a *temporary* increase in taxes to finance a *temporary* increase in war spending. But temporary increases have a way of becoming permanent. The way to meet extra needs is to cut nonwar spending, not to increase taxes.

My fellow economists will tell me also that the major issue is not the level of government spending but whether the economy is overheated and needs higher taxes to restrain it, or, alternatively, is headed into a recession that higher taxes will deepen.

I believe that we are headed for a recession, albeit an inflationary one—but this plays no part in my opposition to a tax increase. Though these days it is like questioning whether two plus two makes four, I do not share the widespread view that a tax increase which is not matched by higher government spending will necessarily have a strong braking effect on the economy.

True, higher taxes would leave taxpayers with less to spend. But this is only part of the story. If government spending were unchanged, more of it would now be financed by the higher taxes, and the government would have to borrow less. *The individuals, banks, corporations or other lenders from whom the government would have borrowed now have more left to spend or to lend to others—and this extra amount is precisely equal to the reduction in the amount available to them and others as taxpayers.* If they spend it themselves, this directly offsets any reduction in spending by taxpayers. If they lend it to business enterprises or private individuals—as they can by accepting a lower interest rate for the loans—the resulting increase in business investment, expenditures on residential building and so on indirectly offsets any reduction on spending by taxpayers.

To find any *net* effect on private spending, one must look farther beneath the surface. Lower interest rates make it less expensive for people to hold cash. Hence, some of the funds not borrowed by the federal government may be added to idle cash balances rather than spent or loaned. In addition, it takes time for borrowers and lenders to adjust to reduced government borrowing. However, any net increase in spending from these sources is certain to be temporary and likely to be minor.

To have a significant impact on the economy, a tax increase must somehow affect monetary policy—the quantity of money and its rate of growth. It clearly need not have any such effect. The Federal Reserve can increase the quantity of money by precisely the same amount with or without a tax rise. However, a tax rise may embolden the Fed politically to hold down the quantity of money, because such a policy would then be more consistent with lower interest rates than if taxes were kept unchanged.

The tax reduction of 1964 had this effect—in the opposite direction. It encouraged the Fed to follow a more expansionary policy. This monetary expansion explains the long-continued economic expansion. And it is the turnabout in monetary policy since April 1966 that explains the growing signs of recession.

The level of taxes is important—because it affects how much of our resources we use through government and how much we use as individuals. It is not important as a sensitive and powerful device to control the short-run course of income and prices.

Fiscal Responsibility
[August 7, 1967]

For the twelve months ending June 30, 1967, the federal government ran a deficit of about $10 billion. And this may be only a mild foretaste of things to come. On present projections, the current year's deficit is likely to be two or three times as large. What does fiscal responsibility call for in the face of these staggering deficits?

At first glance, the answer seems straightforward: restraint in spending and higher taxes. That is why there is a "Rising Consensus for a Tax Hike" (*Newsweek*, July 24).

In my opinion, this is a shortsighted answer. The deficit in the federal budget is only a symptom of a more deep-seated malady: the size of government spending.

When the administration urges higher taxes, it points to Vietnam as the source of the deficit. That is a half-truth. Of course, if military spending were lower—and other spending the same—the deficit would be smaller. But civilian spending too has been rising rapidly—as the administration proudly proclaims when it seeks to calm the liberal critics of its Vietnam policy. And this rise has been reinforced by growing spending by state and local governments.

All in all, we work from January 1 to nearly the end of April to furnish the wherewithal for government spending; only then can we turn to providing for our private needs.

This situation would be dangerous to our liberty even if we were getting our money's worth from present government spending. But there is scarce a man so rash as to say that we are. Most of us regard high military spending as a necessary evil. But even many proponents of big government are having second thoughts about numerous civilian programs— from the agricultural subsidies of the New Deal to the zooming welfare measures of the Great Society. Time and again, extravagant promises have been made that this or that expensive program will solve this or that social problem. And time and again, the result is that both costs and problems multiply.

But what relevance does this have to taxes? If we adopt such programs, does not fiscal responsibility at least call for imposing taxes to pay for them? The answer is that postwar experience has demonstrated two things. First, that Congress will spend whatever the tax system will raise—plus a little (and recently, a lot) more. Second, that, surprising as it seems, it has proved difficult to get taxes down once they are raised. The special interests created by government spending have proved more potent than the general interest in tax reduction.

If taxes are raised in order to keep down the deficit, the result is likely to be a higher norm for government spending. Deficits will again mount and the process will be repeated.

If government spending can be restrained, growth in the economy will, at present tax rates, add enough to revenues in a few years to eliminate the deficit and even to permit tax reduction. This is a big if. But let taxes be raised and there is no if about it at all. The deficits can be temporary; higher taxes are almost certain to be permanent.

If we do not cut spending and do not raise taxes, will not the large interim deficits produce severe inflation?

Deficits have often been connected with inflation, but they need not be. Deficits were large in 1931 and 1932 when prices were falling drastically. There was a surplus in 1919–20 when prices were rising rapidly. Whether deficits produce inflation depends on how they are financed. If, as so often happens, they are financed by creating money, they unquestionably do produce inflationary pressure. If they are financed by borrowing from the public, at whatever interest rates are necessary, they may still exert some minor inflationary pressure. However, their major effect will be to make interest rates higher than they would otherwise be. A short spell of high interest rates is vastly to be preferred to a long spell of high taxes.

Those of us who believe that government has reached a size at which it threatens to become our master rather than our servant should therefore (1) oppose any tax increase; (2) press for expenditure cuts, (3) accept large deficits as the lesser of evils; (4) favor the financing of these deficits by borrowing from the public rather than by undue creation of money; and (5) urge the elimination of artificial ceilings on the rate of interest at which the government may borrow in order to foster this objective.

In the long view, that is the course of true fiscal responsibility.

Regressive Income Tax
[April 22, 1968]

In the boom year 1929, more than 4,000 persons reported a taxable income of more than $250,000. Since then, our population has risen by more than 60 percent and average income has quadrupled—half real, half as a result of a doubling of prices. Hence, today's counterpart would be about 6,500 persons reporting a taxable income of more than $1 million. The actual number of million-dollar taxable incomes reported in 1966 was 626.

Does this dramatic fall in the number of high incomes reported on personal tax returns reflect a major reduction in the inequality of income? The success of a social policy directed at eliminating the extremes of wealth and poverty? Nothing of the sort. It is simply evidence of how successful high-income people have been in getting more and more loopholes introduced into the income-tax law and in taking advantage of them to avoid paying taxes. In 1929, the highest tax rate was 25 percent. It hardly paid then to engage in complicated and expensive transactions to avoid paying taxes. Today, the highest tax rate is 70 percent. It clearly pays to adopt very expensive devices.

The personal income tax professes to adjust the tax to "ability to pay," to tax the rich more heavily and the poor less heavily and to allow for each individual's special circumstances. This is an elaborate facade.

The tax rates are steeply graduated on paper, rising from 14 to 70 percent. But the law is riddled with so many loopholes, so many special provisions, that the high rates are almost pure window dressing. In 1966, total personal income taxes paid amounted to less than 20 percent of total reported taxable income. In other words, all the rates above the very lowest, the 14 percent rate that applies to the first $1,000 of the taxable income of a married couple, accounted for less than 30 percent of total taxes collected. Moreover, had there been a low flat rate, it would not have paid taxpayers to go to the lengths they now do to avoid high marginal rates. They would have reported more income and less deductions. Hence a flat rate well below 20 percent would have yielded as much as the actual steeply graduated rates.

Suppose we classified people by what you and I would regard as their actual income rather than by the taxable incomes they report. Suppose we then expressed the tax they actually pay as a percentage of their actual income. We would find that this percentage is much smaller for persons in very high income classes (and, incidentally, because of exemptions, also in very low income classes) than for persons with incomes of middle size. And within each income class, we would find enormous variation. Two men with the same income may pay vastly different taxes—because one's income is wages and the other's interest on tax-exempt securities or capital gains.

So long as the rates are steeply graduated, it is politically impossible to eliminate the present loopholes and deductions, as is demonstrated by repeated failures to do so. But even if politically possible, it would be undesirable. The present high rates applied to all income would have disastrous effects on incentives. We would lose more in output than we would gain in fairness. Rate reform must accompany other tax reforms.

The personal income tax would come far closer to achieving its professed objectives if we substituted a flat rate on income above personal exemptions for the present graduated rates and, simultaneously, eliminated the present loopholes and deductions that enable so many persons to avoid paying their fair share of the taxes and that require so many more to take tax considerations into account in their every economic decision.

If every deduction were eliminated except occupational expenses strictly interpreted, and if income of all kinds in excess of personal exemptions were subject to a single low flat rate, we could double our present personal exemptions—which are disgracefully low—and still raise as much revenue. That would be more equitable, vastly simpler, and far more efficient.

It would also release all of us from the unpaid bookkeeping we are forced to engage in to satisfy the Internal Revenue Service and make available for productive use the highly skilled accountants and lawyers who now devote their great talents to advising their clients how to avoid taxes under present law, to creating new and ever more complex tax shelters, and to litigating cases in court.

Spend, Tax, Elect
[July 15, 1968]

Harry Hopkins, an intimate of FDR, is reputed to have remarked in the late 1930s, "We shall spend and spend, tax and tax, elect and elect." Whether Hopkins actually said it or not, this formula has proved extraordinarily effective. It has kept the White House firmly in Democratic hands, except only for the eight Eisenhower years.

I doubt that even Hopkins foresaw just how the formula would work—with the Democrats doing the spending and electing and the Republicans doing the taxing. Yet that has proved the division of labor.

The latest example is the 10 percent surcharge recently passed by Congress. Republican votes provided the margin of victory—and not just the votes of a few Democrats in Republican clothing. On the contrary, the Republican leadership in both Senate and House backed the tax increase. It could not have passed without their support.

The largest single source of federal revenue is an individual income tax that automatically imposes heavier taxes as incomes rise—whether the rise be in output or in prices. As a taxpayer's income rises, so does the tax *rate* levied on that income, because the fixed dollar exemption becomes a smaller percentage of income and he moves into higher tax brackets. In order to keep the effective rate constant, nominal tax rates must be lowered. The absence of legislation lowering rates automatically means higher taxes. This is the "fiscal drag" that was made so much of during the Kennedy administration.

In 1940, before our entry into World War Two, individual income taxes amounted to less than 2 percent of total personal income. At their wartime height in 1945, they were just under 10 percent. Postwar tax reductions were followed by rises during the Korean War that carried the effective rate to over 10 percent in 1953. The Eisenhower tax reduction in 1954 brought the rate down to 9 percent—but then economic expansion pushed it up to an all-time high in 1963, well over 10 percent. The Kennedy tax reduction in 1964 again carried the rate back to 9 percent—but the subsequent expansion pushed it back up to around 10 percent. *Even before the surcharge, the effective individual income tax rate was as high as it was at its peak in World War Two.* The surcharge will carry it to a new all-time high.

The standard scenario has been that the Democrats—in the name of the New Deal, the Fair Deal, or the Great Society—push through large spending programs, with the assistance of a few Republicans but generally against the opposition of the Republican leadership. The spending programs not only absorb the increased tax yield generated by "fiscal drag," they go farther and produce deficits. The Democrats then appeal to the Republicans' sense of fiscal responsibility to refrain from cutting tax rates or, as in this case, to raise them. The Republicans cooperate, thereby establishing a new higher revenue base for further spending. The Democrats get the "credit" for the spending; the Republicans, the "blame" for the taxes; and you and I pay the bill.

The current tax increase, like the increase during the Korean War, was sold as a temporary war measure. That is an excuse, not a reason.

Only half of the $53 billion increase in federal spending from 1965 to 1968 went for the military. Not the Vietnam war but the policy of spend and spend produces the need to tax and tax.

The Republicans point to the $6 billion legislated cut in spending to justify their support of the tax increase. That is wishful voting. The tax increase is for real. The spending cut is a hope for the future. And at that, it is window dressing. Even if the full $6 billion cut in the President's proposed budget were achieved, actual spending would go up by $4 billion. And it requires no crystal ball to predict that the full $6 billion will not be achieved.

I honor the Republicans for putting what they regard as the national interest ahead of partisan considerations. But I believe that they have been shortsighted in judging the national interest. True fiscal responsibility requires making the legislators who vote for high spending also vote for the high taxes required to finance it—not bailing them out. True fiscal responsibility requires resisting every tax increase and promoting tax decreases at every opportunity. That is the only way to put an effective ceiling on federal spending.

Can Business Pay Taxes?
[November 29, 1971]

President Nixon's proposals for reductions in taxes have been widely criticized as a "help-the-rich" program "heavily weighted in favor of business at the expense of the individual taxpayer."

This criticism is sheer demagoguery. The elementary fact is that "business" does not and cannot pay taxes. Only people can pay taxes. Corporate officials may sign the check, but the money that they forward to Internal Revenue comes from the corporation's employees, customers, or stockholders. A corporation is a pure intermediary through which its employees, customers, and stockholders cooperate for their mutual benefit. A corporation may be large and control large amounts of capital. Yet it does not follow that a reduction in the check it sends to Internal Revenue benefits wealthy individuals.

Consider, for example, the proposed repeal of the excise tax on automobiles. At first glance, the main beneficiaries are the upper-income people who buy the new cars. But this is too simple. Many cars are purchased for business purposes, and the beneficiaries are the customers, employees, proprietors, and stockholders of the firms buying the cars. More important, increased production of cars will lower prices of secondhand cars, benefiting their purchasers, who are mostly in lower-income classes. The greater sales of new cars will also benefit employees, proprietors, and stockholders of firms producing and selling cars. However, it will harm employees, proprietors, and stockholders of firms producing items for which the demand is now lower because spending has been diverted to new cars.

Or consider the proposed investment-tax credit. Surely, you will say, that benefits corporate stockholders, and we know that they are generally wealthy. True, but misleading. The firms that qualify for the credit will have an incentive to expand. But this adds to the demand for loans, which will tend to raise interest rates, spreading some of the benefits to savers and imposing costs on other users of capital. It will also add to the supply of goods that the firms getting the credit produce, benefiting their customers by lowering prices and their employees by providing better employment opportunities. Stockholders or proprietors of these companies will of course also benefit, but stockholders, proprietors, customers, and employees of firms that do not qualify for the credit will be hurt.

And even this is only part of the story. The rest depends on how the government replaces the revenue, whether by imposing taxes, by borrowing, or by reducing spending, and who is thereby benefited or harmed.

Indirect effects make it difficult to know who "really" pays any tax. But this difficulty is greatest for taxes levied on business. *That fact is at one and the same time the chief political appeal of the corporation income tax, and its chief political defect.* The politician can levy taxes, as it appears, on no one, yet obtain revenue. The result is political irresponsibility. Levying most taxes directly on individuals would make far clearer who pays for government programs.

Under our present tax system, stockholders pay no individual income tax on income that a corporation earns but does not pay out as dividends. Reinvestment of such undistributed income tends to raise the value of the corporation's stock. When and if the stockholder sells his stock, he receives the benefit in the form of a capital gain that is taxed at lower rates than his current dividends. The corporation income tax is defended as a way to prevent such undistributed income from being undertaxed.

A far better way to achieve this objective is to require corporations to attribute undistributed income to their stockholders and to require stockholders to include the undistributed income in their individual income. That is, the XYZ corporation would accompany its dividend check to stockholders with a notice, saying, "In addition to the $1 per share we are now paying you as dividends, we have earned $1.25 per share that we are reinvesting on your behalf." The stockholder would then report $2.25 per share as his income from the stock and pay individual income tax on that amount (and raise his capital gains base by $1.25 per share).

This reform would promote both equity and also greater competition in the capital market. Until it is enacted, and the corporation income tax as such is repealed, the demagogues will continue to have a field day.

A Family Matter
[April 10, 1972]

How would you like to get a letter from your married daughter suggesting that you and your wife of more than thirty years' standing get a divorce? That is what happened to us recently. Wrote our daughter (who, I should add, is a lawyer).

Dear Mom and Dad:

Just a quick note to suggest that you call your tax lawyer about my latest theory for saving income taxes—getting a divorce. (Don't gulp too hard, Mom—how much is it worth to you to be married? Not to live together and have the same name—just to be married?) Under 1971 tax rates, a married couple pays more tax than two single people each with half the income. Since alimony is deductible to the husband and taxable to the wife, if you get a divorce and Dad pays you reasonably high alimony, you can save taxes by making sure you split your total income roughly equally. The saving is pretty sizable.

Love, Jan

My daughter did not know that she was bringing coals to Newcastle. Some thirty years ago, as an employee of the U.S. Treasury Department, I helped devise the tax-splitting provisions that prevailed until the Reform Act of 1969—more accurately described as the Lawyers' and Accountants' Relief Act of 1969.

Those provisions were designed precisely to prevent living in sin from being a tax shelter. Under those provisions, a single person was taxed at the same rates as a married person but each rate applied to half the income, i.e., each rate bracket was half as wide. As a result, if two single persons who had equal incomes married, and continued to have the same incomes after marriage, their tax as a family was precisely the sum of their separate taxes.

This provision also meant, however, that if a man married a woman who had no income, the tax for the family was less than the tax that the single man had paid before. The reason this occurred was because of graduated rates. A single man who has an income of $20,000 pays more in tax than the sum of the taxes paid by two single men each with $10,000 income. His higher income puts him into a higher tax bracket. Similarly, under the earlier rules, a married couple was treated as equivalent to two persons each having half the family income. Hence, it was taxed at a lower rate than that applicable to a single person who had an income equal to the total family income.

Personally, I favor substituting a flat rate on income above a personal exemption for the present graduated rates and at the same time eliminating all deductions other than strictly defined business and occupational expenses. But that is not existing policy. Graduated tax rates were introduced and are defended as a device for equalizing income. There is no more effective means of equalizing income than for Prince Charming to marry Cinderella.

To put this point differently, consider a single man who has an income of $20,000 from, let us say, stocks and bonds. He has a niece who is unable to work and has no income. He gives her half of his stocks and bonds so he retains an income of $10,000 and she has an income of $10,000. The sum of their taxes will be less than the tax he paid before his benefaction. If that reduction in taxes is regarded as equitable, is it not also equitable that the same tax consequences should follow from his marrying his niece?

However, the single persons didn't see it that way. And they persuaded the Congress to revise the law by reducing the tax rates applicable to single persons below those applicable to married persons.

As my daughter said, the resulting tax shelter is by no means negligible. Here are the tax savings from splitting income evenly at various family-income levels.

Here's to April 15 and living in sin!

Family Income	Tax* on basis of		Saving from Living in Sin
	Joint Return	Two Unmarried Persons	
$10,000	$ 1,257	$ 1,114	$ 143
15,000	2,298	2,136	162
20,000	3,582	3,192	390
25,000	5,068	4,356	710
30,000	6,794	5,738	1,056
40,000	10,858	8,902	1,956
50,000	15,635	12,640	$2,995

*Assumes standard deduction throughout.

Can We Halt Leviathan?
[November 6, 1972]

The battle over a ceiling on federal spending has spotlighted the major economic problem facing this country in the coming decade: can we halt the growth of Leviathan—to use Hobbes's expressive term for government? Or will Leviathan crush us?

Until 1930, federal spending was less than 5 percent of the national income except during or just after major wars (the War of 1812, the Civil War, World War One). With the same exceptions, local and state governments spent several times as much as the federal government. For example, in 1930, federal spending was 4 percent of national income; state and local spending, 11 percent. Spending at all levels of government combined thus amounted to roughly 15 percent of the national income.

The New Deal changed all that. Already by 1936, the final year of FDR's first term, federal spending had reached 13 percent of the national income and had passed state and local spending.

World War Two brought an enormous expansion of federal spending, and the end of the war a sharp reduction. But then the New Deal pattern resumed. By 1950, federal spending amounted to 17 percent of national income; by 1960, to 22 percent; and by now, to more than 26 percent. State and local spending—over and above federal grants—has been rising even more rapidly; from 8 percent of national income in 1950 to nearly 14 percent today.

In short, active war apart, from 1789 to 1930, residents of the U.S. never spent more than about 15 percent of their income on the expenses of government. In the past four decades, that fraction has nearly tripled and is now about 40 percent.

War and defense spending have played an important role in the growth of government, but only a supporting role. During each war, federal spending rose sharply and so did federal taxes. After the war, both spending and taxes were reduced, but taxes were reduced less than spending. Instead, following one of Parkinson's laws, peacetime spending rose to exhaust the revenue. As a result, up to 1930, federal spending, as a fraction of national income, consists of a series of steps, each higher than the preceding, though lower than an intervening wartime peak.

The New Deal started a new pattern of ever higher spending and taxes for civilian purposes that has continued ever since. The recent increase in total federal spending has occurred despite a decline in military spending from 12 percent of national income in 1968 to 8 percent today. And certainly the recent rapid rise in state and local spending can hardly be blamed on the military.

The plain fact is that governments are now spending an amount approaching half of our national income not because of war or fear of war, not because of the machinations of a military-industrial complex, but because of a major change in the past 40 years in the role that we, as citizens, have assigned to the government.

Until 1930, citizens of the U.S. viewed the federal government primarily as a keeper of the peace and an umpire. Today, we view it as responsible for treating every social and personal ill, as the source from which all blessings flow.

Senator McGovern is riding this wave. His proposals would boost federal spending from 26 to 31 percent of national income. Mr. Nixon has expressed great concern about the growth in spending, yet his proposals would only hold the line rather than cut sharply federal spending as a fraction of national income.

Neither a legislated ceiling nor any other administrative devices designed to improve the budgetary process—welcome though they would be—will halt Leviathan unless we, as citizens, once again change drastically the role that we assign to government.

There is hardly one among us who believes that he is getting his money's worth for the nearly half of his income that government—federal, state, and local—spends for him. Yet so long as we simply blame waste and bureaucracy, but continue to believe in the omnipotence and beneficence of government, the trend toward ever bigger government will continue.

That trend will stop only when and if we come to recognize that government is the problem, not the solution; that the general welfare requires that we dethrone the federal government from its role as Big Brother and restore it to its historic role as keeper of the peace and umpire.

Chapter Four
Inflation

Inflation has clearly become the major economic problem of the 1970s. It is a problem not only for the United States but also throughout the world. It is a problem that enters into every facet of economic policy—budget policy, tax policy, monetary policy. As a result it has already been dealt with extensively in the preceding three chapters.

Yet it has seemed worth separating out for special consideration the columns in this and the next two chapters: in this chapter, columns that deal with the general issue of inflation and of the relation between inflation and unemployment; in Chapter 5, columns dealing with wage and price controls—in my opinion a wholly false and harmful alleged cure for inflation; and in Chapter 6, columns dealing with the subject of "escalator clauses," or "indexation," the correct way to achieve the one valid objective of price and wage controls, namely, preventing inflationary expectations from being incorporated in future wage and price commitments.

The road to controlling inflation is blocked by widespread misunderstanding of the sources of inflation. Because inflation is reflected in a price quoted by a seller or a wage demanded by a laborer or a trade union, there is a tendency to blame the seller, or the laborer, or the trade union for the inflation. This tendency was manifested in a crude and simple-minded form back in 1966 in a flareup of protest movements by housewives who blamed supermarkets for rising food prices and sought in vain to drive prices down by boycotting the supermarkets. The first column in this chapter analyzes these boycotts. It is manifested also in a more sophisticated form in the widespread belief about the connection between wages and inflation discussed in the third column in this chapter.

To blame the person who records the inflation for producing it is like blaming the thermometer for the heat or the obstetrician for the baby.

The road to recurring bouts of inflation at successively higher levels is paved with a widespread misunderstanding of the relation between inflation and unemployment. It has been widely believed that the two are alternatives, that higher inflation will mean less unemployment and conversely. This "trade-off" doctrine has a valid element but is erroneous as commonly understood. There is, in my opinion, no long-run trade-off between inflation and unemployment; the average rate of inflation over a long period is unrelated to the average rate of unemployment; it is possible to have the same average level of unemployment with prices rising on the average at, say, 5 percent a year, prices constant on the average, or prices falling on the average by, say, 5 percent a year. But there is a trade-off between acceleration or deceleration of inflation and the level of unemployment. A *higher* rate of inflation will temporarily lower the rate of unemployment; a *lower* rate of inflation will temporarily raise the rate of unemployment, but the effect wears off and requires higher and higher doses to maintain. This phenomenon is an underlying theme in most of the remaining columns of this chapter and is discussed more fully in the final item in Chapter 6.

The fifth column in this chapter, "Living with Inflation" (October 8, 1973), is on a rather different level than most of the items in this book. It is devoted to personal rather than public finance.

Boycotts and Prices
[November 28, 1966]

Housewives who are boycotting supermarkets are in an ancient if misguided tradition. "When the price of a thing goes up," wrote the British economist Edwin Cannan in 1915, many people "abuse, not the buyers nor the persons who might produce it and do not do so, but the persons who are producing and selling it, and thereby keeping down its price.... It certainly would appear to be a most extraordinary example of the proverbial ingratitude of man when he abuses the farmer who does grow wheat because other farmers do not.... But have we not all heard the preacher abuse his congregation because it is so small?"

Today, too, the boycotters are attacking the wrong culprit, and their boycotts will be as ineffective as all previous boycotts.

Ask a supermarket operator, "Who sets your prices?"

"I do," he will probably reply.

"In that case, why don't you double them?"

"Don't be silly, I would have no customers."

Press him on the other side, "If you want more customers, why don't you halve your prices?"

"What do you think I am," may be his indignant response, "a philanthropist? If I halved my prices, I would go bankrupt—unless I could get the Ford Foundation to back me. And then they would go bankrupt."

The supermarket operator does not set prices. He simply records the prices that are set by forces outside his control. Blaming him for high prices is like blaming a thermometer for the fever it records. Boycotting him is like breaking the thermometer to cure the fever.

What effects, if any, do boycotts have on the basic forces of demand and supply?

When boycotters spend less at supermarkets, this does impose pressure on supermarkets—witness the rash of lower posted prices, not all of which are sales gimmicks. But if boycotters simply transfer their custom to family grocers, the other side of the coin is a greater demand at those stores and higher prices there. The boycotters lose—because they pay the higher prices at family grocers—and the nonboycotters gain—because they benefit from the lower prices at supermarkets. End the boycott, and you end the temporary stimulus to both the lower and the higher prices.

If boycotters spend less on food by emptying their pantries, there is no current offset to the lower supermarket prices. But when they restock, they will boost demand, which will lead to higher prices then. On the average, they will only have rendered supermarket operations more erratic and costly.

If they spend less on food by eating less and instead spend their money on other items of consumption, their abstinence will reduce the upward pressure on food prices. But the higher demand for other goods will increase the pressure on other prices.

If they spend less in total on all forms of consumption and put the difference in savings and loans, the extra funds available for mortgages will tend to stimulate the building industry. The upward pressure on consumer prices will be less but on construction prices more.

To achieve their objective, boycotters must not only spend less on consumption, they must "hoard" what they save—preferably in mattresses or safe-deposit boxes. That *would* absorb some of the increase in the quantity of money that is the basic source of inflationary pressure.

But this is fantasy. Boycotters want lower prices in order to be able to buy goods. They are not picketing supermarkets to stuff mattresses.

Housewives have a justifiable complaint. But they should complain to Washington where inflation is produced, not to the supermarket where inflation is delivered. Prices have been going up because the quantity of money increased too much from 1961 to the spring of this year. And the quantity of money increased as much as it did because the monetary authorities—primarily the U.S. Treasury and the Federal Reserve System—planned it that way, or, to be less generous, let it happen. The names on the picket signs should be not A&P, but Fowler and Martin.[1]

Unemployment Figures
[October 20, 1969]

Few figures are watched with more fear and trembling than those reported each month on the percentage of the labor force unemployed. The jump from 3.5 to 4 percent reported last week has been seized on by some as the first real sign of success in the battle against inflation, by others, as a portent of economic collapse.

Yet few figures are more misunderstood and misinterpreted.

The unemployment percentage is currently 4 percent. This corresponds to roughly 3.2 million unemployed. Does this mean, as one might suppose from most news stories on unemployment, that more than three million families are wondering where the next paycheck is coming from?

Not at all. Roughly one million unemployed are teen-agers, about half of whom are looking for their first job. Of the remaining unemployed, half are females, many of whom are not regular earners. Of the million unemployed males twenty years and older, only about half are married men.

More important, unemployment is mostly a brief period between jobs—or between school or housework and a job. Nearly two-thirds were

[1] [At the time, Henry Fowler was Secretary of the Treasury, and William McChesney Martin chairman of the Board of Governors of the Federal Reserve System.]

either working in the prior month, or not looking for a job. Only slightly more than a million were unemployed.

Put differently, fewer than half of the currently unemployed have been unemployed for as long as five weeks; only 5 percent—about 150,000—for as long as six months. This is the hard-core group that leaps to mind when we talk about "the unemployed." Their plight is certainly serious—but 150,000 persons in that position is a far cry from three million.

Many persons are unemployed by choice. Some quit one job to look for a better job—more than a third of those who leave jobs in any week do so voluntarily; others have refused a job offered in the belief that a better one will be along; still others left an earlier job some time ago to go to school, or to make a home for their husbands, or to have or raise children, and have only just re-entered the labor force. A rise in unemployment may be a good thing as well as a bad thing—if it means that people have so much confidence in finding another job that they do not hesitate to leave one they do not like.

In some ways, a more meaningful figure than the number of persons unemployed at any one date is the average length of time that persons who become unemployed remain unemployed—the average time between jobs for those who change from one job to another, or the average time it takes to get a job for those who go from school or home to the unemployment rolls. Until the most recent jump in the unemployment rate, that average has been about five and a half weeks—hardly a period long enough to cause acute distress.

What this meant was that each week about 530,000 people started to look for work—because they left or lost a job or because they had just entered or re-entered the labor force. Simultaneously, about 530,000 people each week found jobs or stopped looking. Of the 530,000 people who started to look for jobs each week, about one-fifth found a job within a week; about three-quarters, within a month; and all but about 1 percent, within six months. During a year as a whole, not three million people but around twenty million separate individuals were unemployed at some time or other—the bulk for trivial periods.

Cries of horror go up when it is suggested that the slowing down of the economy as a by-product of policies to stop inflation may mean a rise from 3.5 percent to around 4.5 percent in the unemployment percentage. What, it is said, throw more than a million additional people out of work?

In fact, the number who each week start to look for work would be raised very little—from 530,000 to perhaps 560,000. But these job-seekers would spend on the average an extra week or so finding an acceptable job—the average duration of unemployment would go from about five and a half to about six and a half weeks. The most serious effect would be to raise the number of persons unemployed at any time for more than six months from 180,000 to perhaps 300,000.

These changes are not desirable. But they are not a major catastrophe. They do not spell acute distress. And their avoidance does not justify letting inflation run rampant—which would in any event only postpone higher unemployment temporarily. We badly need less hysteria and dogmatism and more perspective, proportion, and balance in judging these matters.

Inflation and Wages
[September 28, 1970]

I have seldom met a businessman who was not persuaded that inflation is produced by rising wages—and rising wages, in turn, by strong labor unions—and many a nonbusinessman is of the same mind. This belief is false, yet entirely understandable. To each businessman separately, inflation comes in the form of higher costs, mostly wages; yet for all businessmen combined, higher prices produce the higher costs. What is involved is a fallacy of composition. Any one person may be able to leave a crowded theater in two minutes without difficulty. Let everyone try to leave in two minutes and there may be utter chaos. What is true for each separately need not be true for all together.

It is easy to show that the widely held union-wage-push theory of inflation is not correct. If A is *the* cause of B, then whenever A occurs, B will also occur, and whenever B occurs, so will A. *Trade unions* (A) were as strong in the U.S. in 1961–64, when there was no *inflation* (B), as in 1965–69, when there was inflation. Prices in the U.S. more than doubled in the Civil War, when unions were almost nonexistent, in World War One, when unions were weak, and in World War Two, when unions were strong. Prices in the U.S. rose more than 30 percent from 1849 to 1857, and again from 1895 to 1914, both periods when unions were extremely weak. Inflation has plagued countries with negligible trade unions and with strong trade unions; and both kinds of countries have had periods of price stability. Communist countries, like capitalist countries, have experienced both inflation and price stability.

In light of these historical examples, why do businessmen believe so firmly in a wage-push theory of inflation? A simple hypothetical example may explain the puzzle.

Suppose that there was a sudden fad in the U.S. for male footwear. Despite a rush of customers, the shoe stores would not immediately raise the prices they charge. They would, with pleasure and profit, sell more shoes, depleting their inventories. Orders would pour in to wholesalers, who similarly would fill them at list prices, depleting their inventories in turn, and sending on larger orders to manufacturers. The manufacturers, delighted with the flood of business, would try to step up production. To produce more shoes requires more leather. But at any time, there is only a limited stock of leather. To get more leather for themselves, the shoe manufacturers will have to offer higher prices at auctions, in order to bid the leather away from other uses. To produce more shoes, they will also have to hire more labor. How? One way is surely by offering higher wages.

At this point, manufacturers discover that their costs have risen—because of rising wages and the higher cost of leather. They reluctantly raise their prices. Wholesalers discover that their costs have risen and reluctantly raise their prices. Retailers discover that their costs have risen and reluctantly raise their prices.

At each step, prices rise because costs rise—yet the whole process was initiated by a rise in demand.

This example describes accurately a period of inflation. An increase in aggregate money demand leads businessmen to try to increase output. Beyond some limited point, when manpower, equipment, and other resources are fully occupied, they cannot all do so, but the *attempt* to increase output raises costs and makes it look to each businessman as if he must raise his prices because his costs have risen.

The only exception is for a brief period after the turning of the tide. Let an inflationary increase in demand subside. For a time, wages and other costs will continue to rise, reflecting the unspent impetus from the earlier rise in demand. That is what we have been experiencing this past year. But it is a temporary phase that cannot be sustained.

The common element in inflation is not strong unions but an increase in money demand accompanying a rapid increase in the quantity of money. In 1848–1857, the increased quantity of money was produced by gold discoveries in California; in 1896–1913, by the perfection of the cyanide process for extracting gold from low-grade ore; in the Civil War and the two world wars by the creation of money to finance military expenditures; in 1964–1969 by the Federal Reserve System, partly to help finance large government deficits.

Inflation is always and everywhere a monetary phenomenon.

The Hard Truth
[September 17, 1973]

The role of a Cassandra is most uncongenial for a congenital optimist. Yet that is the role that is demanded by the hard facts of inflation and the soft talk about inflation.

The hard facts are that we are faced with at least two more years of inflation in consumer prices at a rate of something like 6 percent a year and probably more; that this is the prospect with or without price controls, with or without tight monetary policy, with or without tight fiscal policy. Past mistakes—too much creation of money, too much government spending, and phases one, two, three and four—have left us that heritage. The soft talk by government and private economists that inflation will be brought down to a "mere" 2.5 or 3 percent by early or mid- or late 1974 without severe economic trauma is wishful thinking pure and simple.[1]

Is there literally no way that the inflation can be broken within a few months? There may be, but not a way that any reasonable man would recommend: step so hard on the monetary and fiscal brakes as to produce a major depression of the 1929–32 variety. That might do it, but the cure would be far worse than the disease.

Should we then simply give up the fight and resign ourselves to indefi-

[1] [And so it proved.]

nite inflation? That, too, is no solution. Inflation is like a drug. It takes bigger and bigger doses to get the same kick. Just as inflation has gone from 2 percent to 4 percent to 6 percent, it would—and very probably will—go to 8 percent, 10 percent and still higher rates. Joining inflation instead of fighting it will at best postpone the evil day but at the cost of making the final cure still more painful.

The best course of action would be to continue indefinitely the moderate rate of monetary growth that seems to have been introduced in the past couple of months, reduce federal spending and abolish the whole kit and kaboodle of mischievous controls that are driving us toward a collectivist society.

This course of action is not a panacea. It will not bring immediate relief. It will mean an economic slowdown and probably a mild recession. But after a couple of years, it will permit vigorous economic expansion without inflation. There simply is no way that we know of to halt inflation without a slowdown or a recession any more than there is a painless way to cure a drug addict.

Are the American people willing to take the cure? Are they—and their political leaders—willing to bite the bullet and take several years of slow growth, of unemployment around 6 percent, in order to make possible a world of steady growth and full employment without inflation? The public, as judged by its political leaders, was not willing to take the cure in 1970, when it would have been less painful than now and was already half completed. I doubt that the political leaders will judge that the public is ready to take the cure now.

We may start on a cure, but when a slowdown or recession occurs, I suspect that the political cry will again be "Damn inflation and full speed ahead." The slowdown or recession will produce some hesitation in the rate of inflation—as occurred in 1971—but then we shall be off again to further inflation—as occurred in mid-1972. This is the ratchet process we have been on now for at least a decade and there seems no end in sight.

Let me warn you not to be misled by a false dawn in coming months. On top of the underlying inflation, there has been a tremendous bubble in food prices and some raw-material prices arising from specific shortages and simultaneous booms in the major countries of the world and spurred on by speculative fever. From October 1972 to July 1973, consumer prices as a whole rose at the rate of 6 percent a year and wholesale industrial prices at the rate of 9 percent, but wholesale prices of farm products and processed foods rose at the astounding rate of 33 percent. This bubble cannot last. It has started to break already and will continue to do so. But the decline in this class of prices will not mean an end to the basic inflation. It will simply mean the elimination of a temporary distortion in the price structure.

If, as I believe, another two years of substantial inflation is now nearly inevitable and a much longer period of inflation is highly likely, is there anything that we can do to reduce the harm from inflation? The answer is clearly yes, as I shall spell out in my next column. [2]

Living With Inflation
[October 8, 1973]

From a reader: "During the past forty-seven years, I have worked and managed to save about $100,000. I have it invested in U.S. Savings Bonds and bank certificates of deposit. . . . Could you give me any idea how I should proceed to protect what I have? . . . Perhaps the only safety one has is to cash his bonds and bury the money." The writer of this moving letter was concerned about the danger of "bankruptcy coming upon the U.S." That danger is illusory, but the threat to his life savings from inflation is real.

U.S. Savings Bonds pay so-called "interest" of 5.5 percent per year if bought since June 1969, less than that if bought earlier, and still less if cashed before maturity. In the past five years, prices have risen at the average rate of 5 percent a year. As a result, if my correspondent cashed in his Savings Bonds, he could buy less with the proceeds today than he could have five years ago. Yet to add insult to injury, he would have to pay income tax on the "interest."

The bank certificates of deposit are a somewhat better investment, but not much. To "protect" him, the government limits the maximum rate that may be paid on the kind of certificates of deposit my correspondent undoubtedly holds. Until recently, the rate was 5.75 percent on commercial-bank deposits, slightly higher on deposits in savings and loan as-

---

[2] [Ultimately extended to two columns: the next one in this chapter was the first. The second, "More on Living with Inflation" (October 28, 1973) has not been reprinted in this book.]

sociations. This interest, too, is subject to tax. The after-tax yield has almost surely been more than eaten up by inflation.

Cashing the bonds and burying the money would be even worse. The pieces of paper that pass for money these days are no safer in any respect than the pieces of paper labeled U.S. Savings Bonds, and they pay no interest at all.

Should he put his money in real property, such as land or houses? *On the average,* real property has been an excellent hedge against inflation. But, as a result, its price has already risen dramatically. More important, properties differ widely in performance. The price of one piece of land may rise tenfold; the price of another may decline sharply. An owned home is an excellent inflation-proof investment for people who do not plan to move. It protects one part of their living standard. Real property in general is sensible only for persons with enough capital to diversify broadly or enough specialized knowledge to choose wisely.

Should he put his money in stocks, perhaps in the form of mutual funds or variable annuities? Again, *on the average,* the market has been a good hedge against inflation and it might well be prudent to have some of his savings in the market. But for the past few years, the market has been a very poor refuge indeed. Here again, the investment is highly risky.

What about gold stocks? Over the past year or so, a magnificent investment. For the prior three decades, a poor investment. For the next ten years, who knows?

High-grade corporate bonds? They provide a higher yield than savings bonds or than bank certificates of deposit, and the yields on them have risen to reflect inflation—though too little and too late. More important, they do not have a predetermined value except at maturity dates. When yields on new bonds rise, prices of existing bonds fall, so you may have to sell at a loss. Anyone who invested in them over the past ten years has probably experienced an even greater loss in real purchasing power than my correspondent.

Perhaps the least bad advice I can give to my correspondent at the present time is to buy six-month Treasury bills (which, unfortunately, are now available only in denominations of $10,000 or more —another measure by the Treasury to "protect" the small investor!), hold them to maturity and replace them. This combines safety of principal, low transactions costs, a higher yield (currently, about 7.5 percent) than he can get on other fixed-value securities of equal safety, and a high degree of flexibility. If inflation speeds up, interest rates will rise, and he will not be locked into existing rates as he would be if he held long-term bonds. Of course, if inflation slows, interest rates will fall, but so will the erosion of his principal.

This is an unsatisfactory answer. But *as things stand*, there is no satisfactory answer. We badly need to develop institutional arrangements that will provide the small saver with an inflation-proof asset with assured real yield and that will reduce in other ways as well the ravages of inflation.[1] But that is fodder for another column.

Perspective on Inflation
[June 24, 1974]

Double-digit inflation is the new scare word. We are warned that it is here to stay. Predictions that inflation will be "only" 6 or 7 percent by the end of the year are greeted as wildly optimistic.

As one who believes that inflation is a serious danger to our society, I deplore this widespread lack of perspective. I fear that exaggerating and misrepresenting the current situation will weaken our will to meet the real problem.

True, computed price-index numbers record double-digit inflation in early 1974. But these computed price-index numbers overstate the "real" inflation. To see why they do, it is necessary to consider the whole period since Aug. 15, 1971, when President Nixon froze prices and wages. Shortly thereafter, I wrote in this space: "Officially computed index numbers . . . will . . . show a dramatic improvement . . . and depart increasingly from reality. . . . How will it end? Sooner or later . . . as all previous attempts to freeze prices and wages have ended . . . in utter failure and the emergence into the open of suppressed inflation" (*Newsweek*, Aug. 30, 1971).

---

[1] [Since this column was written two developments in the private financial markets have provided additional alternatives. One is the establishment of mutual funds specializing in short term market instruments such as Treasury bills, large bank CD's, and commercial paper. The other is the issuance of so-called floating-rate notes by Citicorp and other institutions paying an interest rate linked to the market rate on Treasury bills.]

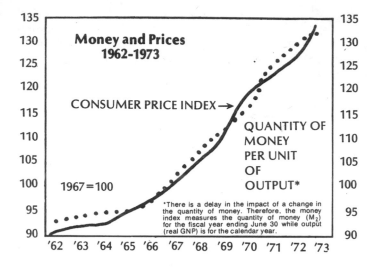

Money and Prices 1962–1973

CONSUMER PRICE INDEX →

QUANTITY OF MONEY PER UNIT OF OUTPUT*

1967 = 100

*There is a delay in the impact of a change in the quantity of money. Therefore, the money index measures the quantity of money (M₂) for the fiscal year ending June 30 while output (real GNP) is for the calendar year.

'62 '63 '64 '65 '66 '67 '68 '69 '70 '71 '72 '73

Precisely that has occurred. The recent explosion in the index reflects largely the unveiling of previously suppressed price increases. The recorded rate of inflation was below the true rate in late 1971 and 1972. It has been above the true rate since mid-1973. This is primarily a catch-up.

The catch-up will no doubt carry too far, but we should shortly be back to the basic underlying inflation of about 6 percent per year. That should be an occasion for concern, not for congratulation. Inflation was running at only 4.5 percent in 1971 when political pressures "forced" President Nixon to freeze prices and wages.

But you will reproach me: what of oil and food to which every government official has pointed? Are they not the obvious immediate cause of the price explosion? Not at all. It is essential to distinguish changes in *relative* prices from changes in *absolute* prices. The special conditions that drove up the prices of oil and food required purchasers to spend more on them, leaving less to spend on other items. Did that not force other prices to go down or to rise less rapidly than otherwise? Why should the *average* level of all prices be affected significantly by changes in the prices of some things relative to others? Thanks to delays in adjustment, the rapid rises in oil and food prices may have temporarily raised the rate of inflation somewhat. In the main, however, they have been convenient excuses for besieged government officials and harried journalists rather than reasons for the price explosion.

The basic source of inflation is the faster growth in the quantity of money than in output. From the fourth quarter of 1970 (the final quarter of the 1970 recession) to the fourth quarter of 1973 (the final quarter of the subsequent expansion) the quantity of money (M_2 = currency plus all commercial bank deposits other than large CD's) grew at the average rate of 10.4 percent per year; output (GNP at constant prices) at 5.5 percent. The growth rate of money exceeded that of output by 4.9 percentage points which, by no coincidence, is almost precisely equal to the rate of inflation in consumer prices (5.1 percent). However, the 5.1 percent is an average of 3.4 percent for the first two years, when inflation was being suppressed by controls, and 8.4 percent for the final year.

The same story is told by the chart that plots for the past twelve years consumer prices and the ratio of the quantity of money to output, both expressed as index numbers with 1967 = 100. Prices have clearly danced to the tune of money. But in 1972, the price index fell below the monetary ratio; in 1973, it overshot the monetary ratio.

For the long pull, averaging booms with recessions, we cannot expect output to grow by more than about 4 percent per year. If the relation that has prevailed between money and prices for the past dozen years continues,[1] and if the Federal Reserve continues to permit the quantity of money to grow by 10 percent a year, inflation will proceed at a rate of about 6 percent. Judged not by pronouncements, not by intentions, but by performance, that is the rate that monetary policy for the past four years has been directed at producing.

Like you, and like the Fed, I regard 6 percent inflation as much too high. I therefore welcome the Federal Reserve's announced intention to reduce the rate of monetary growth. Unfortunately, there is as yet little sign of any change in performance. The widespread impression that the Fed has tightened is based on the mistake of judging monetary policy by interest rates, which the Fed cannot control, rather than by the quantity of money, which it can. The quantity of money is still growing as rapidly as it has for the past four years.

The future well-being of this country depends critically on whether, this time, intentions are translated promptly into performance.

[1] It has prevailed for as far back as the data go, which is more than 100 years for the U.S. and Japan, 90 years for Britain, and shorter periods for other countries. However, the relation in the U.S. for the past dozen years is closer than the average relation.

Dealing With Discontent
[August 19, 1974]

Inflation, 12 percent; unemployment, 5.3 percent; second-quarter economic growth, minus 1.2 percent. These key statistics describe our current economic troubles. Yet they deal only with symptoms. They do not reveal the fundamental economic problem that President Ford inherits.

That problem is reflected in a very different set of statistics:

—From 1955 to 1965, output per person in the U.S. rose by 20 percent; real spendable weekly earnings of the average worker rose by 15 percent.

—From 1965 to the second quarter of 1974, output per person rose by 23 percent—or by more than in the prior decade—but real spendable weekly earnings did not rise at all; they are today actually lower than they were in 1965.

Herein is the real source of our present discontent.

How can it be that output rose yet real spendable earnings fell? Part of the answer is that an ever-higher fraction of the nation's total goods and services has been diverted from producers to nonproducers—through direct government spending and through governmentally imposed private spending for such things as safety and environmental devices.

Inflation has not caused the diversion; it has simply been one means of achieving. it. If producers—the workers who furnish the labor, the managers who coordinate the labor, the investors who provide the tools—have disposed of a declining fraction of total output, some mechanisms must have channeled an increasing fraction into other hands. Explicit taxes were one such mechanism, but legislating higher taxes is not a politically popular pastime. Borrowing from the public is another such mechanism, but that tends to drive up interest rates. Inflation is a third mechanism that no one openly supports yet that political authorities find seductive. It is a hidden tax that no representative or senator needs to vote for. It is collected efficiently, automatically and silently. That is why since time immemorial it has been resorted to by every sovereign who has sought to command a larger share of his nation's output than his subjects would voluntarily spare him.

We could deal with inflation itself—and should have done so long since—by imposing additional explicit taxes and by borrowing more from the public instead of financing government spending by inflationary creation of money. But that would not touch the major problem that makes the one or the other necessary—the diversion of output from producers to nonproducers, which creates widespread dissatisfaction and, by impairing the incentive to produce, threatens future growth.

President Ford can deal with that major problem in only one fundamental way: by persuading Congress to reduce direct and indirect levies on output.

Reduction of direct levies means a reduction in government spending—a real reduction, not a token reduction, a reduction in this year's spending compared with last year's, not a reduction from a proposed $30 billion increase in the budget to a $25 billion increase. There is ample room for reduction, given the will. Every government program is for a "good" objective, but there is hardly one that gives the taxpayer his money's worth.

Reduction of indirect levies means a reduction in government impositions on private spending. The dollars that private enterprises and individuals are required to spend for environmental and other purposes are no less a drain on output because they come from private pockets than they would be if they came directly from government coffers. "Environment" and "safety" are fine objectives, but they have become sacred cows about which it is almost heresy to ask whether the return justifies the cost.

Another indirect levy is the growing tide of government guarantees of credit and direct loans for housing, producers of beef, badly run railroads, banks and other enterprises. This indirect levy is particularly serious because it encroaches on the limited resources available to add to productive capital. Where will the funds come from to pay for the new equipment that we need to continue the growth in total output?

Here is President Ford's challenge. Here too is his opportunity. The public is ahead of its "elected" leaders. It recognizes increasingly that it has been taken to the cleaners, that bigger government is not better government, that there is no magic wand that can produce something for nothing. It is fed up with high explicit taxes. It is fed up also with the hidden tax of inflation. It recognizes that it cannot get rid of these taxes without withdrawal pains. It is ready to bite the bullet. It awaits only strong leadership.

Public Employment
[September 2, 1974]

It is by now widely recognized that there is no way to end inflation without a temporary slowdown in economic growth and a temporary increase in unemployment. In the search for measures to reduce these costs of stemming inflation, "public employment" has been receiving increasing attention. A typical proposal is that Congress appropriate in advance $4 billion to $5 billion or more a year to hire extra government employees, the program to be put into operation automatically when unemployment reaches a designated figure such as 5.5 or 6.0 percent.

The program has great appeal. It appears to offer a way in which the government, while acting to halt inflation, can keep down the higher unemployment that is the most undesirable side effect of such action. But this appeal is spurious. It comes from looking only at the direct effects of the policy and neglecting its indirect effects. When both are taken into account, it turns out that "public employment" would increase, not decrease, the cost of stemming inflation.

The neglect of indirect effects is a common source of economic fallacies. Let me illustrate by an example that is more transparent because by now we have had so much experience with it. In the past several decades we have been troubled by "urban blight." An appealing "solution" is to tear down the slums and rebuild them—whence came the massive "urban renewal" program. What happened? Slums were indeed torn down, which seemed all to the good, but, in the process, housing occupied by lower-income groups was demolished and replaced by nonresidential structures or by a smaller amount of middle- or upper-income housing. The total number of dwelling units was reduced, but the number of people requiring housing was not affected. Persons displaced by urban renewal had to look for housing elsewhere, which created slums where none had existed before. The program deserves the name it received of "Negro removal." It has added to "urban blight," not solved it.

"Public employment" suffers from precisely the same defect. It would in the first instance provide jobs for the unemployed, which seems all to the good. But where would the funds come from to pay their wages?

If the funds came from reducing other government expenditures, new government employees would simply replace other government employees with no gain in total employment and very likely a loss in efficiency.

If the funds came from imposing higher taxes, the taxpayers would have less to spend, which would reduce the number of persons they employ directly or indirectly. New government employees would simply replace persons employed in the private sector. "Make-work" would replace employment that met the private demands of taxpayers.

If the funds came from borrowing from the public, less credit would be available to lend to others. New government employees would simply replace persons employed in building houses or factories or machines that would have been financed by savings now absorbed by the public-employment program. Make-work would replace employment devoted to adding to our productive wealth.

The only other source of finance is printing or creating money. In this case, government demand would add to private demand and could create new jobs. But then it would be inflationary and so would undo with the left hand what the right hand was striving to achieve—namely, less inflation. The whole purpose is, after all, to reduce the rate at which total spending is increasing—for that is the only way that inflation can be stemmed. If extra demand from "public employment" is desirable, then anti-inflation measures are being pushed too hard. It would be better simply to ease up on these measures than to offset one mistake with another.

We have a responsibility to keep to a minimum the costs of ending inflation, and to assure that the disadvantaged do not bear a major part of those costs. The best way to minimize the withdrawal costs is by the widespread use of escalator clauses. The best way to protect the disadvantaged is by improving our system of welfare and of insurance against long-term unemployment. These measures are desirable for the long pull and not only for our present problem.

Throwing some people out of work in order to give jobs to others may have great political appeal. But it makes no economic sense.

Chapter Five
Wage and Price Controls

Wage and price controls were imposed on August 15, 1971, largely in response to widespread dissatisfaction with the slow rate at which inflation was tapering off—or, perhaps more accurately, widespread failure to recognize that inflation was tapering off, at whatever rate. Phase I, a ninety-day freeze, was followed by Phase II, a more flexible system involving a Price Board and a Wage Board which had to approve increases above a specified minimum in industries and concerns subject to their control. As the strains under Phase II began to accumulate, it was replaced in early 1973 by Phase III, which lifted most controls. The simultaneous explosion in food prices, never under controls, produced a very bad press for Phase III, and on June 11, 1973, the President imposed a new wage and price freeze in the form of Phase IV, which I labelled "A Monumental Folly" (June 25, 1973). But, to paraphrase the remark legend attributes to Galileo after the recantation of his heliocentric views ("eppur si muove!"), inflation roared on, oblivious of the passing phases.

The utter failure of price and wage controls finally led Congress to permit the legislation allowing them to elapse. My negative reaction to each imposition of controls, and my applause for each weakening, is recorded in successive columns in this chapter (as also in some columns in earlier chapters). However, it would be premature to suppose that we have truly learned our lesson. Price controls have been imposed repeatedly for more than two thousand years. They have always failed, yet they have been repeatedly resurrected. The reimposition of controls in Britain, discussed in "A Cold Day for Britain" (November 27, 1972), is a recent example and already it has largely followed the pattern of prior examples, ending in an accelerated inflation, widespread industrial distress, and the

120

defeat of the Conservative government. I doubt that we in the United States have seen the last of price and wage controls.

One fairly modern argument given for price and wage controls is that inflation is produced by the concentrated power of business and labor monopolies, so that controlling a small number of strategic prices will suffice to control the price level in general. This argument seems impervious to the evidence that prices of products produced by the concentrated industries have on the average risen less rapidly than other products or indeed may even have fallen. It is equally impervious to the evidence that wages of unionized labor typically lag behind wages of nonunionized labor in the early stages of an accelerated inflation and catch up only later.

Unfortunately, this argument raises issues that are too complex to deal with satisfactorily in a brief column. Hence the reader of this book will not find an adequate explanation of the reasons why I believe that unions and monopolies, which do immense harm to society in many ways, are largely innocent of causing inflation. Mostly they simply respond to inflationary pressure coming from Washington, though they may increase the difficulty of tapering off inflation and may lengthen the transition from a higher to a lower rate of inflation. But even in these respects I believe that their role is minor compared with the part played by governmentally-imposed obstacles.

Most discussions of price and wage controls have dealt with their economic consequences. But controls have also disturbing political and ethical consequences. Indeed, my opposition to them derives even more from their political than from their economic consequences, as I made clear in two columns that I contributed to the Op-Ed page of the *New York Times* in October 1971 and that are here reprinted as a single entry.

Burns and Guidelines
[June 15, 1970]

Arthur Burns has long been an outspoken, principled, and consistent opponent of wage and price guidelines or controls. As a result, he created a sensation when, in a recent speech, he remarked that "an incomes policy, provided it stopped well short of direct price and wage controls and was used merely as a supplement to over-all monetary and fiscal measures, might speed us through this transitional period of cost-push inflation."

Burns's earlier criticisms of wage and price guidelines came during periods of rising excess demand. His support for an incomes policy today comes during a period of declining excess demand. Circumstances do alter cases, yet I remain persuaded that an incomes policy, in any shape or form, is a dangerous expedient.

When excess demand is pulling prices up, wage and price controls work against the basic forces. If firms and unions in some sector of industry are induced or compelled to hold prices or wages down, that is like pinching one corner of a large balloon. The lucky buyers of the goods pay less and have more left to spend elsewhere—driving other prices up still higher and not reducing over-all inflation at all. Jobs in the industry become unattractive, so it will be short of labor. The amount produced will be less than the amount demanded, so buyers will have to be rationed somehow. Distortion of output, black markets, government controls, inefficiency—these are the clearly predictable results. Repressed inflation rolls merrily on, doing far more harm than open inflation. This is the argument that Arthur Burns has always made against wage and price guidelines.

Suppose, however, that monetary and fiscal policies have altered—as they have in the past year in the U.S.—to reduce excess demand. Wages and prices will still rise for a time because of inertia and inflationary expectations. If monetary and fiscal restraint persists, these higher wages and prices will prove inconsistent with the basic forces. They will mean unemployment and underproduction. Yet, the stickiness of wages and prices will make it hard to get them back down. If persuasion, a little judicious arm twisting, could prevent the initial rise in prices and wages, even the persons whose arms were twisted would be grateful afterward. Incomes policy would have contributed to "speed us through this transitional period of cost-push inflation."

This is the intellectual case for "incomes policy." Why do I reject it?

Exhortation by high government officials will not persuade businessmen or labor leaders that inflation is on the way out. They have vivid memories of similar exhortations in the past that were belied by subsequent experience. As a result, an incomes policy that did stop "well short of price and wage controls" would have little effect on anything.

If an "incomes policy" is to have an appreciable effect, it must go beyond talk. We know what that means. Threats of political reprisals or of income tax investigations, withholding of government contracts, and similar politically corrupting exercises of extralegal powers. Or the establishment of formal wage and price controls with arrangements for appeals and all the rest of the cumbrous bureaucratic machinery. In either case, the "transitional period" would be over before the machinery was set up. And how then do we get rid of it?

The way to eliminate inflationary expectations is not by talk but by demonstrating that inflation is tapering off and will continue to do so. The right policy is: (a) moderate monetary expansion; (b) moderate fiscal restraint; (c) complete avoidance of price and wage controls. These policies will work and will bring inflation to an end. They will also provide the basis for a sound expansion without inflation. We need patience and persistence, not gimmicks.

Central banks (like the rest of us) have a tendency to try to shift responsibility and blame to others for economic troubles. The favorite tactic of the Fed in earlier days was "moral suasion" in the field of credit—appeals to banks not to make "speculative" or inflationary loans. Today central bankers worldwide blame fiscal policy, on the one hand, and propose the exercise of "moral suasion" on business and labor, on the other.

It is disheartening to observe so tough-minded, so independent, and so knowledgeable a person as Arthur Burns conform to this pattern so soon after becoming chairman of the Fed.

Imitating Failure
[January 11, 1971]

The Johnson Administration tried wage-price guidelines. The guidelines failed and were abandoned. The British tried a wage-price board. It failed and has just been abolished. The Canadians tried voluntary wage-price controls. Their Prices and Incomes Commission recently announced the program was unworkable and would be abandoned January 1.

Yet, in the U.S., the Committee for Economic Development, an influential organization of businessmen, issues a report recommending (though with some vigorous dissents) a wage-price board on British lines and voluntary wage-price controls on Canadian lines. Arthur F. Burns, chairman of the Federal Reserve Board, supports the recommendation for a wage-price board. The Council of Economic Advisers' second "inflation alert" uses stronger adjectives than the first to describe price developments. Mr. Nixon, in a speech to the National Association of Manufacturers, tries mild jawboning, calling on labor and business to exercise restraint in the national interest.

Surely, this must mean that the experience of the Johnson Administration, of Britain, and of Canada is the exception, that there are other examples of the successful use of incomes policy to slow inflation. Not at all. I do not know a single successful example and the current proponents of an incomes policy do not claim that they do. The refrain is rather, "despite the limited success of these measures elsewhere, they offer promise."

If the promise is not based on direct experience, is it based on economic analysis? Hardly. Economic analysis largely reinforces experience. It suggests that voluntary wage and price controls are likely to be honored in the breach—because those who observe them will suffer at the expense of those who do not—and that compulsory wage and price controls simply repress rather than eliminate inflationary pressure. The only analytical case for wage-price control is to shorten the delayed impact of an inflationary episode after excess demand has been eliminated, not temporarily, but for good (see my *Newsweek* column, June 15, 1970). That case is indeed cited by proponents of incomes policy, but it is a weak reed, since most of them regard the incomes policy as a *substitute* for demand restraint, not a supplement. The policy is based on neither experience nor analysis but simply on the "For God's sake, let's do something" syndrome.

The talk about incomes policy reflects a general tendency: the belief that there is a sugar-coated pill for every economic and social ill, and that only malice and ill will prevent its use. Time and again, I have had anguished letters from sincere readers to the effect, "Since you acknowledge that there is a real problem, it is irresponsible of you to criticize a proposed solution unless you offer an alternative. What is your solution?"

Suppose an expert on cancer criticized a proposed cure. Would any of my correspondents regard him as irresponsible because he did not offer an alternative cure? Why is economics different? In economics, as in medicine, we have imperfect knowledge. Some ills we cannot cure at all, and some only with undesirable side effects. In economics, as in medicine, our knowledge will improve further but there will always remain unsolved problems of both kinds.

We know very well how to cure inflation: by restricting the growth of money demand through monetary and fiscal policy. At present, we know no other way to do it. We know also that this cure has the unpleasant side effect of a recession and of temporarily higher unemployment. We do not know how to avoid this side effect. There have been many inflations in history. I know of none that has ever been stopped in any other way or that has been stopped without temporary economic difficulties.

In the present episode, monetary and fiscal restraint have been working as they always do. The rate of inflation is slowing down and will continue to do so if restraint is maintained. As always, a side effect has been a recession. So far, it has been mild, milder indeed than past experience gave us any reason to expect. We have been attacking the severest U.S. inflation on record except in time of major war; yet we have experienced one of the mildest recessions in our history.

But standards of performance have been driven so unrealistically high that an extremely successful policy, as judged by past experience, is widely regarded as a major failure. What a triumph of rhetoric over reality.

Why the Freeze Is a Mistake
[August 30, 1971]

I applaud President Nixon's proposed reductions in both taxes and federal spending. I applaud also his action in ending the fiction that the dollar is convertible into gold. But I regret exceedingly that he decided to impose a ninety-day freeze on prices and wages. That is one of those "very plausible schemes," to quote what Edmund Burke said in a different connection, "with very pleasing commencements, [that] have often shameful and lamentable conclusions."

Freezing individual prices and wages in order to halt inflation is like freezing the rudder of a boat and making it impossible to steer, in order to correct a tendency for the boat to drift one degree off course. The "price level" has been rising at something like 4 percent per year, or one-third of 1 percent per month, or 1 percent in ninety days. Surely, you will say, preventing so minor a rise can do no harm. Why the outcry? Because the 1 percent is the average of changes in literally millions of individual prices, some rising 10 or 20 percent or more, others falling 10 or 20 percent or more. These price changes reflect changes in conditions of demand and supply affecting particular goods and services. They are the way that we steer the economy. Preventing them leaves the economy rudderless, yet it does nothing to alter the basic force producing the average 1 percent rise in prices. That basic force is a more rapid rise in money demand for goods and services than in the physical supply.

Of course, individual price and wage changes will not be prevented. In the main, price changes will simply be concealed by taking the form of changes in discounts, service, and quality, and wage changes, in overtime, perquisites and so on. Even 60,000 bureaucrats backed by 300,000 volunteers plus widespread patriotism were unable during World War Two to cope with the ingenuity of millions of people in finding ways to get around price and wage controls that conflicted with their individual sense of justice. The present, jerry-built freeze will be even less successful.

But to whatever extent the freeze is enforced, it will do harm by distorting relative prices.

The freeze has reminded me forcefully of a personal experience during World War Two, when I was working for the U.S. Treasury Department. In the course of a presentation to the House Ways and Means Committee on the need for additional taxes to prevent inflation, I was interrupted by one member who exclaimed, "Why do we need to worry about inflation in considering taxes? We have just passed General Max [the measure that put a ceiling on all wages and prices]. It is now up to Leon Henderson [director of the Office of Price Administration] to control inflation." I had barely embarked on a learned discourse about how General Max would not work unless it was reinforced by measures to reduce purchasing power, when he interrupted me again. "I understand that," he said. "Mr. Henderson may fail, but we have discharged our responsibility by giving him the power. Now it's up to him."

Similarly today, every proponent of more government spending who had been restrained by fear that the spending would be inflationary will breathe a sigh of relief and say, "Full speed ahead. The price freeze will hold back inflation." The proponents of tax cuts, and even the Federal Reserve Board, which deserves most of the blame for producing the inflation, will react similarly. The result is likely to be more inflationary pressure, not less.[1]

[1] [And so it was.]

Whatever happens to the *actual* cost of products to customers or of labor to employers, *stated* prices and *stated* wages will be largely frozen. These are the prices and wages that enter into officially computed index numbers. These numbers will therefore show a dramatic improvement —and depart increasingly from reality. If the freeze were simply ended after ninety days, the indexes would spurt, even though the prices actually charged and the wages actually paid did not. This will create a dilemma for Mr. Nixon. He has a tiger by the tail. Reluctant as he was to grasp it, he will find it hard to let go. The outcome, I fear, will be a further move toward the kind of detailed control of prices and wages that Mr. Nixon has resisted so courageously for so long. [1]

How will it end? Sooner or later, and the sooner the better, it will end as all previous attempts to freeze prices and wages have ended, from the time of the Roman emperor Diocletian to the present, in utter failure and the emergence into the open of the suppressed inflation. Fortunately, as Adam Smith once put it, "There is much ruin in a nation."

Will the Kettle Explode?
[October 18, 1971]

The most serious potential danger of the new economic policy is that, under cover of the price controls, inflationary pressures will accumulate, the controls will collapse, inflation will burst out anew, perhaps sometime in 1973, and the reaction to the inflation will produce a severe recession.[2] This go-stop sequence, though not inevitable, is highly likely.

The freeze and the phase-two controls outlined by the President are like putting a brick on top of a boiling kettle to keep the lid from blowing off. If, simultaneously, the flame under the kettle is turned down, the brick may prevent the lid from blowing off. But if the flame is turned up, the pressure will build until the lid blows off or the kettle explodes.

Practically all economists, even those most favorable to price and wage controls, would accept this analogy. Disagreements are about what the

---

[1] [And so it was.]
[2] [To date (July, 1974) this prediction has been fulfilled except that so far, the recession has been mild, not severe.]

flame consists of—whether, as I believe, primarily of monetary expansion, or, as many other economists believe, also of government deficits and union and business power. These disagreements are important for some purposes but they do not affect the analysis of this column, since all agree that money is part of the flame.

One thing is crystal clear. The new economic policy means larger deficits. The President wisely recommended an equal reduction in taxes and spending. But Congress has already moved to cut taxes more, and spending less, than he recommended. The pressure for economy is off. Price, wage, and now also interest, dividend, and profit controls are there to handle inflation. Congress can forget about it. The deficits that were looming before the President spoke on August 15 will become even larger. This flame is surely being turned up.

If monetary policy were also to be highly expansive, the controls would collapse, as they always have under similar circumstances. The repressed inflation would become open inflation. Index numbers of reported prices would start rising rapidly—no matter what happens to actual prices.

I cannot believe that the American public would accept rapid, open inflation without a vigorous reaction. It would demand that something be done. The only possible courses of action are the reimposition of controls, this time far more widespread, detailed, and stringent; or sharply deflationary monetary and fiscal measures. The first would at best be a temporary expedient that would severely strain the economic and social structure; the second would produce a recession. Moreover, the recession would have to be more severe than in 1970 in order to stem inflation. The belief that inflation is the way of the future would be held even more strongly, and the rate of inflation would be even higher.

The only hope of preventing this dismal outcome rests with the Federal Reserve System. We are clearly not going to have fiscal restraint. If the flame under the kettle is to be turned down at all, it will have to be by monetary restraint. If monetary growth could be held to something like 5 percent per year for the next two years, it might be possible to dismantle the controls without unleashing a new burst of inflation.

One encouraging sign is that the quantity of money has grown slowly for the past several months, after exploding earlier in the year. However, this lull may prove temporary. Whenever nonmonetary forces are lowering interest rates, the Fed tends to expand the money supply less than it intends. That was the case these past few months. Whenever nonmonetary forces are raising interest rates, the Fed tends to expand the money supply more than it intends. That was the case earlier this year. Despite the new controls, it is likely to be the case again in 1972 as vigorous expansion and a large federal deficit combine to raise interest rates.[1]

This behavior of the money supply reflects the Fed's continued attempt to ride two horses at once—interest rates and money supply. There have been signs that the Fed was mending its ways and putting more stress on the money supply. But now, in naming Arthur Burns to head the committee on interest and dividends, the President has sharpened the Fed's dilemma. Burns may be able to twist the arms of commercial bankers to hold down the prime rate. But he and the Fed can keep market rates down only by rapid monetary expansion—and even then only temporarily. If the Fed follows this route the kettle is certain to explode.

Morality and Controls*
Part I [October 28, 1971]

Most discussion of the wage-price freeze and the coming Phase II controls has been strictly economic and operational: were they needed, will they work, how will they operate. I have recorded my own opposition to them in three columns in *Newsweek*.

There has been essentially no discussion of a much more fundamental issue. The controls are deeply and inherently immoral. By substituting the rule of men for the rule of law and for voluntary cooperation in the marketplace, the controls threaten the very foundations of a free society. By encouraging men to spy and report on one another, by making it in the private interest of large numbers of citizens to evade the controls, and by making actions illegal that are in the public interest, the controls undermine individual morality.

One of the proudest achievements of Western civilization was the substitution of the rule of law for the rule of men. The ideal is that government restrictions on our behavior shall take the form of impersonal rules, applicable to all alike, and interpreted and adjudicated by an independent judiciary rather than of specific orders by a government official to named

[1] [And so it was.]
*The New York Times.

individuals. In principle, under the rule of law, each of us can know what he may or may not do by consulting the law and determining how it applies to his own circumstances.

The rule of law does not guarantee freedom, since general laws as well as personal edicts can be tyrannical. But increasing reliance on the rule of law clearly played a major role in transforming Western society from a world in which the ordinary citizen was literally subject to the arbitrary will of his master to a world in which the ordinary citizen could regard himself as his own master.

The ideal was, of course, never fully attained. More important, we have been eroding the rule of law slowly and steadily for decades as government has become more and more a participant in economic affairs rather than primarily a rule-maker, referee, and enforcer of private contracts. It was, after all, the development of the private market that made possible the original movement from a world of status to a world of voluntary contract. As government has tried to replace the market in one area after another, it has inevitably been driven to restore a world of status.

The freeze and even more the pay board and price board of the Phase II controls are clearly another massive step away from the rule of law and back toward the rule of men. True, the rule of men will be *under* law but that is a far cry from the rule *of* law—Stalin, Hitler, Mussolini, and now Kosygin, Mao, and Franco all rule under law.

The price that you and I may charge for our goods or our labor or that we may pay others for their goods or their labor will now be determined, not by any set of legislated standards applying to all alike, but by specific orders by a small number of men appointed by the President. And if governmental edict is to replace market contract, there is no alternative. There are millions of prices, millions of wage rates arrived at by voluntary agreements among millions of people. The collectivistic countries have been unable in decades to find simple rules enabling prices and wages to be established by any alternative impersonal mechanism. We are not likely to succeed. And we are not trying. Instead, the appeal is to the patriotism, civic responsibility, and judgment of political appointees, most of whom represent vested interests. How do patriotism and judgment determine that the price of a widget may rise 2.8 percent but the price of a wadget, only 0.3 percent; the wage of a widgeteer by 2 percent but of a wadgeteer, by 10 percent? Clearly they do not. Arbitrary judgment, political power, visibility—these are what will matter.

The tendency for such an approach to violate human freedom is even more clearly exemplified by the present situation with respect to dividends. The President has *requested* firms not to raise dividends—he has no legal power to do more. The request has been accompanied by surveillance, a calling down to Washington and public lambasting of the handful of corporations that did not conform, and a clear implied threat to use extralegal powers. These measures have no legal basis at all. Yet I know of only one small company that has had the courage to refuse to cooperate on grounds of principle.

The full logic of the system will not work itself out this time. Our strong tradition of freedom, the ineffectiveness of the controls, the ingenuity of the people in finding ways around them—these will lead to the collapse of the controls rather than to their hardening into a full-fledged straitjacket. But nonetheless, it is disheartening to see us take this further long step on the road to tyranny so lightheartedly, so utterly unaware that we are doing something fundamentally in conflict with the basic principles on which this country is founded. The first time, we may venture only a small way. But the next time, and the next time?

Part II (October 29, 1971)
Enforcement of the price and wage controls, as of the freeze, must depend heavily on encouraging ordinary citizens to be informers—to report "violations" to government officials.

When you and I make a private deal, both of us benefit—otherwise we do not have to make it. We are partners, cooperating voluntarily with one another. The terms, so long as they are mutually agreeable, should be our business. But not any longer. Big Brother is looking over our shoulders. And if the terms do not correspond with what he says is O.K., one of us is encouraged to turn in the other. And to turn him in for doing something few people have ever regarded and do not now regard as in any sense morally wrong; on the contrary, for doing something that each of us regards, when it affects us, as our basic right. Am I not entitled to sell my goods or my labor for what I consider them worth as long as I do not coerce anyone to buy? Is it morally wrong for Chile to expropriate the property of Anaconda Copper—i.e., to force it to sell its copper mines for a price less than its value; but morally right for the U.S. government to force the worker to sell his labor for less than its value to him and to his employer?

By any standards, the edicts of the pay board and the price board, like the initial freeze, will be full of inequities and will be judged to be by ever increasing numbers of people. You believe that you are entitled to a pay raise, your employer agrees and wishes to give you one, yet the pay board says no. Will there not be a great temptation to find a way around the ruling? By a promotion unaccompanied by any change in duties but to a job title carrying a higher permitted pay. Or by your employer providing you with amenities you formerly paid for. Or by one or another of the innumerable stratagems—legal, quasi-legal, or illegal—that ingenious men devise to protect themselves from snooping bureaucrats.

In general, I have little sympathy with trade unions. They have done immense harm by restricting access to jobs, denying excluded workers the opportunity to make the most of their abilities, and forcing them to take less satisfactory jobs. Yet surely in the present instance they are right that it is inequitable for the government retroactively to void contracts freely arrived at. The way to reduce the monopoly power of unions is to remove the special legal immunities they are now granted, not to replace one concentrated power by another.

When men do not regard governmental measures as just and right they will find a way around them. The effects extend beyond the original source, generate widespread disrespect for the law, and promote corruption and violence. We found this out to our cost in the 1920s with Prohibition; in World War Two with price control and rationing; today with drug laws. We shall experience it yet again with price and wage controls if they are ever more than a paper facade.

One feature of price and wage controls makes their effect on individual morality especially vicious. Because these controls distort the use of resources, the evader benefits not only himself but society. The more rigorously the controls are enforced, the more harm they do. They render behavior which is immoral from one point of view socially beneficial. They thus introduce the kind of fundamental moral conflict that is utterly destructive of social cohesion.

Our markets are far from completely free. Monopoly power of labor and business means that prices and wages are not wholly the product of voluntary contract. Yet these blemishes, real and important though they are, are minor compared to replacing market agreements by government edict, compared to giving arbitrary power to a small number of appointed officials, compared to inculcating in the public contempt for the law.

The excuse for the destruction of liberty is always the plea of necessity—that there is no alternative. If indeed, the economy were in a state of crisis, of a life-and-death emergency, and if controls promised a sure way out, all their evil social and moral effects might be a price that would have to be paid for survival. But not even the gloomiest observer of the economic scene would describe it in any such terms. Prices rising at 4 percent a year, unemployment at a level of 6 percent—these are higher than we would like to have or than we need to have, but they are very far indeed from crisis levels. On the contrary, they are rather moderate by historical standards. And there is far from uniform agreement that wage and price controls will improve matters. I happen to believe that they will make matters worse after an initial deceptive period of apparent success. Others disagree. But even their warmest defenders recognize that they impose costs, produce distortions in the use of resources, and may fail to reduce inflation. Under such circumstances, the moral case surely deserves at least some attention.

Controls: An Exercise in Futility
[May 22, 1972]

The accompanying fever chart of inflation can be used for a parlor game. Just cover up the dates at the bottom and try to guess when the most momentous change in economic policy in the past quarter century was introduced in order to halt inflation. On the basis of the chart alone, you would surely pick October 1970. In the next six months, the rate of inflation fell more sharply than in any other six-month period since the peak of inflation in early 1970 (from 5.8 percent to 4.3 percent, or by 1.5 percentage points). But of course that is the wrong date. The right date is August 1971, when President Nixon froze prices and wages. In the next six months, the rate of inflation fell less than half as much as in the six months after October 1970 (from 4.4 percent to 3.7 percent, or by 0.7 percentage point).

This comparison is not entirely fair, since I picked the first six-month period by hindsight, but it does dramatize two important facts: first, despite all the hoopla in the summer of 1971 about the lack of progress against inflation, there clearly had been a systematic and substantial tapering off of inflation since early 1970; second, despite the extravagant claims for the price and wage controls and the political hurricanes that have swirled about them, the statistics give no sign that price and wage controls have had any appreciable effect on the course of inflation. The recent modest tapering off, like the earlier tapering off, reflects the delayed influence of the restrictive monetary policy of 1969 and the subsequent recession of 1970, not the effect of the controls. (Charts for wholesale prices and for wage rates tell much the same story as the chart for consumer prices.)

Does this mean that the wage and price controls are nothing but a modern Potemkin village that have no real effects on the economy? Hardly. The controls have had appreciable, and adverse, effects on output and on productivity. Most important of all, the controls have significantly eroded your freedom and mine, significantly extended the power of Big Brother over our lives.

The immediate effect of the new economic policy was to chill the recovery then under way by introducing great uncertainty into the calculations of every businessman. The resulting hesitation in the economy during the final months of 1971 seems by now to have been largely overcome. Though further hesitation cannot be ruled out, the incredibly expansive fiscal and monetary policy of recent months almost surely spells a real boom in the final months of 1972. [1]

The controls affect productivity in three ways: (1) millions of manhours in government and industry devoted to administering controls constitute pure and unadulterated waste; (2) insofar as any wage rates are prevented from rising, workers have less incentive to do their best and employers are hampered in hiring as many and as high quality workers as they demand; (3) insofar as profit margins approach the permitted ceilings, businesses lose much of their incentive to keep down costs.

All three effects have been minor so far. Distortions develop only gradually, and the controls have so far been working with the economic tide.

The adverse effects on productivity are almost certain to become much more severe in the coming months. Whatever happens to the basic inflationary forces, distortions will accumulate, so that the backward-looking structure of prices, wages, and profit margins imposed by the price and pay boards will increasingly depart from market requirements.

[1] [And so they did.]

ANNUAL RATE OF INFLATION IN CONSUMER PRICES
(Percentage change in Consumer Price Index from same month a year earlier)

**Percentage changes over a twelve-month
period used to average out irregularities
and avoid problems of seasonal adjustment**

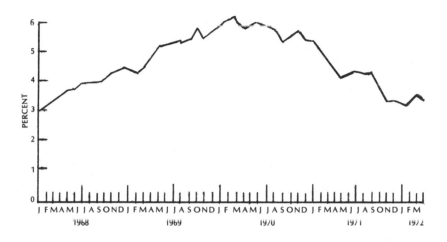

Equally important, it looks from the chart as if the tapering off of inflation has come to an end. For the past six months, the rate of inflation
has been roughly constant. And this observation is consistent with what
has been happening to monetary and fiscal policies. After being contractionary in 1969 and moderately expansive in 1970—which is what
produced the tapering off of inflation that we have had—monetary policy turned highly inflationary in early 1971 and has remained so ever
since, except for a notable interruption during the last five months of
1971. Fiscal policy has become increasingly expansionary throughout the
past year and a half, which will make it even harder for the Fed to restrain monetary growth. As a result, I believe that we are now poised for
a renewed acceleration of inflation. There will be erratic movements
from month to month, but from now on the trend of inflation is far more
likely to be up than down.[2] The controls will from now on be working
against the economic tide, not with it.

[2] [And so it was.]

In short, the worst is yet to come. But the record in the nine months since the imposition of the freeze is enough to show how fully justified President Nixon was in his long-held and courageously defended opposition to government intervention into the setting of prices and wages. What a shame—for himself and the country—that he finally gave in to the widespread, politically motivated pressure to impose controls.

A Cold Day for Britain
[November 27, 1972]

The wage and price freeze just imposed in Britain is almost a duplicate of the freeze that President Nixon imposed in the U.S. on August 15, 1971. But the circumstances under which prices were frozen are very different. As a result, the two actions will have very different results.

When President Nixon froze prices and wages, inflation was already receding in the U.S. The rate of rise of consumer prices had come down from nearly 7 percent in early 1970 to less than 4 percent in mid-1971. Inflation has continued to recede since, but the further improvement has been less than in the year and a half preceding the freeze.

The reduction in the pace of inflation was produced by the monetary and fiscal policies followed in 1969 and 1970—slower monetary growth reinforced by slower growth in government spending. These policies held down the increase in total spending which, in turn, put a damper on inflation, but also produced as an undesirable by-product the recession of 1970. There was no other effective way to stop the accelerating inflation that President Nixon had inherited.

The price freeze and the subsequent wage and price controls seemed to me, at the time, a mistake, and I am of the same opinion still. Yet, in their defense, it can be said that they worked with, not against, the trend of the basic economic forces. Indeed, one of my major objections to them—and one that has loomed ever larger since—is that they would be given credit for results that were attributable to other forces, and that, in consequence, the public would be misled into believing that they really are an effective way to halt inflation.

The U.S. episode was highly unusual. Price and wage controls have almost never been introduced when inflation and the excess demand producing it were tapering off. They have almost always been introduced under precisely the opposite conditions, to try to offset inflationary monetary and fiscal policies when the political will was lacking to change the monetary and fiscal policies themselves.

That is the current British situation. After tapering off from mid-1971 to mid-1972, inflation then started to accelerate rapidly—to a current rate of about 8 percent. The quantity of money has been on an explosive course. The narrowly defined money supply (currency and demand deposits), which was almost constant in 1969, has been rising at a 16 percent rate in the past six months; the broadly defined money supply (including time and savings deposits), which rose at a rate of 3 percent in 1969, has been rising at a 24 percent rate in the past six months. Government spending and deficits have similarly been growing rapidly.

It is one thing to freeze prices and wages when inflation is proceeding at a 3 to 4 percent rate and is already coming down. It is a very different thing to freeze them when inflation is proceeding at an 8 percent rate and heading still higher. Even if the freeze were accompanied by a drastic reduction in the rate of monetary growth and in government spending and deficits, it would be working against the underlying forces, since it takes many months before a change in monetary and fiscal policy can check an accelerating inflation. Yet in that case, there would at least be some restraining forces in the background. So far, however, there is little sign—outside of brave talk—that the Conservative government is prepared to reinforce the freeze with effective monetary and fiscal restraint.

Britain has been through all this before—during and after World War Two, when price and wage controls were used in an attempt to suppress the inflation arising from wartime spending, financed largely by increasing the money supply.

That attempt to bottle up excess demand produced shortages, queues, and rationing. Indeed, they were so prominent that the riddle went around: "Other nations have their national flags, national mottoes, national flowers; Britain is the only Western nation that has a national letter. What is it?" Answer: "Q."

Britain is on its way to repeating that experience[1]—unless the freeze and controls collapse entirely in the next few months, as they well may.

[1] [Which it did. The major economic crisis in early 1974, with the rate of inflation doubling to about 16 percent, led to a general election which the Conservative Party lost, Labour replacing it in power.]

It is hard to find the silver lining in this dark cloud. But perhaps the British experience will shock the public out of the view—which the U.S. freeze has done so much to spread—that controls are an effective—or at least harmless—way to curtail inflation.

Perspective on Controls
[January 29, 1973]

What hath price and wage controls wrought?
—A major reduction in the rate of inflation, to judge from much press commentary and economic pundity.
—A trvial effect on the rate of inflation, to judge from the cold statistics. Here they are for the cost-of-living-index number.

Annual rate of rise

At inflationary peak, early 1970	6.4 percent
First eight months of 1971	3.8 percent
Aug. 1971 to Nov. 1972	3.2 percent

The initial sharp tapering off in the rate of inflation clearly owes nothing to controls, which were introduced in August 1971. The trivial further decline—which came to an end in early 1972—may well have occurred despite rather than because of controls. But it is also possible that it understates the effect of controls. Perhaps, in the absence of controls, inflation would have speeded up instead of tapering off a mite further. Our instruments are too crude to enable us to make such judgments accurately. But one thing is crystal clear: whether controls lowered or raised the rate of inflation, the effect was minor in magnitude—it would be a bold man who would assess the effect at more than one percentage point.

How is it, that, despite all the fuss, the controls had so little effect?
1. Controls were introduced when inflation had already tapered off. Permitted wage and price increases averaged close to those that would have occurred anyway.

2. After the initial freeze, controls were highly selective. They covered, in anything more than name, well under half the economy—as measured by value of output, wages paid or any other broad yardstick. As a result, controls probably had a larger effect on specific sectors of the economy than on the economy as a whole.

For example, the controls clearly contributed to the rapid rise in food prices. Insofar as they held down the prices of automobiles or refrigerators or similar items, they left purchasers of such items with more to spend on other things, and this excess purchasing power naturally flowed to items exempt from control. Defenders of controls have pointed to rising food prices as an excuse for the failure of controls to hold down the cost of living as a whole—as if the rising food prices were independent of the controls!

Another example is the highly adverse effect of controls on the lumber industry. Booming demand has been prevented from raising prices and so has produced shortages, inefficiency, and distorted patterns of distribution.

President Nixon deserves high praise for reading the record correctly and eliminating most mandatory wage and price controls. But, you may ask, does the past impotence of the controls mean that their termination is of equally little moment for the future?

The answer is that what happens to inflation from here on out depends on what happens to total demand and not on controls. And what happens to total demand in turn depends largely on monetary and fiscal policy.

Inflation tapered off in 1970 and 1971 because the rate of monetary growth was reduced sharply from 1968 to 1969. Inflation stopped tapering off in early 1972 because the sharp reduction in the rate of monetary growth ended in 1970 and was followed by a mildly higher rate. Inflation threatens to speed up in 1973 and 1974 because the rate of monetary growth has speeded up sharply in recent months. If recent monetary growth were to continue, no conceivable controls could prevent inflation from accelerating. On the other hand, if the Federal Reserve cuts monetary growth sharply and holds it there, inflation will continue to taper off with or without controls.[1]

[1] [The Fed did not curb monetary growth, inflation accelerated, and controls were reimposed—as the next column reports.]

Lower government spending is important primarily because we are not getting our money's worth for what the government spends. But it is important also because large deficits tend to raise interest rates, which induces people to hold less cash relative to their income and also puts pressure on the Fed to finance the deficits. If the President succeeds in holding down federal spending, he will do the most important single thing he can to hold down inflation. If inflation nonetheless speeds up, the Fed, and the Fed alone, will be responsible. It will have no excuses, no scapegoat to blame. As I put it in an earlier column, it will be "on the spot."

A major cost of controls has been to divert attention from the basic issues to a minor side show.

Monumental Folly
[June 25, 1973]

The new freeze and phase four are a tragic mistake. They take us a long way down the road to rigid and widespread controls. Such controls cannot halt inflation. But they can destroy our freedom and our prosperity.

Are we returning to more rigid controls because our recent experience demonstrates that they are an effective method of stopping inflation? Hardly. Consumer prices rose at annual rates of 5.5 percent in 1970; 3.8 percent in the eight months of 1971 preceding the freeze of August 15; 3.4 percent in the whole seventeen months of the freeze and phase two; and 4.1 percent in the final six months of phase two. Wholesale prices rose at rates of 2.3 percent, 5.3 percent, 5.9 percent, and 8.9 percent in the same periods. The price explosion since the end of phase two has been greatest in foods, never controlled under phase two. For the rest, it mostly continues a trend that started during phase two or unveils price increases concealed by phase two.

Are we returning to more rigid controls because other experience demonstrates that controls are an effective method of stopping inflation? Hardly. The standard life history of controls—documented time and again—is initial apparent success, growing difficulties as distortions accumulate, and a final price explosion when controls collapse or are repealed.

Are we returning to more rigid controls because economic reasoning demonstrates that they are an effective method of stopping inflation? Hardly. A few economists—John Kenneth Galbraith is the most prominent—argue that they are. But for two centuries and more, most economists have regarded controls as an attack on symptoms, not causes; as an interference with the market that creates shortages, distorts production, and breeds further controls; as a desperate expedient for a time of war.

The President, the legislators, and even the shortsighted denizens of Wall Street who cry for controls know this record. They cannot possibly believe that controls are an effective way to stop inflation. Why then do they favor them?

The answer is clear. Any effective policy to stop inflation will be painful. Once inflation gets the start it has here, there is simply no way to stop it without a slowdown in the economy and probably a recession. Three times in the past fifteen years we have taken the cure: in 1960−61, 1966−67, 1969−70. Each time, the cure has started to work. Each time, the policy makers became impatient before the cure had done its work and revved up the monetary and fiscal engines of inflation. Each time, we have suffered the pains in vain.

This time, policymakers do not want to pay any cost. They do not want to stop inflation. But they want to *appear* to be doing something about inflation. Controls look like a way to have their cake and eat it.

In 1971, controls achieved this confidence trick for a time. Perhaps they will again. But conditions are far less favorable. In 1971, surplus capacity was available to increase output; today, we are pressing against capacity limits. In 1971, the public had no experience with wage and price controls in peacetime. It could be gulled into believing that pronouncements were a substitute for policy. Today, the public is less gullible.

The temptation will be strong to try to make the retreaded controls work by piling one intervention on another—the scheduling of production, the allocation of raw materials, the rationing of consumer goods. The proposed export controls are a first portent.

If the U.S. ever succumbs to collectivism, to government control over every facet of our lives, it will not be because the socialists win any arguments. It will be through the indirect route of wage and price controls.

Is there no way to prevent this act of monumental folly?

Chapter Six
Indexation

The introduction of provisions into long-term contracts designed to allow for possible changes in the general level of prices is a very old practice. Already in the sixteenth century (1576) the English Parliament decreed that colleges that granted long-term leases on land they owned had to specify that at least one-third of the rent would be paid in grain or the monetary equivalent thereof. This "purchasing power" provision was the salvation of the colleges. A century or two later the "real" part of the rent was essentially the whole of the rent, the rest having been rendered nearly worthless by inflation.

Similarly, proposals for the widespread use of such clauses to mitigate the evils of inflation date back over a century and a half and have been endorsed by many eminent economists as I point out in the final item in this chapter, "Using Escalators to Help Fight Inflation" (July, 1974). In that article, I urge the widespread use of such clauses primarily as a means of reducing the transitional costs of ending inflation. However, the inclusion of such clauses in governmental tax and borrowing arrangements is called for equally by simple considerations of equity and representative government. I was myself converted to the government issuance of purchasing power securities on a day in 1942 or 1943 when, as an employee of the U.S. Treasury Department, I was asked to draft a speech for a high Treasury official urging the public to buy U.S. government savings bonds. I found that it was impossible to draft a speech suitable for the purpose that was both comprehensive and honest.

Although I have long favored the widespread use of escalator clauses, my writings on that subject attracted little notice, until the inflationary explosion in 1974 created a favorable climate. As a result, when I used the occasion of a visit to Brazil to repeat in "Economic Miracles" (January 21, 1974) a theme I had expressed earlier, the proposal attracted much attention—indeed widespread notoriety. One unfavorable side effect was to give many people the impression that I had been converted by Brazil and that I was proposing for a free society measures that had been able to work only in a military dictatorship—this, despite my reference in the column to Alfred Marshall's support of escalator clauses, a reference I deliberately included in order to avoid any impression that the case for them rested solely on the Brazilian experience.

We can learn from Brazil without necessarily approving what goes on in Brazil. It furnishes one of those experiences that those of us in the social sciences have to use as a substitute for controlled experiments. But learning from one aspect of its experience, and using that aspect to illustrate a general proposition, is a very different thing from approving of the whole of its policy or of its political structure. A visit of some two weeks hardly qualifies me to understand the Brazilian situation, let alone to judge it. As a believer in a free society, I am naturally appalled at the authoritarian aspects of the Brazilian society. But as I look over the countries of South America, it is hard to find any country there that has been able to make our kind of democracy and freedom work. Indeed, this unpleasant reflection applies much more broadly. There are very few countries worldwide which have been able to make our kind of system work.

The future of escalator clauses in the United States depends on the course of inflation. If, by some miracle, inflation were to disappear in the United States in the near future, all talk of such arrangements would also disappear. The more likely development is that inflation will taper off in late 1974, will settle at something like 6 or 7 percent in 1975, and will then start to accelerate in 1976 in response to the delayed impact of overreaction in 1975 to rising unemployment. During this period there will be a steady but unspectacular expansion of escalator clauses. If inflation then accelerates to 10 percent and beyond in 1977 or so, the steady expansion will turn into a bandwagon.

Needless to say, I hope that this scenario is wrong. I hope that the Federal Reserve and the administration will be willing and able to resist the pressure to overreact to the 1974 slowdown or recession, that they will maintain fiscal and monetary restraint, and so avoid another acceleration of inflation. But neither past experience nor the present political climate makes that hope a reasonable expectation.

No Taxation Without Representation
[March 3, 1969]

Congress has not legislated a reduction in the personal exemption under the income tax since 1942. Yet the exemption today is only about half of what it was then. How come? In dollars, the exemption was reduced to $500 per person in 1942. It is now $600. But a dollar is not a dollar is not a dollar. Today, a dollar will buy less than half as much as a dollar would buy in 1942. Rising prices have cut nearly in half the real value of the income tax exemption.

Inflation is not ordinarily considered to be a tax. And yet that is what it is. It is a tax twice over. It is, first, a tax on income because it lowers the real value of personal exemptions, and raises the rate applied to our incomes by pushing us into higher tax brackets. As a result, taxes go up faster than prices, which means that the government collects more in real terms.

Second, inflation is a tax on cash balances. When prices rise, all of us must add to the number of dollars we hold in order to keep the purchasing power of our cash balances constant. To get these extra dollars, we must give up some real resources, in the form of labor or of the goods we could have purchased instead—just as we must in order to get the dollars that we pay in explicit taxes. To whom do we give up the real resources? To the government from whom we get the extra dollars it prints or makes available indirectly through deposits at the Federal Reserve System; and to the banks that create book entries labeled "deposits" over and above the amount they hold as currency or as deposits at the Federal Reserve. The total of these extra dollars is the revenue from the tax on cash balances, a revenue that, under our system, is shared between government and the banks.

The special feature of inflation as a tax is that it is the only tax that can be levied without specific Congressional authorization. It can be and is levied by the U.S. Treasury and the Federal Reserve System on their own say-so, without announcement and without public hearings. That is what has made inflation such a tempting recourse to governments in need of funds. That is why countries that have had their ability to levy and collect explicit taxes destroyed or seriously impaired by defeat in war or by domestic disruption—and only such countries—have experienced hyperinflation that essentially wiped out the value of their money.

What can we do to end such taxation without representation?

We can end taxation of cash balances without representation by adopting a congressional rule to limit the power of the monetary authorities. That is one reason why I have long favored a congressional rule specifying that the money supply should be increased by a fixed percentage year in and year out. However, the main reason I favor this rule is different—to promote economic stability.

We can end the taxation of income without representation by legislating in advance that the exemptions, the maximum standard deductions, and the tax brackets under the personal income tax shall be adjusted each year for the change in the price level.

For example, start with the 1968 dollar exemptions, maximum deductions, and tax brackets. As a measure of price change, use the BLS cost-of-living index number. Suppose that, by this index, prices turn out to average 4 percent higher in 1969 than in 1968. The personal exemption for 1969 would then be 104 percent of the personal exemption for 1968 or $624 per person instead of $600. The maximum standard deduction for a single person would be $312 instead of $300. The first bracket rate of 14 percent would apply to the first $520 for a single person instead of to the first $500, and so on down the line.

This simple and thoroughly practicable reform will not begin to solve all the defects of the income tax. But it will prevent a creeping and automatic increase in the rate of taxation as a result of inflation. It will not prevent Congress from raising or lowering income-tax rates but it will require Congress to do so openly and by explicit action.

The hearings on tax reform that are now being held will be lengthy, complex, and to judge from experience, unproductive. Here is a simple reform that requires no lengthy hearings, no extensive consideration of technical tax provisions, no attack on long-established vested interests.

Will anyone who can find any objection to enacting it at once please step forth?

Economic Miracles
[January 21, 1974]

I have just returned from a brief visit to Brazil, the third major nation in recent history to take off on a period of growth so rapid as to justify the term "economic miracle." The explosion is obvious even to the casual visitor. The cars that jam the streets of São Paulo and Rio are almost all new; multistory buildings, both new and still under construction, crowd the sky; cranes are almost as numerous as TV antennas, and the air of bustle and hustle is unmistakably different from the pre-Christmas shopping rush. Many of the men in responsible positions are surprisingly young; clearly a new generation is taking charge. Their confidence, pride, and high expectations are seasoned with just a tinge of uneasiness about the future. "Will it really last?" is a question that no one asks yet that all seem to have at the back of their minds.

The Brazilian miracle dates from 1967, when output started growing at an average rate of approximately 10 percent a year. The other miracles, in Germany and Japan, started nearly two decades earlier, shortly after the end of World War II. Though the three countries differ greatly in history, culture, resources, and technological sophistication, there are striking similarities among the three miracles.

1. All three miracles were preceded by a period of economic disorganization that was produced or intensified by price and wage controls imposed to suppress inflation.

In Germany and Japan, a productive capacity diminished by war and defeat faced a money supply swollen by wartime spending and postwar fiscal collapse. Wartime price and wage controls were continued by the occupation authorities who enforced them far more rigorously than a native police force could ever have done. The result was economic collapse.

In Brazil, political instability in the late fifties and early sixties produced large government deficits financed by a rapid increase in the quantity of money. Inflation reached a rate of more than 100 percent a year by early 1964. The government attempted to suppress the inflation by measures such as fixing prices and wages, controlling foreign-exchange transactions and introducing multiple exchange rates. As in Germany and Japan, the controls produced widespread waste, inefficiency, and black markets.

2. All three miracles were made possible by monetary reforms that ended most government controls over prices and wages and thereby permitted a market-price system to operate.

In Germany and Japan, the prior economic collapse had been so extreme that the reforms, drastic though they were, were followed almost immediately by recovery and expansion.

In Brazil, where the prior collapse was much less extreme, a "tight" money policy that reduced the rate of inflation from more than 100 percent to about 30 percent in three years was accompanied by recession and increased unemployment. However, after the initial shock was absorbed, the freeing of markets plus political stability unleashed unsuspected dynamic forces.

3. All three miracles relied primarily on private enterprise for their motive power.

In all three countries, government intervened extensively—subsidizing here, taxing there, building roads, ports and similar facilities, taking over part or all of selected industries. Yet these measures, though highly visible, were the trimming on the cake, not the cake itself. I believe that most of them did more harm than good. The government served best when it interfered least with the driving force of private enterprise coordinated by market prices.

The one major difference among the policies that fostered the three miracles is the tactic adopted to permit the price system to operate.

Germany and Japan followed a monetary policy that, until very recently, all but eliminated inflation. They were therefore under no pressure to control prices and wages and could let the price system operate freely.

Brazil followed a different course. After reducing inflation to about 30 percent per year by 1967, it eased off. Simultaneously, however, it introduced purchasing-power escalator clauses into a wide range of contracts. The term used in Brazil is "monetary correction." If a Brazilian deposits money in a savings bank, the bank not only will pay him a stated interest rate, say 5 percent, but also will periodically credit his account with a monetary correction equal to the rate of inflation over the period. Longer-term business loans, government securities, mortgages, and so on are handled the same way: the borrower pays the lender a stated rate plus a monetary correction.

All wage rates are subject to mandatory adjustment by a similar monetary correction—though in fact most wages have been rising much faster than that. The personal exemptions under the income tax and the tax brackets are adjusted by a monetary correction. So also is the value of fixed business assets for purposes of calculating depreciation allowed under the tax laws. The exchange rate is adjusted frequently to allow for inflation. And so on and on.

The use of the monetary correction in some of these ways is mandated by law; in others, it is voluntary. In practice, its use is sufficiently widespread to remove most of the pressure for price and wage controls.

The monetary correction is an accounting nuisance and it cannot be truly universal. A world of zero inflation would obviously be better. Yet, given the inevitable, if temporary, costs of reducing inflation rapidly without such a measure, the Brazilians have been extremely wise to adopt it. I believe that their miracle would have been impossible without the monetary correction. With it, they have been able to reduce inflation gradually from about 30 percent in 1967 to about 15 percent now without inhibiting rapid growth, and they may be able to succeed in gradually bringing inflation down to near zero. With it, they currently experience less economic distortion from a 15 percent inflation than the U.S., without it, experiences from a 9 percent inflation.

Even the most ardent defenders of price and wage controls regard them as at most a "second best," as an expedient to avoid still worse problems. The three major economic miracles—as well as many less dramatic episodes—teach that they are rather a "first worst," a cancer that can destroy an economic system's capacity to function.

The widespread use of purchasing-power escalator clauses as a remedy "for fluctuations of general prices" was proposed by the great British economist Alfred Marshall as long ago as 1887. The Brazilian experience parallels Marshall's proposal with amazing fidelity—by the force of necessity, not design. Theory and practice coincide in demonstrating that a true second best for living with inflation is the widespread use of purchasing-power escalator clauses. It is past time that the U.S. applied the lesson.

Using Escalators to Help Fight Inflation*
[July 1974]

The real obstacles to ending inflation are political, not economic. Ending inflation would deprive government of revenue that it now obtains with-

*Fortune Magazine

out legislation. Ending inflation would also produce a temporary, though perhaps fairly protracted, period of recession or slowdown and relatively high unemployment.

These obstacles to ending inflation can be substantially reduced through what has come to be called "indexation"—the widespread use of price-escalator clauses in private and governmental contracts. Such arrangements are not a good thing in and of themselves. They are simply a lesser evil than a badly managed money. The widespread use of escalator clauses would not by itself either increase or decrease the rate of inflation. But it would reduce the revenue that government acquires from inflation—which means that government would have less incentive to inflate. More important, it would reduce the adverse side effects that effective measures to end inflation would have on output and employment.

From time immemorial, the major source of inflation has been the sovereign's attempt to acquire resources to wage war, to construct monuments, or for other purposes. Inflation has been irresistibly attractive to sovereigns because it is a hidden tax that at first appears painless or even pleasant, and above all because it is a tax that can be imposed without specific legislation. It is truly taxation without representation.

The revenue yield from inflation takes three major forms:

—*Additional fiat money.* Since ancient times, sovereigns have debased coinage by replacing silver or gold with base metals. (Current examples include U.S. dimes and quarters, formerly silver but now copper coated with a nickel alloy.) Later, paper currency supplemented token coins. More recently still, book entries at central banks (misleadingly called deposits) have been added to the repertory. Governments use the fiat money they issue to finance expenditures or repay debts. In addition, the fiat money serves as a base on which the banking system creates additional money in the form of bank deposits. In calendar 1973, the U.S. government realized around $8 billion from these sources.

—*Windfall tax yield.* Inflation increases the yield of the personal and corporate income tax by pushing individuals into higher income brackets; generating paper capital gains on which taxes must be paid; and rendering depreciation allowances inadequate to replace capital, so that a return of capital is taxed as if it were a return on capital. Estimates by the economist George Terborgh of the effect of inflation on the reported profits of nonfinancial corporations imply that the inflation yield from the corporate tax alone amounted to nearly $13 billion in 1973.

—*Reduction in the real amount of outstanding debt.* Much of the federal government's debt was issued at yields that did not allow for current rates of inflation. On a conservative estimate, the government must have realized in 1973 something like $5 billion from this source.

All told, then, the government's revenue from inflation came to more than $25 billion in 1973. Ending inflation would end these sources of revenue. Government would have to reduce expenditures, increase explicit taxes, or borrow additional funds from the public at whatever interest rate would clear the market. None of these courses is politically attractive.

An even more serious political obstacle to ending inflation is the reluctance of the public to tolerate the transitory rise in unemployment that ending inflation would currently entail. To avoid misunderstanding, let me stress that I am not saying an increase in unemployment is a cure for inflation. It is not. There are many ways to increase unemployment that would exacerbate rather than cure inflation. I am saying something very different: that unemployment is today an inevitable *side effect* of curing inflation—just as the need to stay in bed is a side effect of a successful operation for appendicitis but is not itself a cure.

Ending inflation requires a slowing down in the growth rate of total dollar spending. In my opinion, a reduction in the growth rate of the quantity of money is the only reliable instrument available to government for slowing down the growth rate of total dollar spending. But what follows is independent of that proposition. If there is some other way to slow spending growth, the side effects will be essentially the same. Hence this analysis of side effects of ending inflation is relevant even if you do not accept my monetarist view.

When total spending slows down, each producer separately tends to regard the reduction in the demand for his product as special to him, and to hope that it is temporary. He is inclined to meet it primarily by reducing output or accumulating inventory, not by shading prices. Only after a time lag will he start to shade prices. Similarly, any of his workers who are laid off are likely to react by waiting to be recalled or by seeking jobs elsewhere, not by moderating wage demands or expectations.

A slowdown in total spending will therefore tend to be reflected initially in a widespread slowdown in output and employment and an increase in inventories. It will take some time before these lead in turn to widespread reductions in the rate of increase in prices and the rate of increase in wages. It will take still more time before *expectations* about inflation are revised and the revised expectations encourage a resumption of employment and output.

Different activities, moreover, have different speeds of adjustment. Some prices, wages, and production schedules are fixed a long time in advance; others can be adjusted promptly. Accordingly, a slowdown of total spending produces substantial shifts in *relative* prices, which will sooner or later have to be corrected. The corrections, in turn, cause economic disturbances.

For the U.S. the time delay between a change in the rate of monetary growth and a corresponding change in the rate of growth of total spending and total output has averaged six to nine months. The further delay until a braking effect on prices is evident has averaged twelve to eighteen months. Accordingly, the total delay between a change in monetary growth and a change in the rate of inflation comes to about two years.

After inflation has continued for a time, inflationary expectations are reflected in interest rates, union contracts, and other long-term arrangements. Then a drop in the inflation rate imposes severe strains and hardships. The employer who granted very large wage increases in the expectation of continued inflation finds his real wage costs higher than he bargained for. The borrower who agreed to pay a very high interest rate finds his real borrowing cost higher than he expected. For example, a homeowner who took out a mortgage at 10 percent would be in a bad fix if the prevailing rate dropped to 5 percent, while the lender on that 10 percent mortgage would have received a bonanza.

Such side effects constitute, I believe, the most important political obstacle to ending inflation, given the commitment on the part of most modern governments to "full employment," the failure of the public at large to recognize the inevitable if temporary side effects of ending inflation, and the unwillingness or inability of political leaders to persuade the public to accept these side effects.

Some years back, when the rate of inflation was much lower than now, I believed that the readjustment required was sufficiently mild and brief to be politically feasible. But, unfortunately, the opportunity was cast aside on August 15, 1971, when President Nixon reversed economic policy by imposing a price and wage freeze and encouraging expansive monetary and fiscal policy.

At the time, we were well on our way to ending inflation without severe side effects. At the cost of the mild 1970 recession, the annual rate of inflation had been reduced from over 6 percent to 4.5 percent and was still declining. The economy was slowly recovering from that recession. Had the nation had the will—for President Nixon was reflecting a widespread national consensus when he reversed policy—another year of continued monetary restraint and of slow expansion would probably have turned the trick. As it was, the 1970 recession was a masochistic exercise rather than a side effect of a successful cure.

As everyone certainly knows, inflation is now far worse than in August, 1971. The very high rate in the first half of 1974 was doubtless a temporary bubble, but even on the most optimistic view, inflation is not likely to fall below 6 percent during the next twelve months. Starting from that level, and with inflationary expectation ever more deeply entrenched, an effective policy to end inflation would entail as a side effect a considerably more severe and protracted recession than we experienced in 1970. The political will to accept such a recession, without reversing policy and restimulating inflation, is simply not present.

What then? If we do nothing, we shall suffer ever higher rates of inflation—not continuously, but in spurts as we overreact to temporary recessions. Sooner or later, the public will get fed up, will demand effective action, and we shall then have a really severe recession.

How can we make it politically feasible to end inflation much sooner? As I see it, only by adopting measures that will reduce the side effects from ending inflation. These side effects fundamentally reflect distortions introduced into *relative* prices by *unanticipated* inflation or deflation, distortions that arise because contracts are entered into under mistaken perceptions about the likely course of inflation. The way to reduce these side effects is to make contracts with prices, wages, or interest rates stipulated in *real* terms, not nominal terms. This can be done through the widespread use of escalator clauses.

Indexation is not a panacea. It is impossible to escalate all contracts (consider, for example, currency in circulation), and widespread escalation would be cumbersome. A great advantage of using money is precisely the ability to carry on transactions cheaply and efficiently, and universal escalator clauses reduce this advantage. Far better to have no inflation and no escalator clauses. But that alternative is not now available.

Let me note also that the use of escalator clauses is not a new idea or an untried idea. It dates back to at least 1707, when a Cambridge don, William Fleetwood, estimated the change in prices over a six-hundred-year period in order to get comparable limits on outside income that holders of fellowships should be permitted to receive. The use of escalator clauses was explicitly suggested a hundred years later by an English writer on money, John Wheatley. In 1886 the concept was spelled out in considerable detail, and enthusiastically recommended, by the great English economist Alfred Marshall.

The great American economist Irving Fisher not only favored the "tabular standard"—as the proposal for indexation was labeled nearly two centuries ago—but also persuaded a manufacturing company that he had helped to found to issue a purchasing-power security as long ago as 1925. Interest in the tabular standard was the major factor accounting for the development of index numbers of prices. In recent years, indexation, as the tabular standard is now called, has been adopted by Brazil on a wider scale than I would recommend for the U.S. It has been adopted on a lesser scale by Canada, Israel, and several other countries.

For the U.S., my specific proposal has two parts, one for the federal government, one for the rest of the economy. For the federal government, I propose that escalator clauses be legislated; for the rest of the economy, that they be voluntary, but that any legal obstacles be removed. The question of which index number to use in escalator clauses is important but not critical. As Alfred Marshall said in 1886, "A perfectly exact measure of purchasing power is not only unattainable, but even unthinkable." For convenience, I would use the cost-of-living index number calculated by the Bureau of Labor Statistics.

The U.S. government has already adopted escalation for social-security payments, retirement benefits to federal employees, wages of post-office employees, and perhaps some other items. Taxes that are expressed as fixed percentages of price or other value base are automatically escalated. The government should now proceed to adopt escalator clauses in the personal and corporate income tax and in government securities. (The following proposed revisions in the federal government's taxing and borrowing arrangements are contained in a pending bill introduced by U.S. Senator James Buckley of New York.)

The Personal Income Tax. Minor details aside, four changes are called for:

—The personal exemption, the standard deduction, and the low-income allowance should be expressed not as a given number of dollars, but as a given number of dollars multiplied by the ratio of a price index for the year in question to the index for the base year in which indexation starts. For example, if in the first year prices rise by 10 percent, the base amounts should be multiplied by 1.10.

—The brackets in the tax tables should be adjusted similarly, so that, in the example given, $0-500 would become $0-550, and so on.

—The base for calculating capital gains should be multiplied by the ratio of the price index in the year of sale to the price index in the year of purchase. This would prevent the taxing of purely paper capital gains.

—The base for calculating depreciation on fixed capital assets should be adjusted in the same way.

The Corporate Tax.

—The present $25,000 dividing line between normal tax and surtax should be replaced by that sum multiplied by a price index number.

—The cost of inventories used in sales should be adjusted to eliminate book profits (or losses) resulting from changes in prices between initial purchase and final sale.

—The bases for calculating capital gains and depreciation of fixed capital assets should be adjusted as for the individual income tax.

Government Securities.

—Except for short-term bills and notes, all government securities should be issued in purchasing-power form. For example, Series E bonds should promise a redemption value equal to the product of the face value (calculated at an interest rate of, say, 3 percent per year) and the ratio of the price index in the year of redemption to the price index in the year of purchase. Coupon securities should carry coupons redeemable for the face amount multiplied by the relevant price ratio, and bear a maturity value equal to the face amount similarly multiplied by the relevant price ratio.

These changes in taxes and in borrowing will reduce both the incentive for government to resort to inflation and the side effects of changes in the rate of inflation on the private economy. But they are called for also by elementary principles of ethics, justice, and representative government, which is why I propose making them permanent.

As a result largely of inflation produced by government, personal income taxes are today heavier than during the peak of World War Two financing, despite several legislated "reductions" in tax rates. Personal exemptions in real terms are at an all-time low. The taxes levied on persons in different economic circumstances deviate widely from the taxes Congress explicitly intended to levy on them. Congress has been in the enviable position of actually imposing higher taxes while appearing to reduce taxes.

As for government borrowing, the savings-bond campaigns of the Treasury have been the largest bucket-shop operation ever engaged in. This is not a recent development. In 1951, in responding to a questionnaire of the Joint Economic Committee of Congress, I wrote:

"I strongly favor the issuance of a purchasing-power bond on two grounds: *(a)* It would provide a means for lower- and middle-income groups to protect their capital against the ravages of inflation. These groups have almost no effective means of doing so now. It seems to me equitable and socially desirable that they should. *(b)* It would permit the Treasury to sell bonds without engaging in advertising and promotion that at best is highly misleading, at worst, close to being downright immoral. The Treasury urges people to buy bonds as a means of securing their future. Is the implicit promise one that it can make in good faith, in light of past experience of purchasers of such bonds who have seen their purchasing power eaten away by price rises? If it can be, there is no cost involved in making the promise explicit by adding a purchasing-power guaranty. If it cannot be, it seems to me intolerable that an agency of the public deliberately mislead the public."

Surely the experience of the nearly quarter century since these words were written reinforces their pertinence. Essentially every purchaser of savings bonds (or, indeed, almost any other long-term Treasury security) during that period has paid for the privilege of lending to the government. The supposed "interest" he has received has not compensated for the decline in the purchasing power of the principal, and, to add insult to injury, he has had to pay tax on the paper interest. And the inflation that has sheared the innocent lambs has been produced by the government that benefits from the shearing!

It is a mystery to me, and a depressing commentary on either the understanding or the sense of social responsibility of businessmen (note that I say of *businessmen,* not of business), that year after year eminent and honorable business leaders have been willing to participate in this bucket-shop operation by joining committees to promote the sale of U.S. savings bonds, or by providing facilities for payroll deductions for that purpose.

Private use of escalator clauses is an expedient that has no permanent role if government manages money responsibly. Hence I favor keeping such private use voluntary in order to promote its self-destruction if that happy time arrives.

No legislation is needed for the private adoption of escalator clauses, and such clauses are now widespread. More than five million workers are covered by union contracts with automatic escalator clauses, and there must be many non-union workers who have similar implicit or explicit agreements with their employers. Many contracts for future delivery of products contain provisions for adjustment of the final selling price either for specific changes in costs or for general price changes. A great many rental contracts for business premises are expressed as a percentage of gross or net receipts, which means that they have an implicit escalator clause. This is equally true for percentage royalty payments and for automobile-insurance policies that pay the cost of repairing actual damage. Some insurance companies issue fire-insurance policies under which the face value is automatically adjusted for inflation. No doubt there are many more examples of which I am ignorant.

It is highly desirable that the practice of incorporating escalator clauses be extended to a far wider range of wage agreements, contracts for future delivery of products, and financial transactions involving borrowing and lending. The first two are entirely straightforward extensions of existing practices. The third is more novel.

The arrangements suggested for government borrowing could apply equally to long-term borrowing by private enterprises. Instead of issuing a security promising to pay, say, interest of 9 percent per year and to repay $1,000 at the end of ten years, XYZ Corp. could promise to pay 3 percent plus the rate of inflation each year, and to repay $1,000 at the end of ten years. Alternatively, it could promise to pay each year 3 percent times the ratio of the price index in that year to the price index in the year the security was issued, and to repay at the end of ten years $1,000 times the corresponding price ratio for the tenth year.

One question has invariably been raised when I have discussed this kind of arrangement with corporate executives: "Is it not too risky for us to undertake an open-ended commitment? At least with fixed nominal rates we know what our obligations are." This is a natural query from businessmen reared in an environment in which a roughly stable price level was taken for granted. But in a world of varying rates of inflation, the fixed-rate agreement is the riskier agreement. The dollar receipts of most businesses vary with inflation. If inflation is high, dollar receipts are high, and business can afford to pay the escalated rate of interest. If inflation is low, dollar receipts are low, and they will find it easier to pay the low rate with the adjustment for inflation than a fixed but high rate. And similarly at the time of redemption.

What is crucial is the relation between assets and liabilities. For many enterprises, their assets, including goodwill, are real in the sense that the dollar value will rise or fall with the general price level. But their liabilities tend to be nominal, i.e., fixed in dollar terms. Accordingly, these enterprises benefit from inflation at a higher rate than was anticipated when the nominal liabilities were acquired, and they are harmed by inflation at a lower rate than was anticipated. Match assets and liabilities, and such enterprises would be hedged against either event.

A related yet somewhat different case is provided by financial intermediaries. Consider savings-and-loan associations and mutual-savings banks. Both their assets (primarily home mortgages) and their liabilities (due to shareholders or depositors) are expressed in nominal terms. But they differ in time duration. The liabilities are in practice due on demand; the assets are long term. The mortgages now in the portfolios were mostly issued when inflation and therefore interest rates were much lower. If the mortgages were revalued at current yields—i.e., at the market prices they could be sold for in a free secondary market—every savings-and-loan association would be technically insolvent.

So long as the thrift institutions can maintain their level of deposits, no problem arises because they do not have to liquidate their assets. But if inflation speeds up, interest rates on market instruments will rise further. Unless the thrift institutions offer competitive interest rates, their shareholders or depositors will withdraw funds to get a better yield (the process inelegantly termed disintermediation). But with their income fixed, the thrift institutions will find it difficult or impossible to pay competitive rates. (This situation is concealed but not altered by the legal limits on the rates they are permitted to pay.)

Further acceleration of inflation threatens a major crisis for this group of financial institutions. And the crisis is no minor matter. Total assets of these institutions approach $400 billion. As it happens, they would be greatly helped by a deceleration of inflation, but some of their recent borrowers who are locked into high rates on mortgages would be seriously hurt.

Consider how different the situation of the thrift institutions would be with widespread escalator clauses. The mortgages on their books would be yielding, say, 5 percent plus the rate of inflation; they could afford to pay their shareholders or depositors 3 to 4 percent plus the rate of inflation (assuming that legal limits were removed or modified). They, their borrowers, and their shareholders or depositors would be fully protected against changes in the rate of inflation.

Similarly, an insurance company could afford to offer an inflation-protected policy if its assets were in inflation-protected loans to business or mortgages or government securities. A pension fund could offer inflation-protected pensions if it held inflation-protected assets.

To repeat, none of these arrangements is without cost. It would be far better if stable prices made them unnecessary. But they seem to me far less costly than continuing on the road to periodic acceleration of inflation, ending in a real bust.

Note that the suggested governmental arrangements will stimulate the private arrangements. Today one deterrent to issuance of private purchasing-power securities is that the inflation adjustment would be taxable to the recipient along with the real interest paid. The proposed tax changes would in effect exempt such adjustments from taxation, and so make purchasing-power securities more attractive to lenders. In addition, government issuance of purchasing-power securities would offer effective competition to private borrowers, inducing them to follow suit.

How would widespread adoption of the escalator principle affect economic policy? Some critics say that indexation would condemn us to perpetual inflation. I believe that, on the contrary, indexation would enhance the government's ability to act against inflation.

To begin with, indexation will temper some of the hardships and distortions that now follow from a drop in the rate of inflation. Employers will not be stuck with excessively high wage increases under existing union contracts, for wage increases will moderate as inflation recedes. Borrowers will not be stuck with excessively high interest costs, for the rates on outstanding loans will moderate as inflation recedes. Indexation will also partly counteract the tendency of businesses to defer capital investment once total spending begins to decline—there will be less reason to wait in expectation of lower prices and lower interest rates. Businesses will be able to borrow funds or enter into construction contracts knowing that interest rates and contract prices can be adjusted later on in accord with indexes of prices.

Most important, indexation will shorten the time it takes for a reduction in the rate of growth of total spending to have its full effect in reducing the rate of inflation. As the deceleration of demand pinches at various points in the economy, any effects on prices will be promptly transmitted to wage contracts, to contracts for future delivery, and to interest rates on outstanding long-term loans. Accordingly, producers' wage costs and other costs will go up less rapidly than they would without indexation. This tempering of costs, in turn, will encourage employers to keep more people on the payroll, and produce more goods, than they would without indexation. The encouragement of supply, in turn, will work against price increases, with additional moderating feedback on wages and other costs.

With widespread indexation, in sum, firm monetary restraint by the Federal Reserve System would be reflected in a much more even reduction in the pace of inflation and a much smaller transitory rise in unemployment. The success in slowing inflation would steel the political will to suffer the smaller withdrawal pains, and so might make it possible for the Fed to persist in a firm policy. As it became credible that the Fed would persist, private reactions could reinforce the effects of its policy. The economy would move to noninflationary growth or high levels of employment much more rapidly than now seems possible.

The major objection to indexation is the allegation that escalators have an inflationary impact on the economy. In this form, the statement is simply false. An escalator goes into effect only as the result of a prior price increase. Whence came that? An escalator can go down as well as up. If inflation slows, and hence so do wage increases, do escalators have a deflationary impact?

Escalators have no direct effect on the rate of inflation. They simply assure that inflation affects different prices and wages alike, and thus they moderate distortions in relative prices and wages. With widespread use of escalators, inflation will be *transmitted* more quickly and evenly, and hence the harm done by inflation will be less. But why should that raise or lower the rate of inflation?

On a more sophisticated level, it has been argued that by reducing the revenue yield from any given rate of inflation, indexation would induce the government to speed up the rate of inflation in order to recoup the lost revenue. Furthermore, it has been suggested that the general public would interpret the adoption of escalator clauses to mean the government has given up the fight against inflation, and is seeking only to live with it—which in turn would reinforce inflationary expectations. To me, these objections do not seem weighty. If the public does not wish to stop inflation, but is content to have the government use inflation as a regular source of revenue, the sooner we adapt our institutions to that fact the better.

On a still more sophisticated level, it can be argued that, by removing distortions in relative prices, indexation will make it easier for the public to recognise changes in the rate of inflation, will thereby reduce the time lag in adapting to such changes, and so will make the nominal price level more sensitive and variable. It is certainly possible that indexation would have this effect, though it is by no means demonstrated. But if so, the *real variables* would be less sensitive and more stable—a highly beneficial trade-off. Moreover, it is also possible that by making accurate estimates of the rate of inflation less important, indexation will reduce the attention devoted to such estimates, and thereby provide greater stability.

An objection of a very different kind is that inflation serves the critical social purpose of resolving incompatible demands by different groups. In this view, the participants in the economy, to put it crudely, have "non-negotiable demands" for more than the entire output. These demands are reconciled because inflation fools people into believing that their demands have been met when in fact they have not been. Escalator clauses, it is argued, would bring the inconsistent demands into the open. Workers who would accept a lower real wage produced by unanticipated inflation will not be willing to accept the same real wage in explicit negotiations. If this view is correct on a wide enough scale to be important, I see no other ultimate outcome than either runaway inflation or an authoritarian society ruled by force. Perhaps it is only wishful thinking that makes me reluctant to accept this vision of our fate.

The conventional political wisdom holds that the citizenry may mutter about inflation but votes on the basis of the level of unemployment. Nobody, it is said, has ever lost an election because of inflation; Hoover in 1932 and Nixon in 1960 lost because of unemployment. But as we leave the Depression decade further and further behind, and as we experience more and more inflation, this conventional wisdom becomes increasingly questionable. Edward Heath surely lost an election because of inflation. Prime Minister Tanaka's popularity is at an all-time low because of inflation. Throughout the world, inflation is a major source of political unrest.

Perhaps indexation is not the best expedient in this time of trouble. But I know of no other that holds out as much promise of both reducing the harm done by inflation and facilitating the ending of inflation. If inflation continues to accelerate, the conventional political wisdom will be reversed. The insistence on ending inflation at whatever cost will lead to a severe depression. Now, before that has occurred, is the time to take measures that will make it politically feasible to end inflation before inflation ends not only the conventional wisdom but perhaps also a free society.

Chapter Seven
International Economic
Policy

The columns in this chapter present a series of reports on a sequence of events that unfolded with all the inevitability of a Greek tragedy. These events had two key origins: (1) President Franklin D. Roosevelt's action on March 6, 1933, ending the internal convertibility of dollars into gold; (2) the World War Two Bretton Woods agreement which established after the war a system of fixed exchange rates that were to be changed only by official action.

Once the United States government terminated its commitment to its own citizens to exchange gold for currency and currency for gold at a fixed rate, it was inevitable that—whether for good or ill—gold would lose its role as an effective determinant of the quantity of money and as an effective element in United States economic policy. The only question was when and by precisely what route. As things turned out, it took a little over thirty-eight years, from March 6, 1933, to August 15, 1971, and there are still vestigial remains of the earlier reign of gold in the international sphere.

Similarly, from the time Bretton Woods became effective, it was inevitable that it would break down. The Bretton Woods system gave the dollar a unique role—the United States and the United States alone had no obligation to support the price of its currency in terms of foreign currencies; the United States and the United States alone was committed to convert its currency into gold at a fixed price on demand of foreign central banks or other official agencies.[1] Other countries committed themselves to keep the exchange rates of their currencies in terms of the dollar

[1] Technically, the rules were symmetrical. Any country was free to adopt the same role but only the United States did so, and it was intended and expected that this would be the case.

within a specified band (plus or minus 1 percent of the officially stated parity), though they were free to change the parity by up to 10 percent on their own volition and by larger amounts with the approval of the International Monetary Fund.

This arrangement was designed to solve a simple, yet fundamental and little understood, problem in foreign exchange—the so-called n-country problem. Given n currencies, there are only n-1 independent exchange rates. To take the simplest case, let there be just two currencies, say the dollar and the pound. Then there is only one exchange rate—the price of the pound in terms of the dollar or of the dollar in terms of the pound. There is no way in which *both* Britain and the United States can be free to determine that rate, no way in which Britain can make the price of the pound $2.40 and the United States can simultaneously make the price of the dollar .25 pounds, i.e., the price of the pound $4. The two countries either have to agree on a single price or agree to let the single price be determined on the free market or agree that one country will be passive and let the other country fix the price at its volition. In effect, the Bretton Woods agreement solved the problem by making the United States the passive country, letting other countries set their prices but requiring them to support the prices they set. Other countries accepted this because the United States agreed to convert its currency into gold. [2]

This system was bound to break down because it tried to achieve incompatible objectives: freedom of countries to pursue an independent internal monetary policy; fixed exchange rates; and relatively free international movement of goods and capital. The incompatibility of these objectives was brilliantly demonstrated by John Maynard Keynes in one of his earliest and, in my minority opinion, best books, *A Tract on Monetary Reform* (1923). As one of the architects of Bretton Woods, Keynes tried to resolve the incompatibility by providing for flexibility of exchange rates through what he intended to be frequent and fairly easily achieved changes in official parities. In practice, this hope was doomed because maintaining the announced parity became a matter of prestige and political controversy. Countries therefore held on to a parity as long as they could, in the process letting minor problems grow into major crises and then making large changes. In practice, the system was a system of rigid parities rather than of rates fixed at any point in time but subject to frequent change.

[2] One way of looking at this is that gold constituted an additional currency.

The only countries that were able for a long period to maintain the fixed exchange rate were those, such as Japan and Germany, which were willing to let internal policy be dominated by the needs of the balance of payments.

This system in effect broke down in March 1968 when a two-tier system for gold was adopted. Under that system, the price of gold was free to find its own level in private markets (this is one tier) but was fixed at $35 an ounce for transactions among central banks (this is the second tier). In addition, the central banks agreed not to buy or sell gold in the free market. However, the formal announcement of its death was delayed until August 15, 1971, when President Nixon officially suspended the United States commitment to buy and sell gold at a fixed price from and to foreign official agencies. Since then, the international financial system has been in flux. The countries were initially unwilling to accept a system of freely floating exchange rates of the kind that I have supported for over two decades; yet in practice that is the direction in which they were forced to move as demonstrated by the floating of the British pound on June 23, 1972, and the exchange crisis in the spring of 1973, as noted in the column, "The Crisis that Refreshes" (March 12, 1973). The subsequent crisis produced by the Arab-Israeli War in October 1973 and the oil embargo and rapid rise in oil prices which followed sealed the doom of the continuing attempts to reestablish something like the old order. Finally, in mid-1974, the representatives of the major financial countries ("Committee of Twenty") formally accepted the continuation of a system of floating exchange rates though they continued to express the pious hope that it would be possible to return to a system of fixed exchange rates at a later date.

The sequence of developments is a beautiful example of how much more potent are basic economic forces than the prejudices of central bankers and government officials. That this is not simply hindsight can be readily demonstrated. In my book, *Capitalism and Freedom,* published in 1962, I specified in detail the measures that I believed the United States should take to promote a truly free market in both gold and foreign exchange.

1. The U.S. should announce that it no longer commits itself to buy or sell gold at any fixed price.
2. Present laws making it illegal for individuals to own gold or to buy or sell gold should be repealed. . . .

3. The present law specifying that the Reserve System must hold gold certificates equal to 25 percent of its liabilities should be repealed.

4. A major problem in getting rid completely of the gold price-support program . . . is the transitional one of what to do with accumulated government stocks. . . . [M]y own view is that the government should immediately restore a free market by instituting steps 1 and 2, and should ultimately dispose of all of its stocks. . . . Hence, I propose that the government auction off its gold stocks on the free market over a five-year period. . . .

5. The U.S. should announce also that it will not proclaim any official exchange rates between the dollar and other currencies and in addition that it will not engage in any speculative or other actions aimed at influencing exchange rates. . . .

6. These measures would conflict with our formal obligation as a member of the International Monetary Fund. . . . However, the fund found it possible to reconcile Canada's failure to specify a parity with its Articles and to give its approval to a floating rate for Canada. There is no reason why it cannot do the same for the U.S.

7. Other nations might choose to peg their currencies to the dollar. That is their business and there is no reason for us to object so long as we undertake no obligations to buy or sell their currency at a fixed price. . . . [pp. 69 – 70]

A decade later, five and one half of these seven points have been realized, and one more will almost surely be realized soon.

Points one and five were realized on August 15, 1971, when President Nixon closed the gold window. Unfortunately, however, the Fed backslid in July 1972 by selling some German marks, and has since continued to do so by engaging in exchange speculation from time to time. See "Speculation and Speculation" (April 23, 1973).

Points six and seven were realized subsequently.

Point three was realized in a series of legislative enactments, the final one in 1968.

Point four was half realized when the United States gold stock declined from roughly $20 billion in 1959 to less than $10 billion today (valued at the initial legal price of $35 an ounce), though this occurred at a fixed price rather than at an auction price and over twelve years instead of five years.

Point two is the only one so far not achieved at all. However, Congress has voted the President the authority to end the ban on private ownership of gold at his discretion. I predict that he will do so in the near future.[3]

This record does not bespeak my powers of persuasion. Far from it. It bespeaks rather the strength of the basic economic forces that were embedded both in the measures I specified and in the actual sequence of events.

Exchange Controls
[March 24, 1969]

In the course of their attempt to stem the outflow of gold, Presidents Kennedy and Johnson imposed numerous controls on foreign payments. The three key items were:

1. The interest-equalization tax on the purchase of foreign securities by U.S. residents. Enacted in 1964 at a rate of 15 percent as a "temporary" measure, this tax has been renewed several times and the rate is now 18.75 percent.

2. "Voluntary" restriction of foreign loans by banks begun in 1965 and administered by the Federal Reserve System. It took a special act of Congress to exempt the agreement among banks from the antitrust laws.

3. Restriction of foreign investment by U.S. corporations. This "voluntary" program, also begun in 1965, was made compulsory by President Johnson on January 1, 1968. It is administered by the Department of Commerce.

Candidate Nixon strongly criticized these controls as inconsistent with a free society and promised to end them as soon as possible.

3 Since this was written Congress has passed, and President Ford has signed, a bill legalizing gold ownership on January 1, 1975.

Recent congressional testimony indicates that the administration plans to honor this campaign promise by relaxing the controls gradually over a period of years. Commerce Secretary Stans spoke of "the first step toward some type of relaxation" of the control over business investment in "the next thirty to sixty days." Abolition, he said, should be discussed "in terms of years." Treasury Under Secretary Volcker said that the Treasury would "like" to reduce, "if possible," the interest-equalization tax.

So timid a policy is a serious mistake. These controls should be ended at one fell swoop. And they should be ended at once. We are not likely to have a better opportunity.

Tapering the controls off gradually is like cutting a dog's tail off by inches. Each time a relaxation is suggested, civil servants administering the controls will find reason to caution delay, or a milder relaxation. Abolition rather than relaxation of the controls would end such bureaucratic obstruction. It would also end the ever-present temptation to turn to controls when difficulties arise rather than to adopt more fundamental remedies.

Experience teaches that the longer controls stay in effect, the stronger are the vested interests that develop to keep them. The banks that have large loan quotas will, if they do not already, recognize that the credit restriction is a cartel device that enables them to keep this profitable business to themselves. Corporations that have large allocations of investment, or that have found ways to get around the controls, will come to look at the investment controls as highly desirable.

The time to end the controls is now because we are in an extraordinarily favorable position to do so. Capital is currently flowing into, not out of, the country. Commercial banks are borrowing abroad, not expanding their foreign loans. Their foreign loans are well under the ceiling permitted by current controls. The boom in the U.S. plus difficulties abroad have reduced the attractiveness of foreign investment. As a result, it is doubtful that any of the three controls has a real bite at the present time. Eliminating them now would simply get rid of unnecessary nuisances.

Compulsory restriction of foreign investment has in any event almost surely hurt rather than helped our balance of payments—certainly for the long run and possibly even for the short run. Its imposition must have spurred every corporation with extensive interests abroad to accumulate extra foreign balances in order to be prepared for a further tightening of the control screws. Abolition would reverse this tendency; relaxation would not. More fundamentally, foreign investment is accompanied by exports and produces a return stream of income later.

Finally, and most important of all, the U.S. dollar is in a very strong position. A run on our gold by private sources is impossible, thanks to the decision last March to let the London price of gold be a free-market price. A run on our gold by foreign central banks is technically possible but politically almost inconceivable. The strong flow of capital into the United States has at least temporarily eliminated the balance-of-payments deficit. If the Administration succeeds in slowing down inflation, the trade balance should improve rapidly to offset any future slackening in the capital inflow.

Here is also one bold campaign promise that can and should be honored by bold action. [1]

Free Trade
[August 17, 1970]

We have heard much these past few years about using the government to protect the consumer. A far more urgent problem is to protect the consumer from the government.

The immediate occasion for these remarks is the bill that is being considered by the House Ways and Means Committee to impose import quotas on textiles, shoes, and other products. Such a bill will, like present tariffs, raise prices to customers and waste our resources. Unlike present tariffs, it will not even yield any revenue to the government. The higher prices will all go to the producers—mostly simply to pay for higher costs. The consumer will be forced to spend several extra dollars to subsidize the producers by one dollar. A straight handout would be far cheaper.

The proponents of quotas say, "Free trade is fine in theory but it must be reciprocal. We cannot open our markets to foreign products if foreigners close their markets to us." Japan, they argue, to use their favorite whipping boy, "keeps her vast internal market for the private domain of Japanese industry but then pushes her products into the U.S. market and complains when we try to prevent this unfair tactic."

[1] [It was finally honored five years later, in early 1974, but only after further unnecessary foreign exchange crises. See final column in Chapter One, "A Dramatic Experiment" (April, 1974).]

The argument sounds reasonable. It is, in fact, utter nonsense. Exports are the cost of trade, imports the return from trade, not the other way around.

Suppose Japan were incredibly successful in her alleged attempt to restrict imports into Japan, managing to dispense with them entirely. Suppose that Japan were incredibly successful in her alleged attempts to push exports to the U.S., managing to sell us large quantities of assorted goods. What would Japan do with the dollars she received for her exports? Take crisp greenbacks back to Tokyo to stash in the vaults of the Bank of Japan? Let deposits at U.S. banks pile up? Jolly for us. Can you think of a better deal than our getting fine textiles, shiny cars, and sophisticated TV sets for a bale of green printed paper? Or for some entries on the books of banks? If the Japanese would only be willing to keep on doing that, we can provide all the green paper they will take.

The Japanese might accumulate, as they have been doing, a moderate sum in greenbacks or dollar deposits or dollar securities as a reserve for possible future needs. But they are too smart to do so indefinitely. Very soon Japan would take steps either to reduce exports or to use the dollars to buy imports (by changes in trade restrictions, or in the internal price level, or in the exchange rate between the yen and the dollar). We would again be under the unfortunate necessity of having to pay in real goods for real goods.

But, you may say, what if the Japanese asked for gold? Like greenbacks, gold would be useful to them only as a reserve for future purchases. They would derive no current services from the gold any more than we do from the gold buried at Fort Knox. I for one would rather have the useful goods than the idle gold. But if the U.S. authorities thought differently, they could readily refuse to sell the gold for the dollars at a fixed price of $35 an ounce. In that case, Japan would again have only the alternatives of greenbacks, deposits, dollar securities—or buying U.S.-produced goods.

Japan does impose numerous restrictions on trade—though in recent years she has been reducing them. Those trade restrictions hurt Japan and they hurt us—by denying them and us mutually profitable trade. In Japan no less than in the U.S., concentrated producers exert a greater influence on government than widely diffused consumers and are able to persuade the government to fleece the consumer for the benefit of the producers.

However, we only increase the hurt to us—and also to them—by imposing additional restrictions in our turn. The wise course for us is precisely the opposite—to move unilaterally toward free trade. If they still choose to impose restrictions, that is too bad but at least we have not added insult to injury.

This is clearly the right course of action on economic grounds. But it is also the only course of action that is in keeping with our political position in the world. We are a great nation, the leader of the free world. Yet we squander our political power to appease the textile industry in the Carolinas! We should instead be setting a standard for the world by practicing the freedom of competition, of trade, and of enterprise that we preach.

The Mark Crisis
[May 24, 1971]

Few things are so puzzling to the ordinary person as an international currency crisis. Herewith a hypothetical dialogue between an innocent reader (R) and myself (F).

R Why was there a dollar crisis?

F There wasn't a dollar crisis. There was a mark crisis. A widespread belief developed that the price of the mark was likely to rise from the 27.3 cents at which the West German government had been pegging it. Hence, many people wanted to buy marks. Since the dollar is the international currency, marks were purchased with dollars, just as a widespread belief that the price of silver was going to rise would lead people to buy silver with dollars.

R Isn't this a quibble? A distinction without a difference?

F Not at all. A dollar crisis would mean a widespread desire by holders of dollars to reduce their dollar balances. That would lead to purchases of all currencies—not just the mark and currencies closely linked to the mark. In fact, there was no great rush into French francs, British pounds, Canadian dollars, or even Japanese yen, despite the fact that the yen, like the mark, is widely regarded as undervalued at existing exchange rates. The selective character of the money flows confirms that this episode was a mark, not a dollar, crisis.

R Why was it widely believed that the mark would rise in price?

F Because West Germany had been selling or borrowing abroad more than it was buying and investing abroad. Hence, it was accumulating dollars.

R But why should Germany object to accumulating dollars? Isn't that a good position to be in?

F Not at all. It means that Germany is shipping abroad more than it is receiving from abroad. It means that people are earning incomes without having goods to buy. That part of their incomes must be immobilized—by taxes, by government borrowing, or by inflation.

R How would a higher price for the German mark affect the situation?

F If a mark costs 30 cents, say, rather than 27.3 cents, then German goods, priced in marks, would be more expensive in terms of dollars, which would reduce exports from Germany. Foreign goods, priced in dollars, would be cheaper to Germans because they could get more dollars for a given number of marks. Germany would export less and import more.

R Why then was there opposition in Germany to a higher price of the mark?

F Because the Germans, like most of us, would like to have their cake and eat it too. Exporters object to anything that would reduce exports; domestic producers object to competition from imports; the consumers who would benefit are, as in most countries, not aware of their stake. Put differently, some Germans would like to export more, other Germans would like to import less, yet both groups would like to avoid the accumulation of dollars. But Germany cannot suspend the laws of arithmetic.

R How does all this explain the sudden massive flood of funds? It is reported that purchases of marks totaled over $2 billion in just two days.

F The system under which Germany was operating, of exchange rates that are temporarily pegged by the government but are subject to change from time to time, is a wide-open invitation to massive speculation whenever a change in the exchange rate seems likely. There never was any doubt that, if the price of the German mark changed at all, it would rise. Yet, until the German central bank stopped selling them, marks were for sale at a fixed price. That gave speculators a free ride. At worst, if the mark was not revalued, they lost commissions on the purchase and sale of marks. At best, they made a handsome profit.

R Was the German central bank forced to suspend the sale of marks?

F No. As a technical matter, it could have sold an indefinite amount since it prints them.

R But wouldn't it have been inviting open inflation if it had printed all the marks that the speculators wanted to buy?

F Not at all. The speculators wanted marks to hold for future resale, not to spend in Germany. That is the key difference between the speculative flow of dollars and the accumulation of dollars in the ordinary course of trade.

R Why then did the German central bank suspend the sale of marks?

F The only answer that makes sense is that the German authorities were in fact contemplating a rise in the price of the mark, and they did not want to have to buy back the marks they printed at a price higher than the price at which they sold them.

R Is there an alternative that would avoid massive speculative swings?

F A free-market exchange rate—the system Canada returned to in 1970. Under such a system, if there is a belief that the price will rise, and speculators start buying Canadian dollars, the price rises at once, which discourages speculation because there is no longer a one-way option.

When the German central bank stopped selling marks, that did not mean that you could not buy marks, but only that you could no longer buy them from the central bank *at a fixed price*. On Monday, May 10, Germany explicitly adopted a floating exchange rate.

R Is that bad?

F I believe that it is good. It provides an effective automatic mechanism that will eliminate crises—provided the German central bank doesn't try to manipulate the rate. I have myself been in favor of floating exchange rates for more than twenty years. Incidentally, an article that I wrote at that time stating the case for floating rates was a by-product of a study of the problems facing Germany and other continental countries under the so-called Coal and Steel Community—a precursor to the Common Market.

R If the price of the mark rises, isn't that equivalent to a devaluation of the U.S. dollar?

F Vis-à-vis the mark, yes. At the same time, the dollar was not de-valued vis-à-vis the French franc, British pound, etc. With floating ex-change rates, the U.S. dollar would appreciate every day vis-à-vis some currencies, depreciates vis-à-vis other currencies.

R What should the U.S. have done to avert or ease the crisis?

F Nothing. For domestic reasons we should continue a monetary policy directed at slowing down inflation while at the same time encouraging moderate expansion. That is also the best policy for the world. The dollar has become *the* international currency. The world, like the U.S., will be served best by a currency that remains stable in value.

R In sum, has the crisis seriously impaired the world monetary system?

F On the contrary, it has strengthened it. A system of fixed exchange rates subject to change from time to time is not a viable system. The sooner it is replaced by floating exchange rates, the better.

R Can I now consider myself a fully qualified expert on international monetary arrangements?

F Afraid not. No area in economics is so complex and full of pitfalls. Despite the length of this column, I have not even mentioned interest arbitrage, futures markets, official price of gold, special drawing rights, IMF, exchange controls or Eurodollars.

Gold
[August 16, 1971]

The West Coast Commodity Exchange recently initiated public trading in gold futures. The exchange thought it had found a loophole in the Treasury Regulations issued under the Gold Reserve Act of 1934, which prohibits U.S. residents from owning, buying or selling gold except for industrial and numismatic purposes. The Treasury objected and after a few days the exchange suspended trading. The matter will now be decided in the courts.

There never was, and there is not now, any valid reason to prohibit individuals from owning, buying or selling gold. Individuals should have the same right to trade in gold as they have to trade in silver, copper, aluminum, or other commodities.

It was widely believed that the prohibition had a valid monetary justification when it was first imposed. That is false. When President Roosevelt severed the link between the dollar and gold on March 6, 1933, the U.S. gold stock was higher relative to the total quantity of money than at any time since the Federal Reserve System was established in 1914.

There was no major run on gold in 1933, separate from the run on banks which led holders of deposits to try to convert them into currency, including gold coin and gold certificates. FDR severed the link between the dollar and gold and then deliberately raised the price of gold—first in 1933 by manipulating the market and then in early 1934 by fixing the price at $35 an ounce under the Gold Reserve Act of 1934—in order to devalue the dollar relative to other currencies, and thereby raise the dollar prices of farm products and other internationally traded goods. He did not raise the price to protect a dwindling official stock of gold or in order to permit monetary expansion. The rise in the price of gold produced a flood of gold into the U.S. The U.S. gold stock more than tripled from 1934 to 1940.

Why then did President Roosevelt forbid the private ownership of gold and require all holders of gold to deliver their holdings to the government? This "nationalization" of gold was for one purpose and one purpose only: to keep private individuals from profiting by the rise in the dollar price of gold that the government deliberately engineered. Private holders of gold were required to turn their gold over to the U.S. Treasury at $20.67 an ounce when the market price was well above this sum.

This was an act of expropriation of private property in no way different in principle from Castro's nationalization of U.S.-owned factories and other properties without compensation or from Allende's nationalization of U.S.-owned copper mines in Chile at a price well below market value. As a nation, we do not have a leg to stand on when we object to these acts of expropriation. We did precisely the same thing to residents of the U.S.

Of course, holders of gold resisted the expropriation. Those who held gold certificates were helpless, since the Treasury would no longer honor them. But those who held coin were in a different position. Of the gold coin estimated to be held by the public in February 1933 ($571 million), only half was ever turned in—and much of this was probably turned in by commercial banks whose holdings were a matter of official record.[1]

[1] To maintain the fiction that the law had been obeyed, the official statistics were "revised" to exclude the $287 million not turned in, on the ground that this amount must have been lost, destroyed, exported without record or held in numismatic collections. In its official statistics, the Federal Reserve System went so far as to subtract this amount from its estimates of the quantity of money all the way back to 1914. This revision cannot be justified. It can be demonstrated conclusively that the maximum error on this score was trivial. Accordingly, in estimates of the U.S. money stock made by Anna J. Schwartz and myself, we have eliminated the spurious revision.

Whatever arguments there might once have been for prohibiting the private ownership of gold, there are none today. The reduction in the monetary role of gold that President Roosevelt began has now been completed. Gold-reserve requirements for Federal Reserve notes and deposits have been abolished. The attempt to maintain the world market price of gold at $35 an ounce has been abandoned. There is a free market in London on which the price is currently more than $40 an ounce. The official price is wholly symbolic, and so is the monetary role of gold.

Congressman Philip Crane has introduced a bill repealing the prohibition on the ownership, purchase, or sale of gold by private individuals. That bill should be passed promptly.[1] Let us end once and for all an utterly unnecessary and shameful, if niggling, restriction on individual freedom.

Keep the Dollar Free
[December 20, 1971]

Rumor hath it that the U.S. is on the verge of agreeing to a rise in the official dollar price of gold (or of SDR's) as part of an international agreement to establish a new structure of fixed exchange rates. If this rumor proves correct, we shall have squandered a great opportunity.[2] The actions of August 15 set the dollar free—from gold and from other currencies. We should keep the dollar free—from gold and from other currencies.

So long as the U.S. neither buys nor sells gold, a change in the official price of gold (or SDR's) is a purely bookkeeping change that need have no technical effects whatsoever. What conceivable difference can it make to the U.S., or to other countries, if we don't sell gold to foreign governments at $35 an ounce or if we don't sell gold to them at $38

[1] [A bill giving the President power to end the ban passed in 1973. After his failure to do so, both houses of Congress have now (July, 1974) passed bills to end the ban on a definite date. In August President Ford signed a bill legalizing private ownership on January 1, 1975.]

[2] [It did prove correct in part. The United States raised the official price to $38 an ounce early in 1972, and to $42.22 in 1973. However, the rumor proved false in the sense that the rise in the official price was not accompanied by any commitment on the part of the U.S. to convert dollars into gold at the new price.]

an ounce? Yet other countries want us to take this step. It looks as if we can make them happy at no cost to us. As the *Morgan Guaranty Survey* recently put it: "One can perhaps marvel that other countries would place so much importance on what is really a token action on the part of the U.S. but the fact is that they do. And if that's what it takes to break the international stalemate . . . it seems extremely questionable for the U.S. to hold back."

The fallacy in this argument is that it treats foreign central bankers as utter fools, which they clearly are not. If raising the official price of gold is simply "a token action," why do they "place so much importance" on it? The answer, I submit, is that *in a longer-run context,* it is very far indeed from a token act.

Over the past decade, other countries—France and Germany in particular—have exerted an influence on us out of all proportion to their true political and economic strength because of an unwise commitment to convert dollars into gold at $35 an ounce. By undervaluing the franc, de Gaulle accumulated dollars that he could threaten to present to us for gold; by undervaluing the mark, Germany did the same thing, though without the public gestures that de Gaulle gloried in. The demeaning result, as I put it in congressional testimony as early as 1963, was that we "send our officials hat in hand to make the rounds of foreign governments and central banks; we put central banks in a position to determine whether or not we can meet our obligations and thus enable them to exert a great influence on our policies."

Foreign central banks and governments naturally regret our ending a commitment that gave them so much power. They are desperately anxious to induce us to undertake a new commitment—be it to convert dollars into gold or into SDR's or into some other international asset. They recognize that they cannot do so at once. But if they get us to take the first step—to proclaim publicly that the dollar does have a fixed relation to gold that is only temporarily suspended—they will be well on the road to persuading us once again to fasten a rope around our neck. That—and not stupidity, or ignorance, or irrationality—is why they set such a high value on our changing the official price of gold.

What do they have to offer us in return? Not a single thing in the monetary area. The President's dramatic actions of August 15 broke an ice jam and jarred exchange rates loose. It is not in our interest—or in the world's interest—to have them fixed again. That will simply once again set the stage for monetary instability, balance-of-payments crises, and exchange controls. We cannot, on our own, establish a flexible exchange rate between the dollar and any other currency. It takes two to make that bargain. But so long as we do not commit ourselves to converting the dollar into any other currency or asset at a fixed rate, we have done our part. If other countries wish to avoid surpluses, they can let the market set exchange rates that will balance payments. In that case, we shall not have a deficit. If other countries choose to peg their currencies to the dollar, they must bear the consequences.

Public pressure at home and abroad to reestablish a system of fixed exchange rates largely reflects the fear that flexible rates will mean unstable exchange rates that will hamper foreign trade. These fears are not justified. The postwar period demonstrated that supposedly fixed exchange rates are unstable exchange rates. When they change, they change by a lot. Flexible exchange rates change frequently but by much less. Gradual changes produce gradual adjustments that prevent big problems from arising. In practice, flexible exchange rates are more stable, and more favorable to the healthy and vigorous expansion of foreign trade and investment, than temporarily rigid rates subject to large changes from time to time. The past three months is too short a time to demonstrate the full effects of a system of flexible rates but surely it is long enough to discredit the prophets of doom.

Monetary neutrality would liberate trade policy from balance-of-payments problems. Trade policy could and should be directed at promoting the freer movement of goods, services and capital. The current emphasis on stimulating exports is misguided. The *imports* we get from other countries are the gain to us from foreign trade. Exports are the price we pay. The less we must export to acquire imports the better off we are. Producing exports simply to give them away is a make-work project strictly on a par with hiring people to dig holes.

The 10 percent surtax succeeded beyond expectation in shaking exchange rates loose. Once it did that, it should have been abolished promptly. Its continuation has been fostering the new wave of mercantilism that is sweeping the U.S. and the rest of the world. What does it profit us to hurt ourselves simply in order to hurt other countries as well? We are a great nation and should act like one. We should move on our own to eliminate exchange controls and barriers to the movement of goods and capital. A bold and farsighted U.S. example is likely to produce a healthier response from other countries than threats of retaliation.

At home, the dollar is a dollar is a dollar. The U.S. government makes no commitments to its own citizen to exchange dollars for anything else at a fixed rate. He cannot turn them in for SDR's or any other funny money, let alone for gold or silver. President Nixon's action on August 15 put citizens and governments of other countries precisely on a par with U.S. citizens. That is as it should be. However, if the rumored agreement becomes fact, our government will once again be making commitments to foreign countries that it is unwilling to make to its own citizens. Secretary Connally and President Nixon will have snatched defeat from the jaws of victory.

The Crisis That Refreshes
[March 12, 1973]

The crisis that closed foreign-exchange markets in many countries last week is good for the U.S. and the world. It is another nail in the coffin of the obsolete system of fixed exchange rates that has produced such crises repeatedly in the past few years. It is another step toward a system of exchange rates determined in free markets, the arrangement that is best for both the U.S. and the world. That has been my view for more than two decades and the events of the past few years have confirmed me ever more strongly in that view. They have also increased the number of fellow believers from a meager platoon to an army.

The present crisis was triggered largely by the mistaken policy of Germany. In May 1971, Germany faced a similar run into the mark. It purchased something like $5 billion or $6 billion in a vain attempt to keep the mark exchange rate fixed. After a week, it let the exchange rate float. The mark appreciated by about 10 percent, so Germany had to sell back the $5 billion for fewer marks than it paid for them—thereby losing something like $500 million on the deal.

I said at the time that such an episode would not recur, that never again would Germany pay so high a price for the trivial gain of postponing the floating of the mark for a week. I was wrong. Apparently, governments do not learn. Only people do. Mr. Schiller was the German economics minister in 1971. He resigned and was replaced by Mr.

Schmidt, who, determined to be different, announced that Germany would neither float nor appreciate the mark. When a crisis emerged, he simply repeated the earlier mistake, forcing the German people to pay a still higher tuition fee this time. The U.S. took Mr. Schmidt off the hook in February by agreeing to devalue by 10 percent, which enabled the exchange rate of the mark to rise without any explicit action by Germany. But then another crisis emerged.

As I write this, it is not clear how the present crisis will end. There is much talk of a coordinated float by the Common Market countries in terms of the dollar, with fixed exchange rates among the separate Common Market currencies. By the time this column appears in print, you may know whether that approach was adopted. If it was, I predict that the fixed rates within the Common Market will break down within the next year or so, as has happened after every previous attempt to fix exchange rates among the Common Market countries.[1] Such a breakdown will demonstrate that still another variant of a fixed-rate system is not viable either, and so will take the world another step on the road toward freely floating exchange rates.

What should the U.S. do? Follow a stable monetary policy at home and take no specific action whatsoever with respect to the international crisis. Naturally, we regret the disturbances other countries are experiencing, but the crisis raises no direct problem for us, since we have no commitment to peg the price of gold or of other currencies. We have in effect said to the world: a dollar is a dollar. You are free to buy or sell dollars at any price you wish, to use them for purchases or investment in the U.S., or to hold them. We shall not interfere with your use of them. We shall not try to fix the price of the dollar in terms of other currencies.

That is the right policy. It is also the policy that President Nixon has been following (for example, note his recent commitment to remove all controls on capital movements by the end of 1974).

The U.S. economy is strong. We have been restraining inflation more successfully than almost any other nation in the world. We remain the leading economic power in the world. Under these circumstances, the U.S. can serve the world best by keeping its own economy healthy and by preventing inflation. If we do that, the dollar will remain the major international currency.

As the world is gradually coming to learn, so-called fixed exchange

[This is precisely what happened.]

rates mean unstable exchange rates and repeated crises. Floating exchange rates mean stable exchange rates and orderly markets. Fixed exchange rates mean great uncertainty for traders and travelers—because any day the rate may be changed drastically or exchange controls may be imposed or altered. Floating exchange rates mean far less uncertainty because free markets adjust promptly and thereby eliminate the need for large changes.

Speculation and Speculation
[April 23, 1973]

During the recent international monetary crisis, governments in all lands blamed currency speculators for their troubles. At the same time, the governments themselves engaged in currency speculation—though of course they called it by a different and more dignified name. They engaged in "intervention."

The private speculation that the governments deplored was socially useful and had desirable effects. The official speculation in which the governments engaged was socially harmful and had undesirable effects.

Private speculation forced governments to face up to reality, to recognize that the exchange rates they were seeking to peg were artificial. It forced Japan and Germany in particular to recognize that their currencies were undervalued. It forced them and other countries to give the market a greater role in setting exchange rates. Reality would have conquered in any event, sooner or later. Speculation made it sooner rather than later and thereby reduced the harm done by the artificial exchange rates.

Official speculation was very different. Its aim was to preserve artificial exchange rates, to postpone the recognition of reality. Had it succeeded, it would have permitted economic distortions to cumulate to still more harmful proportions.

Private speculators are far from omniscient. This time, they happened to be right and so made handsome profits. Next time, they may be wrong and suffer grievous losses. But in either case, they speculate at their own risk with their own money.

Official speculators, too, are far from omniscient. This time, they were wrong; next time, they may be right. But there is an important reason why they are more likely to be wrong than right. They speculate not with their own money but with the taxpayers' money. As a result, there is little pressure on them to control their natural impulse to resist change.

Regrettably, the U.S. participated in the official speculation. Prior to the so-called U.S. devaluation on February 12, 1973, the Federal Reserve sold marks that it held and marks that it borrowed from Germany in a vain attempt to hold down the dollar price of the mark. It sold the marks for about $320 million. After the devaluation, it would have cost more than $350 million to buy back the same number of marks. The result? A negligible postponement of mark appreciation, at a cost of at least $30 million to the U.S. taxpayer and a worsening of the balance of payments, since that $30 million also had to be financed. The U.S. taxpayer got off cheaply. Official German and Japanese speculation probably cost German and Japanese taxpayers more than $1 billion—to equally little avail.

But we have not always gotten off so cheaply. And we may not do so in the future. Official U.S. speculation before the closing of the gold window on August 15, 1971, cost the American taxpayer a much larger sum. And Secretary of the Treasury George Shultz, at the end of the recent European negotiations, announced that although the U.S. was not "committed" to intervening to support the new price of the dollar, it would do so at its discretion from time to time.

As U.S. citizens, we cannot and should not prevent German and Japanese governmental officials from speculating with their taxpayers' money. That is a task for German and Japanese citizens. But we can and should restrain our own officials.

It would be nice if we could simply forbid U.S. government purchase of foreign currencies. But that is not practicable. Foreign currencies must be purchased to pay government expenses abroad. But Congress could at least forbid the purchase or sale of foreign currencies to influence exchange rates.

Moreover, the Federal Reserve speculates via so-called swap agreements under which we agree with other countries to lend them dollars on demand for a short period and they agree to lend us their currency. These swap agreements now total something like $12 billion.

The swap agreements serve no useful function and Congress should terminate the Fed's authority to enter into them. Their only role is to enable the U.S. government to "intervene" in order to affect exchange rates. We and the world would be better off if exchange rates were determined in a free market. And whatever other countries do, the U.S., as the source of the key international money, has no business engaging in currency manipulation to affect exchange rates.

Alexander Hamilton on the Common Market
[June 4, 1973]

I recently treated myself to a re-reading of the Federalist Papers—that remarkable collection of newspaper columns by Alexander Hamilton, James Madison, and John Jay written in 1787 and 1788 during the campaign to replace the Articles of Confederation by the Constitution. I was astounded to discover that Paper no. 15, written by Hamilton, contains a more cogent analysis of the European Common Market than any I have seen from the pen of a modern writer.

How can that be? Because the Common Market has almost the same political structure as the Confederation of the original thirteen states—Hamilton's explicit target. Hence, his analysis applies equally to both.

"The great and radical vice in the construction of the existing Confederation," wrote Hamilton, "is the principle of LEGISLATION for STATES or GOVERNMENTS, in their CORPORATE or COLLECTIVE CAPACITIES, and as contra-distinguished from the INDIVIDUALS of which they consist . . . . Though in theory [the Confederation's] resolutions . . . are laws constitutionally binding on the members of the Union, yet in practice they are mere recommendations which the States observe or disregard at their option."

A striking example is a Common Market agreement in 1972 to maintain a narrower range of exchange rates among Common Market currencies than between them and other currencies (the short-lived "snake in the tunnel"). The agreement specified that each country was to settle net debts to other Common Market countries monthly in gold, dollars, and other currencies in the proportions they constituted of the country's own reserves. Italy came into deficit. The rules called on it to settle roughly half the debt in gold at an official value of $38 an ounce. Naturally, Italy was reluctant to do so, since gold was selling in London at about $70 an ounce. The result: the rules were changed as Hamilton had predicted and Italy settled without transferring any gold.

"There is in the nature of sovereign power," says Hamilton, "an impatience of control that disposes those who are invested with the exercise of it to look with an evil eye upon all external attempts to restrain or direct its operations. From this spirit it happens that in every political association . . . of lesser sovereignties, there will be found a kind of eccentric tendency in the subordinate or inferior orbs by the operation of which there will be a perpetual effort in each to fly off from the common center. This tendency is not difficult to be accounted for. It has its origin in the love of power. Power controlled or abridged is almost always the rival and enemy of that power by which it is controlled or abridged."

"If we still will adhere to the design of a national government . . . we must resolve to incorporate into our plan those ingredients which may be considered as forming the characteristic difference between a league and a government; we must extend the authority of the Union to the persons of the citizens—the only proper objects of government. . . ."

This was the decisive difference between the Articles of Confederation and the Constitution. The Articles were an agreement among sovereign states, under which laws passed by the national government were to be enforced on individuals by the state governments. That is today the situation in the Common Market. The Constitution gave both national and state governments authority over persons. The result was a strong and stable nation instead of the unstable, quarreling league that it replaced.

The many proponents of a true United States of Europe favor the same development. They wish to make the Common Market a true government with authority over persons and not simply a league of nations. But national loyalties are vastly stronger in Common Market countries than state loyalites were in the thirteen states, and cultural differences are vastly greater. The thirteen states accepted the Constitution only after a bitter fight and by a narrow margin. There is little chance that the Common Market countries will accept similar restraints on national sovereignty.

I infer that no real United States of Europe is in the cards, that instead we shall see, in the words of Hamilton again, "how impossible it must be to induce a number of assemblies, deliberating at a distance from each other, at different times and under different impressions, long to cooperate in the same views and pursuits."

The Price of Gold
[April 22, 1974]

From the time of King Croesus to the present, few diseases have been more virulent than gold fever. An epidemic is again raging, as the price of gold in London has doubled from 1971 to early 1973, and then doubled again in the past year—from $90 an ounce to $180. The gold bugs regard this as only a beginning. A recent front-page story in a French weekly economic paper was headlined: "The price of gold, $500 an ounce?"

Herewith, in question-and-answer form, an attempt at a sober evaluation of gold's present role and future prospects.

Q. The "official" price of gold is $42.22 an ounce. Exactly what does that mean?

A. Before August 15, 1971, the official price (then $35 an ounce) was the price at which the U.S. government was committed to trade gold with foreign central banks. Since August 15, 1971, when President Nixon closed the gold window, the official price is the price at which the U.S. will *not* buy or sell gold. It serves purely the bookkeeping function of putting a value on the gold owned by the U.S. government.

Q. Many gold bugs expect the U.S. and other countries to fix a much higher "official" price and to restore the convertibility of paper moneys into gold at that higher price. Is this likely?

A. Not as far as the U.S. is concerned. And I doubt that any other country will do so if the U.S. does not.

The U.S. has little to gain, and much to lose, by accepting the obligation to buy and sell at a fixed price, whatever its level. It should have suspended the commitment to do so much sooner than it did.

The French, of course, would like us to resume convertibility into gold. Our earlier unwise commitment to that effect gave them far greater political power over us than they otherwise would have had. They dream of recovering that power. I trust that we shall not oblige.

The only relic of the earlier commitment, apart from the artificial bookkeeping price, is that it is still illegal for U.S. citizens to buy, sell or hold gold for other than commercial or numismatic purposes. Congress has already given the President authority to remove this prohibition. The sooner he exercises the authority the better.

Q. Does that mean that gold no longer has any real monetary role?

A. Exactly. Gold is today a highly speculative commodity. However, its past monetary role is reflected both in public attitudes toward gold and in the huge stocks of gold still held by central banks of the world. These stocks are now simply national assets like our own strategic stockpiles of copper and other metals.

Q. Do you foresee any future monetary role for gold?

A. Lip service, yes. A meaningful role, no. I see one and only one possibility of a future monetary role for gold. If governments follow completely irresponsible monetary policies, private individuals could conceivably contract with one another in terms of gold, so producing something of a private gold money. However, even this possibility is hampered for the U.S. by legal obstacles. After the Civil War, a gold clause became a standard feature of long-term bonds as well as of many other contracts. In 1933, a joint congressional resolution abrogated the gold clause in all public and private contracts, past and future, and in 1935, the Supreme Court in effect upheld, by a five-to-four decision, the constitutionality of that resolution.

Q. As commodity, what is gold worth?

A. Whatever the market says, which is today $180 an ounce.

Q. That's an evasion. Can that price be expected to continue? Does it reflect simply general inflation?

A. In 1929, the official, and effective, price of gold was $20.67 an ounce. At that price, most gold production was being absorbed into monetary reserves. Commercial use alone was far less than current production. In 1933, President Roosevelt started raising the price of gold and he fixed it at $35 an ounce on January 31, 1934. At that price, the U.S. was flooded with gold, so in 1934, $35 was decidedly above an effective market price. Wartime inflation converted $35 into an artificially cheap price, so that by the late 1950s, U.S. gold reserves started declining.

From 1929 to date, dollar prices in general have tripled; from 1933 to date, they have quadrupled. Applying these multiples to the 1929 and 1934 price of gold gives $60 to $140 as a price range for gold today that fully allows for the inflation since 1929 and 1933—and the upper limit of $140 is clearly too high.

I conclude that inflation alone cannot justify today's market price for gold.

Q. What about commercial and monetary uses?

A. Commercial uses have expanded rapidly, encouraged by the artificially low level at which the price of gold was held for many years by the U.S. The present abnormally high price is likely to reverse that effect.

Official monetary reserves are a major overhang on the gold market They are worth more than $200 billion at today's market prices—or more than twenty-five times the present value of estimated world annual production. Central banks will probably continue to hold on to this gold, but present prices must be very tempting. Even a moderate release from monetary stocks could have a major influence on the market price.

Q. What about the demand by private persons as a reserve?

A. This demand derives from two sources: first, as an emergency reserve; second, as a hedge against inflation.

Holding some gold as an emergency reserve is certainly a prudent policy for many people in many parts of the world. For example, the Indians who were unceremoniously expelled from Kenya some years ago could not benefit from houses, factories, or other similar property they owned. They could sell them, if at all, only at distress prices. If they had gold or diamonds that they could take with them, they were in a much better position.

As a hedge against inflation, gold was useless from 1935 to 1971. In the past three years, gold has more than quadrupled in price. That was a bonanza for holders of gold, but it was hardly a reliable hedge.

Q. Your net conclusion?

A. Over the long term, the market price of gold can be expected to rise along with prices in general. But the price today is sharply above the level that could be justified by either past inflation, or by present and foreseeable monetary or commercial demand. That does not mean that the price of gold may not soon go still higher. Almost anything is possible over short periods for a highly speculative commodity, such as gold has become. But, in my opinion, it does mean that the price of gold is also likely to take a sharp tumble in the not too distant future—after all, sooner or later, prices do tend to reflect the basic underlying forces rather than temporary speculative moves. [1]

[1] [As of this writing (July 1974), the price of gold on the London market had fallen to $129 an ounce.]

Chapter Eight
A Volunteer Army

It would be nice to record that this chapter has only historical interest, that the move from conscription to an all-volunteer armed force, completed on June 30, 1973, can be regarded as a *fait accompli*. Unfortunately, that would be premature. The draft did end on June 30, 1973, both because President Nixon and Secretary Laird had committed themselves to that outcome and also because Congress was unwilling to enact a further continuation of conscription. But sad experience has taught me that there is many a slip between initial acceptance of a policy and its full implementation and retention. The final column in this chapter documents the divided views in the armed services about the volunteer army and the difficulty of inducing the armed forces to implement it vigorously and effectively.

Despite these doubts, the record does give real ground for optimism. We have come a long way from the period when the draft was routinely and with hardly a murmur of opposition renewed for four years at a clip (always in odd-numbered years when there were neither congressional nor presidential elections). There is widespread, informed, and vigorous opposition to the draft, and despite all their hesitancy, the leaders of the armed forces are making a determined and intelligent effort to implement a volunteer force. After my column, "Volunteer Armed Force: Failure or Victim?" (February 11, 1974) appeared, I received a number of letters from high officials in the armed forces assuring me that they were determined to make the volunteer army a success and that the problems I had referred to in my column had been resolved.

Though this issue is outside my major field of professional interest, it happens to be one in which I have been passionately involved for many years—indeed, it is almost the only issue on which I have engaged in any extensive personal lobbying with members of the House and Senate (as contrasted with testifying before relevant congressional committees on subjects in my fields of competence).

My interest has been on two grounds: first, and most obvious, because conscription is such a blatant and serious restriction on individual freedom—it is the most extreme form of compulsory servitude practiced in the United States since the Civil War; and second, public acceptance of a strong armed force seems to me essential to maintain the freedom of the United States. Conscription undermined that acceptance and has played a major role in bringing the military into the low public estate to which it has fallen.

In the course of my involvement in this issue, I have come into contact with many other persons concerned with the draft—both in favor of it and opposed to it. I have observed many persons initially in favor of the draft change their opinions as they have looked into the arguments and studied the evidence; I have never observed anyone who was initially in favor of a volunteer force reverse his position on the basis of further study. This greatly enhances my confidence in the validity of the position I have taken.

For the reader who is interested in a comprehensive summary of the arguments pro and con, I recommend *The Report of the President's Commission on an All-Volunteer Armed Force* (Macmillan Company, 1970). This commission was headed by Thomas Gates, and I was a member of it, so this is not an unbiased recommendation even though I believe that the report is unbiased.

A Volunteer Army
[December 19, 1966]

A military draft is undesirable and unnecessary. We can and should man our armed forces with volunteers—as the United States has traditionally done except in major wars.

Only a minority of young men now enter the armed forces. Hence, some method of "selective service"—of deciding which young man should serve and which two or three should not—is inevitable. But our present method is inequitable, wasteful, and inconsistent with a free society.

On this point there is wide agreement. John K. Galbraith and Barry Goldwater, the New Left and the Republican Ripon Society, have all urged that conscription be abolished. Even most supporters of the draft regard it as at best a necessary evil.

The draft is inequitable because irrelevant considerations play so large a role in determining who serves. It is wasteful because deferment of students, fathers, and married men jams colleges, raises the birth rate, and fuels divorce courts. It is inconsistent with a free society because it exacts compulsory service from some and limits the freedom of others to travel abroad, emigrate, or even to talk and act freely. *So long as compulsion is retained, these defects are inevitable.* A lottery would only make the arbitrary element overt. Universal national service would compound the evil—regimenting all youth to camouflage the regimentation of some.

Two principal objections are made to a volunteer force:

1. That a "professional" army endangers political freedom. There *is* a real danger, but it arises from a strong armed force not from the method of recruiting enlisted men. Napoleon and Franco both rose to power at the head of a conscript army. However we recruit, the essential need is to maintain close links between the officer corps and the body politic.

2. That a volunteer army is not feasible because, at present terms, too few men volunteer. Little wonder: the starting pay, including cost of keep, is about $45 a week! We could readily attract more volunteers simply by paying market wages. Estimates of how much total military pay would have to go up vary from $4 billion to $20 billion a year.

Whatever the extra amount, we are now paying a larger sum in concealed form. Conscription is a tax in kind—forced labor exacted from the men who serve involuntarily. The amount of the tax is the difference between the sum for which they would voluntarily serve and the sum we now pay them—if Joe Namath were drafted, his tax might well run into hundreds of thousands of dollars. The real cost of manning the armed forces now, *including this concealed tax,* is greater than the cost of manning a volunteer force of the same size because the volunteers would be the men who find military service the most attractive alternative.

Moreover, a volunteer force would need fewer recruits. We now waste manpower by high turnover, unnecessary training and retraining, and the use of underpaid servicemen for menial tasks.

Adding to cost, low pay for men in service encourages extravagant veterans' bonuses—currently more than $6 billion a year (over 40 percent as much as total military pay). Young men seeking shelter from the draft impose unnecessary costs on colleges and universities. Other young men fritter away their time in stopgap jobs awaiting conscription, while industry seeks men to train.

The monetary savings that would come from abolishing conscription are dwarfed by even greater nonmonetary advantages: young men could arrange their schooling, careers, marriages, and families in accordance with their own long-run interests; draft boards could be freed from the appalling task of choosing which men should serve, deciding claims for conscientious objection, ruling whether young men may leave the country; colleges and universities could be free to pursue their proper educational function; industry and government could hire young men on their merits not their deferments.

One of the greatest advances in human freedom was the commutation of taxes in kind to taxes in money. We have reverted to a barbarous custom. It is past time that we regain our heritage.

The Draft
[March 11, 1968]

The arbitrariness and deficiencies of our present method of manning the armed forces are highlighted by the recent directive ending automatic exemption for hitherto protected occupations and automatic deferments for most graduate students (the exceptions are students already in their second year or beyond, and students going into medicine, dentistry and related fields or into the ministry).

Academic administrators are expressing great concern that graduate-student enrollments will decline sharply and that teaching assistants will be scarce. This concern would be fully justified if all the young men who would have been deferred or exempted under earlier rules will in fact now be drafted—except of course for those who do not meet physical or mental standards or are granted status as conscientious objectors.

But arithmetic plus the needs of the military assure that this will not occur. The number of young men added to the eligible rolls is at least double the number who will be drafted. Supposedly, the oldest are to be drafted first. If that were done, all of the new draftees would be in their middle twenties, and most would be college graduates. Not one of the roughly two million young men turning eighteen would be taken. Would the military be satisfied with this outcome? If there be conscription, it is certainly inequitable to give special treatment to young men who go to college. But, on the other hand, is soldiering one of the occupations for which college graduation should be a prerequisite? Is that a reasonable use of our manpower?

What is likely to happen is that, by one expedient or another, most college graduates and persons now exempt on occupational grounds will continue to be deferred. Public pronouncements will be one thing, practice another. But that does not mean that the pronouncements do no harm. On the contrary, hundreds of thousands of young men will be subjected to needless uncertainty and distress. They will find it more difficult to get employment because of the risk that they will be drafted. Employers will be induced to get along with less satisfactory employees. Thousands of colleges will take measures that will prove unnecessary or harmful. We shall have another striking example of the defect of compulsion as a method of deciding which young man shall serve in the armed forces and which two or three or four shall not.

Over a year ago, I wrote in this column that "a military draft is undesirable and unnecessary. We can and should man our armed forces with volunteers—as the United States has traditionally done except in major wars" (*Newsweek,* Dec. 19, 1966).

In the interim, Congress has passed a bill extending conscription for another four years, yet there has also been increasing recognition of the defects of conscription. The case for a voluntary system has been presented in testimony before congressional committees. Several bills have been introduced in both the Senate and the House providing for the early transition to a fully voluntary system of manning the armed forces.

Three books on the subject have recently appeared: *The Draft,* which summarizes a conference held at the University of Chicago in December 1966 and presents evidence on all the alternatives (edited by Sol Tax, University of Chicago Press); *How to End the Draft,* by five congressmen (edited by Douglas Bailey and Steve Herbits, National Press, Inc.); and *Why the Draft?* by seven young men connected with the University of Virginia (edited by James C. Miller III, with an introduction by Senator

Brooke, Penguin Books). These books demonstrate that conscription is neither necessary nor desirable, that it is entirely feasible to man our armed forces by voluntary means provided the military stop underpaying new recruits and take effective steps to make a career in the services more attractive. These books consider and meet every objection that has been raised to a voluntary army.

Draft or no draft, this country would be now engaged in a searching debate over Vietnam. But the virulence and the divisiveness of the debate have been greatly increased by the draft, with its threat to civil liberties and with its closing of all alternatives except open revolt to young men who disagree strongly with our policy. Must we continue to add to the strain on our society by using a method of manning our armed forces that is inequitable, wasteful, and basically inconsistent with a free society?

The End of the Draft?
[March 16, 1970]

At long last, the end of the draft is in sight.

Two months after his Inauguration, President Nixon appointed a commission "to develop a comprehensive plan for eliminating conscription and moving toward an all-volunteer armed force." That commission has now unanimously recommended a plan that it believes would permit conscription to end on June 30, 1971, when the present legal authority expires. It would retain only a standby draft to be put into effect in case of emergency by action of Congress on the recommendation of the President.

As a member of the President's commission, I was much impressed by the emergence of unanimity out of initial disagreement. As our deliberations proceeded, and especially as our knowledgeable staff developed a growing body of factual evidence, it became ever clearer to all of us how superficial are most arguments in favor of conscription and how inefficient conscription is both as a method of taxation and as a method of recruiting manpower.

The often hysterical claims that an all-volunteer force is undesirable because it would be all black or all this or all that or because it would strengthen militarism or because . . . all these claims are contradicted by one simple yet overwhelmingly important fact: *our armed forces today consist predominantly of true volunteers.*

Many men "reluctantly" volunteer for a first term of service because of the threat of the draft. But we know that all men beyond the first term of service are true volunteers, and they alone number nearly 40 percent of the total forces. In addition, our best estimates are that at least one-third of the first-termers are also true volunteers. In all, therefore, at least 60 percent of the armed forces are true volunteers. A change in the method of recruiting the remaining 40 percent—mostly enlisted men in the very lowest ranks—cannot produce drastic changes in either the composition or character of the armed forces.

Enforced service by a conscript is a tax imposed on him no less than the check you send to Internal Revenue is a tax imposed on you. The size of his tax is the difference between the sum of money for which he would have served voluntarily and the pay he actually receives. Currently, this tax amounts to about 50 percent of the potential civilian income of draftees. So unfair a tax imposed on so small a minority would never be passed explicitly by Congress. It persists only because it is hidden.

The tax is not only unfair, it is also inefficient. Every tax involves costs in addition to the amount of the tax itself. For conscription, these indirect costs are the heavy burdens imposed on actual and potential draftees, their families, universities, employers—and most important, on all of us through the weakening of the political fabric of society.

Most of these costs cannot be assigned a money value. But for those that can, the commission estimates that "for each $1 in tax-in-kind collected, an average of $2.50 is foregone by the public"—i.e., that it costs $1.50 to collect $1. That is one reason why, when the books are kept properly to show all costs and all returns, a volunteer force is far less costly than a mixed force of conscripts and volunteers. But it is not the only reason.

A young man is conscripted for two years. He spends the first six months or so being trained, the last few months being processed for his discharge. We are lucky if he spends one year in active service. In addition, the time of other men must be used to train him and move him in and out of service.

To man a mixed conscript-volunteer force of 2.5 million men (the middle of the range of force levels considered by the commission) requires recruiting each year about 440,000 enlisted men (excluding officers). Even with today's low first-term pay and conditions of service, at least 250,000 would be true volunteers, leaving 190,000 who would have to be conscripted or induced to volunteer by threat of the draft.

An all-volunteer force of equal effectiveness has less turnover and uses manpower more efficiently. As a result, it requires recruiting each year about 325,000 enlisted men, or only 75,000 in addition to the present number of true volunteers.

Compel 190,000 men per year to serve. Or improve pay and conditions of service to attract an additional 75,000 volunteers out of the 1.5 million who each year turn nineteen. These are the real alternatives.

Volunteer Armed Force: Failure or Victim?
[February 11, 1974]

The end of the draft has not ended controversy about the draft. In recent months the news media have carried story after story alleging that the volunteer armed force is a failure. Volunteers, it is said, are too few and of poor quality, despite substantial pay raises for first-termers. Representatives of the armed forces have warned that national security may be in danger unless conscription is reinstated.

As a longtime proponent of an all-volunteer armed force, I regard the end of the draft as one of President Nixon's and then-Secretary of Defense Melvin Laird's finest hours. No other measure has done so much to end the divisions that were threatening to tear this nation apart. No other measure has done so much to reduce the real cost of defending the nation.

The draft was ended despite the opposition of the military. I have wondered whether the military, encouraged by Watergate and Laird's departure from Defense, may not have been feeding the stories to the media in an attempt to reverse the decision.

Accordingly, I have probed more deeply into the facts about the actual performance of the volunteer force. I have been greatly heartened—but also appalled—by what I have found.

The Air Force, Navy, and to a lesser extent, the Marines, have had no significant problems. On the contrary, they not only have met their quotas but also have raised the average quality of the enlisted force. Their 1973 recruits are better educated, and score higher on intelligence tests, than the men they recruited in earlier peacetime years under conscription. In addition, the average term of service has lengthened, still further raising quality via experience.

The alleged failures have all been in the Army. They have been significant, though fairly small. At the end of 1973 the Army conceded that it had met 89 percent of its 1973 recruiting goal. Far more important, the failures have been the result of either gross incompetence or deliberate sabotage by some middle-rank Army officers, including some retired officers in civilian positions. This is a harsh judgment, so let me document it.

1. In July 1972, when the draft was still in effect, the Army was authorized to have 6,552 recruiters. It had 6,550 on station. The number of recruiters authorized remained about the same throughout 1973, but the number on station fell sharply, especially after the draft was ended. In September 1973, for example, 6,662 were authorized but only 5,425 were on station.

2. The Army kept changing recruiting standards with dizzying frequency. Recruiters were demoralized and many potential recruits lost.

3. Officers in the recruiting command were not promoted or rewarded. Eighteen colonels were eligible for promotion to general, eight lieutenant colonels for promotion to colonel, and 103 officers for assignment to a senior service school.

Not a single one was either promoted or sent to a service school!

True, few officers in general were promoted or sent to service schools. But, based on the number that were, the chance that three goose eggs would have occurred for the recruiting command simply as a result of accident is about 1 in 700.

Either the Army assigned low-quality officers to the recruiting command—hardly a sign that they were meeting effectively the challenge of the all-volunteer force—or the Army discriminated against the officers in the recruiting command—hardly a course of action designed to attract able men into the recruiting command.

4. Until it was stopped by the Assistant Secretary of Defense for Manpower, William Brehm, the Army reported results in a way that grossly overstated shortfalls. If in January 1973, the Army fell 1,000 men short of its quota, it added that sum to its quota for each succeeding month. For example, suppose it had a quota of 12,000 men for each month. Suppose it recruited 11,000 men in January and 12,000 men in each of the next eleven months. You and I might say it fell short 1,000 men in one month. But the Army would have reported twelve successive shortfalls of 1,000 men each because after January it would have raised its quota to 13,000.

I have limited myself to points that are objective and readily checked. They are nevertheless adequate to demonstrate that the Army has chiefly itself to blame for its failure. They suggest also that the Army cannot be counted on to reform itself. Civilian leadership is essential to make an all-volunteer armed force work.

Chapter Nine
Social Security and Welfare

The two programs discussed in the columns of this chapter are part of a much more extensive set of programs enacted in the name of alleviating poverty. These programs include, in addition, farm price supports, public housing, urban renewal, model city programs, the assorted projects in President Johnson's mislabeled "war on poverty," and much else besides, some of which are discussed in later chapters.

Of all these programs, the welfare program is the only one that clearly transfers money to people who are in lower income classes than those who pay the taxes to finance the program—and perhaps for that reason is the program that is most widely regarded as a "mess" and failure.[1] As the columns on Social Security indicate, that program very likely does precisely the opposite—that is, transfers income from lower to higher income classes. For many other so-called poverty programs (like farm price supports and urban renewal), "very likely" can be replaced by "certainly." I hasten to add that in addition to transferring income from some persons to others, all these programs involve much pure waste, so that the "benefit" to the recipient, whoever that may be, is far less than the cost to the taxpayer.

How misleading is the poverty label is sharply etched by the calculation that total governmental expenditures (federal, state, and local) on programs justified on grounds of alleviating poverty exceeded $75 billion in 1969–1970. If this money were really going to the "poor," they would be among the well-to-do! But of course most of it is going to people who by no stretch of the imagination can be regarded as

[1] See M. Friedman and Wilbur Cohen, *Social Security: Universal or Selective*, American Enterprise Institute, Washington, 1972, pp. 48–49.

"poor." The label is "poverty." The contents are waste and subsidy to special interests.

Negative Income Tax—I
[September 16, 1968]

The negative income tax, as Paul Samuelson remarked in one of his recent columns (*Newsweek*, June 10), is a striking example of an idea whose time has come. First suggested decades ago, it has attracted widespread interest only in the past few years as the defects of present methods of assisting the poor have become more obvious and more flagrant.

The widespread interest is remarkable. But the appearance of growing agreement—of support for a negative income tax by the right and the left, by businessmen and professors, by Republicans and Democrats—is highly misleading. In large part, it reflects the use of the same term to describe very different plans. For example, some months ago, more than 1,200 economists from 150 different colleges and universities signed a petition favoring a negative income tax. Despite my longtime advocacy of a negative income tax, I found it impossible to join in sponsoring the petition or even to sign it because I did not agree with the plan it advocated or the arguments it presented.

The basic idea of a negative income tax is to use the mechanism by which we now collect tax revenue from people with incomes above some minimum level to provide financial assistance to people with incomes below that level.

Under present law, a family of four (husband, wife and two dependents) is entitled to personal exemptions and minimum deductions totaling $3,000 ($2,400 personal exemptions, $600 deductions).

If such a family has an income of $3,000, its exemptions and deductions just offset its income. It has a *zero taxable* income and pays no tax.[1]

If it has an income of $4,000, it has a *positive taxable income* of $1,000. Under current law, it is required to *pay* a tax of 15.4 percent, or $154. Hence it ends up with an income after tax of $3,846.

If it has an income of $2,000, it has a *negative taxable income of* −$1,000 ($2,000 minus exemptions and deductions of $3,000 equals

[1] [The no-tax income has since been raised. For 1973, it was $4,300 for a family of four.]

—$1,000). This negative taxable income is currently disregarded. Under a negative income tax, the family would be entitled to *receive a fraction* of this sum. If the negative tax rate were 50 percent, it would be entitled to receive $500, leaving it with an income after tax of $2,500.

If such a family had no private income, it would have a negative taxable income of —$3,000, which would entitle it to receive $1,500. This is the minimum income guaranteed by this plan for a family of four.

Let me stress the difference between the *break-even income* of $3,000 at which the family neither pays taxes nor receives a subsidy and the *minimum guaranteed income* of $1,500. It is essential to retain a difference between these two in order to preserve an incentive for low-income families to earn additional income.

Let me stress also that these numbers are all for a family of four. Both the break-even income and the minimum guaranteed income would be higher for larger families and lower for smaller families. In this way, a negative income tax automatically allows for differences in need because of differences in family size—just as it does for differences in need because of differences in income.

This plan is intended to replace completely our present programs of direct relief—aid to dependent children, public assistance, and so on. For the first year or two, it might cost slightly more than these programs—because it is so much more comprehensive in coverage. But, as the incentive effects of the plan started to work, it would begin to cost far less than the present exploding direct-assistance programs that are creating a permanent class of people on welfare.

By varying the break-even income and the negative tax rate, by adding the negative income tax to present programs rather than substituting it for them, it is possible to go all the way from the rather modest and, I believe, eminently desirable plan just outlined to irresponsible and undesirable plans that would involve enormous redistribution of income and a drastic reduction in the incentive for people to work. That is why it is possible for persons with so wide a range of political views to support one form or another of a negative income tax.

In my next column, I shall try to answer some of the objections to a negative income tax that I have encountered most frequently in the more than two decades since I first began recommending its adoption.

Negative Income Tax—II
[October 7, 1968]

The proposal to supplement the incomes of the poor by paying them a *fraction* of their unused income-tax exemptions and deductions, which I termed a *negative income tax* years ago, has many advantages over present welfare programs:

1. It would help the poor in the most direct way possible.

2. It would treat them as responsible individuals, not as incompetent wards of the state.

3. It would give them an incentive to help themselves.

4. It would cost less than present programs yet help the poor more.

5. It would eliminate almost entirely the cumbrous welfare bureaucracy running the present programs.

6. It could not be used as a political slush fund, as so many current programs—notably in the "war on poverty"—can be and have been used.

In the course of advocating a negative income tax like the one outlined in my preceding column (*Newsweek*, Sept. 16), I have repeatedly encountered the same objections time and again. Let me try to answer a few of them.

1. By removing a means test, the negative income tax establishes a new principle in the relation between citizens and the government. This is simply a misunderstanding. The negative income tax retains a means test—the straightforward numerical test of income rather than the present complex and demeaning test. It uses the same means test to decide who shall receive assistance from the government as the one we now use to decide who shall pay the expenses of government.

True, it guarantees a minimum income to all. But that is not a new principle. Present welfare arrangements guarantee a minimum income in practice, and in some states, even in law. The trouble is that these present welfare programs are a mess.

2. The minimum levels of income proposed are too low. We are talking about a federal program and a *nationwide* minimum. The levels of assistance are decidedly higher than current levels in most states. They are decidedly lower than current levels in states like New York, Illinois, California. It would be absurd to enact such high levels as national standards. But there is every reason to encourage the more affluent states to supplement the federal negative income tax out of state funds—preferably by enacting a supplementary state negative income tax.

3. The poor need regular assistance. They cannot wait until the end of the year. Of course. The negative income tax, like the positive income tax, would be put on an advance basis. Employed persons entitled to negative income tax would have supplements added to their paychecks, just as most of us now have positive taxes withheld. Persons without wages would file advance estimates and receive estimated amounts due to them weekly or monthly. Once a year, all would file a return that would adjust for under- or over-payments.

4. The negative income tax destroys incentives to work. Under present programs, persons on welfare who obey the law generally lose a dollar in relief for every additional dollar earned. Hence, they have no incentive whatsoever to earn the dollar. Under the negative income tax plan that I propose, such a person would keep 50 cents out of every additional dollar earned. That would give him a far greater incentive than he now has.

One additional point. A welfare recipient now hesitates to take a job even if it pays more than he gets on welfare because, if he loses the job, it may take him (or her) many months to get back on relief. There is no such disincentive under a negative income tax.

5. The negative income tax will foster political irresponsibility. If we adopt an open and aboveboard program for supplementing the incomes of people below some specified level, will there not be continued political pressure for higher and higher break-even incomes, for higher and higher rates on negative income? Will the demagogues not have a field day appealing to have-nots to legislate taxes on haves for transfer to them?

These dangers clearly exist. But they must be evaluated in terms of the world as it is, not in terms of a dream world in which there are no governmental welfare measures. These dangers are all present now—and have clearly been effective. The crucial question is, how do we get out of the mess into which these pressures have driven us? The negative income tax offers a gradual and responsible way to work ourselves out of this mess. No other way of doing so has as yet been suggested.

Welfare Reform Again
[September 7, 1970]

In an earlier column (*Newsweek*, May 18), I applauded the Senate Finance Committee for asking the administration to redraft the Family Assistance Act of 1970, which passed the House in April. "The bill in its present form," I wrote, "is a striking example of how to spoil a good idea."

The primary defect of the House bill was that a person on welfare could not add much to his income by going to work. Any extra earnings were largely offset by reductions in welfare payments and other benefits, and in some cases more than offset, so that going to work actually lowered total income.

The revised version, on which the Senate Finance Committee is now holding hearings, is free from most of the egregious anomalies of the House bill, but unfortunately it does not come much closer to redeeming the bold promise of the President's initial TV speech—to end the relentless rise of the welfare rolls by giving people on welfare both opportunity and incentive to become self-supporting.

The provisions are incredibly complex. However, their incentive effects can be summarized simply without serious inaccuracy: a person on relief who goes to work has about 60 cents left for himself out of each dollar of the first $720 of earnings per year, but only about 20 cents out of each additional dollar until he is entirely off relief (which occurs for a family of four at $3,920 of earnings in some states but not until $7,000 of earnings in New York). For most levels of income, and particularly at the lower levels, this is a smaller incentive to work than exists under the present law—which is uniformly, and correctly, regarded as a mess.

How is it that such a promising initiative has fizzled out? The reason is that the administration has tried to implement a bold idea without seriously disturbing any existing program. If food stamps, state supplements to existing federal welfare, medical and housing assistance, and the entrenched welfare bureaucracy are all to remain largely undisturbed, there is no way to construct a sensible family-assistance program.

President Nixon's bold initiative can still be rescued but it will take equally bold action by the Senate Finance Committee to do so. The key objectives of welfare reform should be:

1. To establish a minimum national welfare standard, reducing the incentive for poor people to move in order to qualify for higher welfare.

2. To give persons on relief a strong incentive to work themselves off relief.

3. To end the present division of the nation into two classes—welfare recipients and taxpayers—by treating all alike and all impersonally. This requires a single objective test—best provided by income—to determine who pays taxes and who receives benefits; and cash payments to recipients to eliminate the present paternalistic welfare bureaucracy.

The minimum changes in the present bill required to achieve these objectives are:

1. Eliminate food stamps. The bill now provides a maximum federal payment of $1,600 in cash plus $820 in funny-money food stamps to a family of four which has no other income. Both components are reduced as the other income of the family rises. This is one major reason why so little is left out of additional dollars earned. Relief recipients and taxpayers would both benefit if the minimum payment were raised to, say, $2,100 in cash with no food stamps, and the combined payment were reduced by 50 cents for every dollar of earnings after the first $720. The farm bloc, not the poor, are the real political force behind food stamps.

2. Eliminate the provisions about the supplementary payments that states must pay to welfare families. These provisions are a second major reason why so little is left out of additional dollars earned. Instead, let the federal government fix definite dollar grants to each state on the basis of present commitments. Let these grants taper off over a period of years to fixed future levels. Then leave every state free to do whatever it wishes about supplementing federal family-assistance payments. Each state separately will have an interest in maintaining work incentives. We need more true federalism as part of the New Federalism.

3. Assign administration of the program to Internal Revenue and not to HEW. This will be a step to a single integrated tax system covering both those who pay taxes and those who receive benefits.

Radical surgery, not face-lifting, is required to end the welfare mess.

Truth in Advertising
[June 14, 1971]

I recently came across an egregious example of misleading advertising. Yet that watchdog of truth in advertising, the Federal Trade Commission, has issued no complaint and is not likely to. Why not? Because the culprit is the U.S. Department of Health, Education, and Welfare.

A widely circulated booklet, *Your Social Security,* begins:

"The basic idea of social security is a simple one: during working years employees, their employers, and self-employed people pay social security contributions which are pooled in special trust funds. When earnings stop or are reduced because the worker retires, dies, or becomes disabled, monthly cash benefits are paid to replace part of the earnings the family has lost."

This is Orwellian doublethink:

—Payroll taxes are labeled "contributions" (or, as the Party might have put it in the book *1984*, "Compulsory is Voluntary").

—Trust funds are conjured with as if they played an important role. In fact, they are small (less than $35 billion) and consist simply of promises by one branch of the government to pay another branch. A decade ago, the Social Security Administration estimated that the present value of the pensions already promised to persons covered by social security (both those who had retired and those who are not) was more than $300 billion. The corresponding sum must be far larger today. That is the size of the trust fund that would justify the words of the booklet. ("Little is Much.")

—The impression is given that a worker's "benefits" are financed by his own "contributions." The fact is that currently collected taxes are being used to pay current benefits. No trust fund in any meaningful sense is being accumulated. ("I am You.")

What assurance do current workers have that they will receive the benefits promised? Solely the confidence that our children will be willing to impose taxes on themselves to pay benefits being promised by us to ourselves. This one-sided "compact between the generations," foisted on generations that literally cannot give their consent, may be sufficient assurance, but it is a very different thing from a "trust fund"—a "chain letter" would be a more accurate designation.

The booklet goes on: "Nine out of ten working people in the United States are now building protection for themselves and their families under the social security program."

More doublethink.

What nine out of ten working people are now doing is paying taxes to finance benefits to persons who are not working. An individual working person is in no sense building his own protection—as a person who contributes to a private vested pension system is building his own protection. Persons now receiving benefits are receiving much more than the actuarial value of the taxes that were paid on their behalf. Young persons are now being promised much less than the actuarial value of the taxes that are being paid on their behalf.

More fundamentally yet, the relationship between taxes paid and benefits received is extremely loose. Millions of people will never receive any benefits attributable to their taxes because they have not paid for enough quarters to qualify, or because they receive benefits as spouses rather than on their own account. Two persons may receive the same benefit, yet have paid very different taxes over their working lives because they worked different numbers of years. Conversely, two persons may have paid precisely the same taxes at the same times yet receive very different benefits because one is married and the other is single. A man who continues working after age sixty-five will be required to pay additional taxes, yet may receive no benefits at all.

Social security is not in any meaningful sense an insurance program in which individual payments purchase equivalent actuarial benefits. It is a combination of a tax—a flat-rate tax on wage income up to a maximum—and a program of transfer payments, in which all sorts of considerations other than the amount paid determine the amount received.

The tax is almost surely far and away the most regressive element in our tax system. The benefits are capricious and inequitable. Hardly any student of social security approves of either part separately. Yet the two combined have become a sacred cow. I know of no greater triumph of imaginative packaging and Madison Avenue advertising.

Is Welfare a Basic Human Right?
[December 18, 1972]

In a recent *Newsweek* column on poverty, Shana Alexander wrote, "Access to food, clothing, shelter, and medical care is a basic human right."

The heart approves Ms. Alexander's humanitarian concern, but the head warns that her statement admits of two very different meanings, one that is consistent with a free society, and one that is not.

One meaning is that everyone should be free to use his human capacities to acquire food, clothing, shelter, and medical care by either direct production or voluntary cooperation with others. This meaning is the essence of a free society organized through voluntary cooperation.

This meaning is far from trivial. Indeed, I conjecture that most hardship and misery in the U.S. today reflect government's interference with this right. You cannot earn your livelihood by becoming a plumber, barber, mortician, lawyer, physician, dentist, or by entering a host of other trades, unless you first are licensed by the government. And the granting of a license is typically in the hands of practitioners of the trade you desire to enter, who find it in their self-interest to restrict entry.

You will have difficulty getting a highly paid job as a carpenter, mason or electrician unless you can persuade a union to let you join, and that may not be easy if your brother or father or uncle is not a member of the union. It will be especially difficult if you are black and poor, however competent. Like the American Medical Association, the unions can enforce their tight monopoly only with the support of the government.

If you are a black teen-ager whose services are currently worth only $1.50 an hour, it is illegal for most employers to hire you, even though you are willing to accept that wage.

And I have only scratched the surface of existing restrictions on your basic human right to use your capacities as you wish, provided only that you do not interfere with the right of others to do the same.

But this is not Ms. Alexander's meaning, as is clear from her next sentence: "When lawmakers attempt to convert welfare into workfare ... this is less conversion than perversion of that basic idea."

Ms. Alexander apparently believes that you and I have a "basic human right" to food, clothing, shelter, and medical care without a quid pro quo. That is a very different matter.

If I have the "right" to food in this sense, someone must have the obligation to provide it. Just who is that? If it is Ms. Alexander, does that not convert her into my slave? Nothing is changed by assigning the "right" to the "poor." Their "right" is meaningless unless it is combined with the power to force others to provide the goods to which Ms. Alexander believes they are entitled.

This is clearly unacceptable. But neither can we rely solely on the "right to access" in the first sense. Protecting that right fully would reduce poverty and destitution drastically. But there would still remain people who, through no fault of their own, because of accidents of birth, or illness, or whatever, were unable to earn what the rest of us would regard as an acceptable minimum income. I believe that the best, though admittedly imperfect, solution for such residual hardship would be voluntary action on the part of the rest of us to assist our less fortunate brethren.

But our problem is far more serious. Restrictions on access in the first sense, plus ill-conceived welfare measures, have made millions of people dependent on government for their most elementary needs. It was a mistake to have permitted this situation to develop. But it has developed, and we cannot simply wipe the slate clean. We must develop transition programs that eliminate the welfare mess without unconscionable hardship to present welfare recipients.

That is why, for three decades, I have urged the replacement of our present collection of so-called poverty programs by a negative income tax that would guarantee a minimum to everyone and would encourage recipients to become self-supporting.

I favor a negative income tax not because I believe anyone has a "right" to be fed, clothed, and housed at someone else's expense but because I want to join my fellow taxpayers in relieving distress and feel a special compulsion to do so because governmental policies have been responsible for putting so many of our fellow citizens in the demeaning position in which they now find themselves.

Chapter Ten
Government vs. the People

This chapter and, to a considerable measure, also the two that follow deal with the difference between the intentions of disinterested persons who support specific government interventions and the outcome of these interventions. The range of cases in which noble intentions produce ignoble results gives reason to believe that this outcome is not accidental.

Why is it that well-intentioned reformers so often end up as front men for special interests they would never knowingly represent? The underlying reason is the difference between the way the market operates and the way a political mechanism operates. In a market, I can get command over your money only if you agree. You are free to buy or to refuse to buy what I have to sell. It is therefore in my interest to try to figure out what you are willing to pay for and make it available to you. Of course, if I can, it is also in my interest to prevent other people from competing with me in providing whatever it is that I have to sell. But unless I can get the government to help me, it is very difficult for me to succeed. I may for a time get some other producers to join an agreement to fix at a high level the prices we charge, but the more successful we are, the greater the incentive for participants in the agreement to "chisel," or for outsiders to go into the business. In short, the market makes it in the interest of other people to serve you. You are protected from being overcharged not only by your own efforts but also by the efforts of other customers whose threat, implicit or explicit, to divert their custom induces sellers to keep prices down. You are protected even more effectively by the efforts of other sellers, who have a real interest in letting you know if you are being overcharged. In highly simplified form, this is the essence of Adam Smith's famous passage: although "every individual . . . intends only his own gain, . . . he is in this, as in many other cases, led by an invisible hand to promote an end which was no part of his intention. . . . By pursuing his own interest he frequently promotes that of the society more effectively than when he really intends to promote it."

A political mechanism is very different. It is a means for exercising power, including getting money, without the case-by-case agreement of the person over whom the power is exercised or whose money is being spent. I am required by law to buy specified "safety" equipment on cars "for my own good" whether I want to or not. Some of my money is spent by the National Traffic Safety Agency. I would rather not spend my money that way, yet I have no way to opt out. You may say that I had the choice to vote for it or not. But that is a very different choice than I have in the market. If I vote in the market for a belt, I get the belt I vote for; if I vote in the market not to buy a belt, I don't get the belt. If I vote in the polling booth for auto-safety legislation, and my side wins, I get the seat belt that the National Traffic Safety Agency specifies. If I vote against auto-safety legislation and my side loses, I still get the seat belt that the NTSA specifies. And, even the side that appears to win in the polling booth may not get what it wants. Clearly the connection between what I vote for in the polling booth and what I get is far looser than between what I vote for in the market and what I get.

This difference introduces a marked bias into the results. Since there is in general little relation between my vote or my political action and the outcome, it does not pay me to give much attention to the matter unless I have an unusually large interest in it. To shift examples, let me vote as a public-spirited citizen for "public housing" because I have an interest in the poor and am willing to see some of my taxes go to benefit the poor. Once I have voted, I have done my duty. I have a clear conscience, and can enjoy the pleasing glow of rectitude. I can and will now go about my business. I have little incentive to monitor the outcome, to keep close tabs on how the money is spent. But people who have property that they would like to sell or improve are in a different position. To them, activity has just begun. Here is a plush source of revenue available —and available without having to persuade individuals to part with their own money. They have a strong incentive to go after the public funds, to see that it is spent to benefit themselves. Who is going to stop them? The poor? In considerable part they are poor because of limited ability to carry through such activities, and they are likely to be even more disadvantaged in politics than in the market—where they can benefit more directly from other people's greed and ability.

If the misuse of the housing money becomes particularly blatant, an ambitious politician may find it an effective issue to arouse public indignation and support. He may even be able to generate enough interest to get a change in the law or the program. But once the interest dies down, the basic pressures will resume and the changed program will again be dominated by special interests.

This is the fundamental reason why governmental agencies set up to regulate a particular industry are inevitably dominated by that industry; why program after program set up to help the "poor," or to promote "safety," or to raise "standards," ends up doing the opposite. There is an invisible hand in politics that operates in the opposite direction to the invisible hand in the market. In politics, individuals who seek to promote only the public good are led by an invisible hand to promote special interests that it was no part of their intention to promote.

Examples of this tendency keep being documented—for example, the perverse effects of the FDA reported in "Frustrating Drug Advancement" (January 8, 1973) and in "Barking Cats" (February 19, 1973). Yet the well-meaning people who serve as unwitting front men for the special interests seem incapable of learning from experience. How much more evidence do we need?

The Bank Depositor
[November 7, 1966]

Do you have a bank deposit? If so, I trust you are aware of how solicitous Congress has been of your welfare. Over thirty years ago, Congress made it illegal for banks to pay you any interest at all on your checking deposits and gave the Federal Reserve System power to fix the maximum interest rate that member banks may pay you on your savings or time deposits. Needless to say, the Fed promptly exercised this power.

However, there was a loophole in the law. Savings-and-loan associations and banks that were not members of the Federal Reserve System were free to pay any rate on savings deposits. As these associations and banks, anxious to exploit the helpless depositor, offered higher and higher interest, the Fed reluctantly raised the ceiling on the rates member banks could pay in order to keep them from losing their time deposits.

This loophole has now been closed. A month ago, Congress authorized the Federal Reserve, the Federal Deposit Insurance Corporation, and the Federal Home Loan Board to fix maximum rates for all banks and savings-and-loan associations and these agencies promptly exercised their power. So you are now fully protected against being induced to save too much by the lure of high interest or to spend too much out of ill-gotten interest.

Of course, the small man needs the most protection. Aware of this, Congress gave the Fed power to discriminate among depositors. The Fed promptly set a lower ceiling for small than for large deposits. If you can deposit more than $100,000, or buy a certificate of deposit for more than that sum, banks may offer you up to 5.5 percent. But for the rest of us, the most they are now permitted to offer is 5 percent.

The new law is a tribute to the social conscience of the banking fraternity, especially the men who run savings and loans. It was they who pressed Congress to protect the small saver—and, incidentally, their own deposits—from the competition of commercial banks. To my knowledge, no small depositor even testified in favor of the bill, let alone lobbied for it. Perhaps this is not surprising. Bankers clearly know best what depositors need to be protected from.

One flaw remains in the protective ceiling. The new powers were granted for only one year. However, you need have no concern. I have little doubt that a year from now, Congress will see its duty plain and renew these powers so that you will continue to be protected from the temptation of high interest rates on your saving deposits.[1]

Federal and state governments have been vigilant to protect your welfare not only as bank depositor but also as consumer. Are you a milk drinker? Federal milk marketing authorities set minimum prices at which farmers can sell milk and thereby protect you from the temptation to carry this good habit too far. Do you imbibe hard liquor? State liquor commissioners perform a similar service for you. Only the soft-drink addict has so far been overlooked.

State fair-trade laws curb the cupidity of retailers by keeping them from cutting prices to you on branded items price-fixed by manufac-

---

[1] [As, of course, did occur. As of July, 1974, there is no ceiling on deposits of $100,000 or more; ceilings on other member bank time and savings deposits vary from 5 percent to 7.25 percent.]

turers—indeed, men have gone to jail for selling headache remedies at
too low a price. The Federal Trade Commission makes it hard for chain
stores to offer you bargains by using their buying power to get quantity
discounts. The Interstate Commerce Commission sees to it that railroads
do not undercharge you for riding on their trains—when you can find
one—and that truckers do not cut prices when they move your goods.
Airlines must get permission from the Civil Aeronautics Board to cut
fares—and the CAB has not been easy to persuade.

The protecting hand of the law extends to some items most of us have
never heard of. The other day, a newspaper story reported that "American Telephone said it won't appeal a U.S. Court of Appeals decision holding that it is charging too little for its 'Telpak' service." Public spirited of
Mother Bell, isn't it?

Do you recall the *New Yorker* cartoon in which the blowzy blonde in
the back seat of a cab tells her butter-and-egg companion as he hands her
a glittering bauble, "You're so kind to me, and I'm so tired of it all."

Auto-Safety Standards
[June 5, 1967]

Now that the furor over car safety has subsided, it is instructive to consider some little-noticed aspects of the federal legislation it produced.

1. Cost: The recently issued safety standards will raise the cost and
hence the price of new cars. According to some estimates, consumers will
pay about $1 billion a year extra.

Suppose Congress had been asked to appropriate this sum for the identical safety equipment, raising the money by a special excise tax on automobiles. Would Congress have enacted this proposal as readily as it
enacted the safety legislation? Yet the two are identical except in form.

2. Delegation of power to tax: Congress has been jealous of its pre-
rogative to impose taxes. Time and again it has rejected proposals that
the President be granted discretion to alter tax rates. Yet in this case,
as in other similar cases, Congress has delegated to an administrative
official near-absolute power to decide how large a tax to impose.

3. Failure to compare alternatives: The basic issue before Congress
was safety, not requiring automobile manufacturers to build their cars

in specified ways. Yet, so far as I know, there was no discussion whether $1 billion a year would contribute more to safety if spent in this way than if spent in other ways—on improved highways, or driver education, or better enforcement of speed limits, or more intensive investigation of causes of auto accidents.

4. *Who will set the standards?:* The National Traffic Safety Agency has already been criticized for yielding to the demands of manufacturers in drawing up its final safety standards for 1968 cars. Mr. William Stieglitz resigned as consultant to the agency on roughly these grounds. Such complaints will be even more justified in the future—though the complaints themselves may become less shrill.

How else can it work out? Safety standards are a peripheral matter to most car owners. A Ralph Nader may get them or the politicians aroused enough to pass a law; but once the law is passed, the consumers will return to somnolence, from which only an occasional scandal will reawaken them. The car manufacturers are in a very different position. They have billions at stake. They will assign some of their best talent full-time to keep tabs on the standards. And who else has the expertise? Sooner or later they will dominate the agency—as, despite well-publicized tiffs, railroads and truckers have dominated the ICC; radio and TV networks, the FCC; physicians, state medical licensure boards; and so on.

5. *Effect on competition:* Several small specialty-car manufacturers have already complained that compliance with the new safety requirements would put them out of business—the 1931 Ford that one company replicates has less glass in total in its windshields than the windshield wiper standards require the wipers to clear! No doubt, special exemptions will be granted to these companies. But how shall we ever know about the innovations that might have been made, or the companies that might have been established, without this additional handicap?

The effect on foreign producers will be even more important. Any extra cost will be more of a burden on them than on U.S. producers because they sell a much smaller fraction of their output in the U.S. Beyond this, it will become clear to the agency—staffed as it must be by men trained in the U.S. industry and in daily touch with it—that our cars are really safer and that the way to promote safety is to require foreign cars to meet American specifications.

The result will be a sheltered market for U.S. producers—and higher costs to U.S. consumers that have little to do with safety requirements.

6. *The effect on safety:* To begin with, the standards may well make cars safer. But, as administrative rigor mortis sets in, they will soon slow up product improvement, so that a decade from now cars may well be less safe. Reduced competition will reinforce this tendency. In addition, the higher price of new cars will raise the average age of cars on the road.

7. *An oft-told tale:* Time and again, laws passed to protect the consumer have ended up by restricting competition and so doing the consumer far more harm than good. Is it too much to hope that one of these days we shall learn this lesson before we enact a new law rather than after?

Moonlighting
[September 18, 1967]

Far away in the backwoods where the writ of the unions does not run, workers and employers have been fashioning ingenious arrangements under the spur of federal wages-and-hours legislation.

The legislation requires that any worker who is employed for more than forty hours a week must be paid time-and-a-half for hours in excess of forty (with some exceptions for a few occupations that are subject to a highly volatile demand—like longshoremen). Employers are understandably reluctant to employ men more than forty hours a week—though many of their workers would prefer to work extra hours at straight time if they could.

One somewhat surprising reaction has been a move to a ten-hour day. This enables workers to put in their forty hours in four ten-hour days, leaving them a long three-day weekend. Another is to separate the number of hours worked from the number paid for. Workers are paid for forty hours each week but actually work five ten-hour days a week for four weeks and then take a full week off. This device may not be strictly within the letter of the law but it seems clearly consistent with the spirit of the law—and besides, it is mutually advantageous to employer and employee.

To many a worker, the three-day weekend, or the one week off in five, is more leisure than he desires, except in hunting and fishing season—

given the state of his finances and the demands of his wife and children. So he moonlights by taking on additional jobs.

Mostly, I have been told, the moonlighting is catch-as-catch-can, arranged by individuals on an individual basis. But I have every confidence that this situation will change. There is ample evidence that imagination and innovation are not stilled by restrictive legislation—only diverted to figuring out ways around it.

The obvious development to be expected is what might be dubbed "cooperative moonlighting" and, for all I know, it may already be in operation. Let two employers use the same work force, each worker working four ten-hour days for one employer and two ten-hour days for the other. This will put the matter on a regular basis, for both employer and employee, and fully satisfy the law. Moreover, it will have the advantage for the employers that the division of time between the two employers can readily be varied. They can thereby jointly achieve flexibility of hours worked without having to pay time-and-a-half.

As this practice spreads, the law will no doubt cooperate by reducing straight-time hours still further—say to thirty hours a week. That would permit the employers to share men equally and so remove one problem that might now be a source of friction.

Of course, the men may not want to work sixty hours a week, but that could easily be arranged. The cooperative arrangement permits wide variation to suit every taste. And, of course, the hunting season does come and fishing is often excellent. But that too can readily be handled. The law does not prevent men from taking vacations—it seeks only to prevent them from taking nonvacations.

Needless to say, it might be more efficient for the men to work longer hours for the same employer than to straddle two employers to stay inside the letter of the law. But that is a subversive thought that you must stifle at birth lest it undermine our whole system. Start on this line, and soon you will be spoiling all the fun.

Eliminate restrictions and simplify laws, and what will happen to all the lawyers now busily engaged in plugging loopholes on the one side and opening them on the other? To all those accountants employed in keeping the records required for compliance, or in advising clients how to keep their books to reduce the costs of compliance? To those business advisory services that regularly issue fat volumes codifying government regulations in various areas, and giving the latest information about how the administration and courts have interpreted them?

To come closer to home, what would this cooperative moonlighter have left to write about? Perish the thought!

"The state," said Frédéric Bastiat, in 1848, "is that great fiction by which everyone seeks to live at the expense of everyone." Were Bastiat alive today, he would see no reason to alter this definition but he might be led to add to it—"and everyone can be employed either imposing legislative restrictions on his fellows or figuring out how to get around them."

The Negro in America
[December 11, 1967]

Newsweek's remarkable cover story on the Negro in America (Nov. 20) is depressing for what it reveals about the present position and attitudes of the Negro minority in these United States. It is more depressing for what it reveals about the views of well-intentioned liberals.

Negroes have made great progress in the past century, thanks to their own efforts and to the opportunities offered them by a market system—and despite widespread prejudice and governmentally enforced discrimination. Liberals have generally disparaged this progress, encouraged Negroes to look primarily to government for relief, and assured them that the white community, by waving its magic legal wand and opening its purse, could and shortly would eliminate their disabilities and drastically raise their standard of living.

In my opinion, this liberal view is tragically wrong. Many of the problems that the Negro faces in America today were produced or aggravated by governmental measures proposed, supported, and executed by liberals holding the views that dominate the *Newsweek* story. The drive for further legislative measures, and particularly the techniques adopted, have awakened the sleeping giant of racial prejudice among the whites in the North. The encouragement of unrealistic and extravagant expectations has produced frustration, outrage, and a sense of betrayal among the Negroes in the North. Unwittingly, the liberals have set race against race.

Let me turn to specifics. Says *Newsweek*, "welfare, job, and housing are the three main spokes of the wheel of poverty." Consider each.

1. Welfare: We have adopted paternalistic governmental arrangements for dispensing more than $7 billion a year that impair the freedom, independence, and dignity of the recipients, and demean the so-cial workers administering the program. These arrangements have weakened family structure and have produced a permanent class of persons on relief.

2. *Jobs:* Unemployment among Negro teen-agers is running around 25 percent or more. Why? Largely because minimum-wage legislation has declared that it is better for a youngster to be unemployed at $1.40 an hour than employed at $1 an hour (see my column, Sept. 26, 1966). In the absence of legal minimum wages, unemployment among Negro teen-agers would now be under 10 percent, not over 25 percent. Other governmental measures—particularly those favoring unions—have restricted the job opportunities of Negroes.

3. *Housing:* Public housing and urban renewal programs have destroyed more dwelling units than they have constructed. Concentration of the poor, many of them broken families, in public housing has reinforced despair and fostered juvenile delinquency. Urban renewal has destroyed viable neighborhoods, driven the poor from their homes to even less satisfactory and more expensive housing, and created slums where none existed before. It deserves the invidious label of a "Negro removal program."

4. *Schools:* To *Newsweek*'s three spokes, I would add a fourth, schooling. Inferior slum schools help to perpetuate the Negroes' present disabilities. Yet these are wholly provided by government.

Government programs have shackled the forces of self-reliance, independence, and private enterprise that alone can produce a permanent solution. Progress toward our common objective requires less government intervention, not the major expansion *Newsweek* calls for.

In welfare, we could substitute a negative income tax for present welfare arrangements. This would reduce government interference in the lives of the poor yet help them more.

In jobs, we could set free the most effective machine for eliminating low incomes that the world has ever seen—competitive private enterprise.

In schooling, parents who choose not to use public schools could be given a voucher for an equivalent sum of money to be used to purchase schooling. This would give slum children a real alternative. And competition would force improvement in public schools.

It is not an accident that government measures have produced results that are the opposite of those intended by their well-meaning sponsors. I am tempted to address to my liberal friends Oliver Cromwell's plea to his enemies: "I beseech you, in the bowels of Christ, think it possible that you may be mistaken."

Book-Burning, FCC Style
[June 16, 1969]

The Federal Communications Commission, which now requires radio and TV stations to provide time to anti-smoking ads at no cost, has voted to go still further and prohibit entirely the advertising of cigarettes on radio and television—if the present congressional ban on such action is not renewed. The Federal Trade Commission favors strengthening the present required health-hazard warning on cigarette packages. The U.S. Public Health Service and other federal agencies spend sizable sums on campaigns against smoking.

As it happens, I am an ex-smoker. I quit some dozen years ago when the evidence started piling up on the adverse effects of smoking. That evidence persuaded me that I was paying too high a price for the dubious pleasure of smoking. Like most ex-es, I can be counted on to recite the dreary statistics at the drop of an ash.

Nonetheless, I object strongly to the government's measures because I believe that they are hostile to the maintenance of a free society. Government censorship and thought control are no less censorship and thought control when they are exercised for purposes that I approve of.

The evidence on the harmful effects of smoking, though certainly strong, is not conclusive. Reasonable men who have studied the evidence believe that the statistical association between smoking and a shorter life may have a more subtle explanation than that smoking shortens life. But even if the evidence were conclusive, that would not justify present policies. Every time we take an automobile ride—or cross the street—we knowingly risk our lives because we think that the gain from the ride or from crossing the street justifies the risk. Just so, a smoker may view the pleasures of smoking as justifying the cost in length of life. We may wish to cajole him, plead with him, try to change his tastes. Do we have the right to do more? To use his money, extracted in taxes, to persuade him that he has reached the wrong decision?

Marx's *Das Kapital* and Hitler's *Mein Kampf* have caused far more deaths than all the cigarettes ever smoked. Should we therefore ban their sale? Should we prohibit their being advertised over the radio and TV? Should we require them to carry a warning: READING IS DANGEROUS TO MENTAL HEALTH AND MAY CAUSE DEATH FROM REVOLUTION AND OTHER DISTURBANCES? Should we spend millions of taxpayers' money to "educate" the public to the viciousness of the doctrines they spread?

In a free society, a government has no business using the power of the law or the taxpayers' money to propagandize for some views and to prevent the transmission of others. Freedom of speech includes the freedom to preach for or against communism, for or against fascism—and also for or against smoking. Freedom of speech includes freedom to promote particular views out of religious zeal or altruism or humanitarianism—or plain selfishness. Freedom of speech is for the listener as well as the speaker—to enable him to make his own choice among as wide an assortment of views as his fellows are inclined, for whatever reasons, to set forth.

But, you will say, where do you draw the line? How can we justify imposing taxes on opponents of the Vietnam war to pay for that war? The answer is that the one decision—to smoke or not to smoke—is divisible and affects us individually. Each person can have what he wishes without preventing others from having what they wish. The other decision is indivisible and affects us collectively. The country is at war. There is no way some of us can be at peace, others of us at war. Unfortunately, one or the other group must be overruled. Just because many collective decisions are unavoidable, it is all the more important that we lean over backward to preserve individual choice where we can, that we decide borderline cases in favor of individual freedom.

Part of the duty of elected officials is to lead and not simply to follow—to try to persuade the rest of us that the policies they favor are in the national interest. Yet, let them go too far in that direction, and the threat of government indoctrination, financed by the taxes we pay, becomes very real indeed, held in check only by the division of powers, the multiplicity of governmental units, and the offsetting pressures of different groups.

If we are to preserve a free society, we must reinforce these fragile checks with the unremitting pressure of an enlightened citizenry.

Defense of Usury
[April 6, 1970]

In 1787, Jeremy Bentham published a lengthy pamphlet entitled, "Defense of Usury; Shewing the Impolicy of the Present Legal Restraints on the Terms of Pecuniary Bargains." The pecuniary bargains he was concerned with were loans between individuals or business enterprises. The legal restraints were limits on interest rates paid or received. Usury was and is the popular term for charging interest rates in excess of legal limits.

Bentham makes an overwhelmingly persuasive case for the proposition he sets forth at the beginning of the pamphlet, "viz. that *no man of ripe years and of sound mind, acting freely, and with his eyes open, ought to be hindered, with a view to his advantage, from making such bargain, in the way of obtaining money, as he thinks fit: nor* (what is a necessary consequence) *any body hindered from supplying him, upon any terms he thinks proper to accede to.*"

During the nearly two centuries since Bentham's pamphlet was published, his arguments have been widely accepted by economists and as widely neglected by politicians. I know of no economist of any standing from that time to this who has favored a legal limit on the rate of interest that borrowers could pay or lenders receive—though there must have been some.[1] I know of no country that does not limit by law the rates of interest—and I doubt that there are any. As Bentham wrote, "in great political questions, wide indeed is the distance between conviction and practice."

Bentham's explanation of the "grounds of the prejudices against usury" is as valid today as when he wrote: "The business of a moneylender . . . has no where, nor at any time, been a popular one. Those who have the resolution to sacrifice the present to future, are natural objects of envy to those who have sacrificed the future to the present. The children who have eaten their cake are the natural enemies of the children who have theirs. While the money is hoped for, and for a short time after it has been received, he who lends it is a friend and benefactor: by the time the money is spent, and the evil hour of reckoning is come, the benefactor is found to have changed his nature, and to have put on the tyrant and the oppressor. It is an oppression for a man to reclaim his own money: it is none to keep it from him."

[1] [Since I wrote this, my attention has been directed to favorable comments on usury laws by J.M. Keynes in his *General Theory*.]

Bentham's explanation of the "mischief of the anti-usurious laws" is also as valid today as when he wrote that these laws preclude "many people, altogether, from the getting the money they stand in need of, to answer their respective exigencies." For still others, they render "the terms so much the worse. . . . While, out of loving-kindness, or whatsoever other motive, the law precludes a man from *borrowing*, upon terms which it deems too disadvantageous, it does not preclude him from *selling*, upon any terms, howsoever disadvantageous." His conclusion: "The sole tendency of the law is to heap distress upon distress."

Developments since Bentham's day have increased the mischief done by usury legislation. Economic progress has provided the ordinary man with the means to save. The spread of banks, savings-and-loan associations, and the like has given the ordinary man the facilities for saving. For the first time in history, the working class may well be net lenders rather than net borrowers. They are also the ones who have fewest alternatives, who find it hardest to avoid legal regulations, and who are therefore hardest hit by them.

Under the spur of Wright Patman and his ilk, the Federal Reserve now limits the interest rate that commercial banks may pay to a maximum of 4.5 percent for small savers but to 7.5 percent for deposits of $100,000 or more.[2] And the deposits of small savers have been relatively stable or growing, while those of large depositors have been declining sharply because they have still better alternatives.

That is the way the self-labeled defenders of the "people" look after their interests—by keeping them from receiving the interest they are entitled to. Along with Bentham, "I would . . . wish to learn . . . why the legislator should be more anxious to limit the rate of interest one way, than the other? Why should he set his face against the owners of that species of property more than of any other? Why he should make it his business to prevent their getting *more* than a certain price for the use of it, rather than to prevent their getting *less?* . . . Let any one that can, find an answer to these questions; it is more than I can do."

Migrant Workers
[July 27, 1970]

The old saw is that the Quakers went to the New World to do good and

[2][As noted above, in July, 1974, the limits are 5 percent for small savers, nonexistent for deposits of $100,000 or more.]

ended up doing well. Today, well-meaning reformers go to Washington to do good and end up doing harm.

A recent *Wall Street Journal* story gives a striking example—the effects in Michigan of stricter federal and state standards for housing migrant farm workers. The intent: to improve the conditions of a group of low-paid workers. The result: to hurt the workers, the farmers, and consumers.

"Higher labor costs," says the story, "have prompted many growers . . . to switch to mechanized harvesting in recent years, lessening demand for migrant workers. That trend has intensified in the last two years, as government agencies have implemented stricter housing regulations for growers participating in their migrant-worker placement programs. . . .

"State and federal officials estimate that mechanization could eliminate from 6,000 to 10,000 jobs in Michigan this summer that were previously done by migrants. . . . License applications [for migrant camps] are down 11 percent so far this summer. . . .

"Nonetheless, approximately 50,000 migrant workers, mostly Mexican-Americans from Southwest Texas, are expected to come into Michigan looking for work this summer. That's about the same number that came through last year."

Mechanization is a good thing if it is a response to a decline in the number of persons seeking jobs as migrant workers at low wages. That would mean that the former migrant workers have found better employment opportunities. Mechanization is a bad thing if it is a response to higher labor costs imposed arbitrarily from the outside. That simply wastes capital to replace people who are forced into unemployment or even less desirable jobs.

Migrant workers are clearly hurt. It is small comfort to an unemployed migrant worker to know that, if he could get a job, he would have better housing. True, the housing formerly available may have been most unsatisfactory by our standards. However, the migrant workers clearly regarded it, plus the accompanying jobs, as the best alternative available to them, else why did they flock to Michigan? It is certainly desirable that they have better alternatives available to them, but until they do, how are they helped by eliminating alternatives, however unsatisfactory, that are now available? That is simply biting off their noses to save our faces.

Farmers are clearly hurt. The cost of migrant labor has been raised. That is why they are mechanizing. The machines limit the rise in cost but do not eliminate it. Costs would be lower if farmers could hire migrant labor on *terms that would be mutually satisfactory to them and the laborers*. But they are not permitted to do so.

Consumers are clearly hurt. At the higher costs, less food will be harvested, so making food prices higher than they otherwise would be.

Producers of mechanized farm equipment are helped by having a larger market. But in the main, they simply produce harvesting equipment instead of other equipment.

The only other people who are helped are the do-gooders responsible for this type of legislation and for these effects. They have the high-minded satisfaction of promoting a noble cause. The good intention is emblazoned forth for all to see. The harm is far less visible, much more indirect, much harder to connect with the good-hearted action. Besides, the harm is mostly to someone else.

This case is not in any way unique, except that it happens to be more obvious than most. I know hardly any do-gooder legislation of this kind—whether it be minimum-wage laws or rent control or urban renewal or public housing or fair-employment legislation—which, on examination of its full consequences, does not do more harm than good—and more harm as judged by the intentions of the well-meaning people who sponsor such legislation.

Will the liberals ever learn this lesson of experience? So far, the clear failure of government program after government program to achieve its objective has simply led to a clamor for still larger, still more expensive, still more far-reaching programs—to do still more harm. It is about time that the liberals asked themselves whether the fault may not be in the system they favor—doing good at other people's expense—rather than in the way the system is operated. It is about time that they appealed to their heads as well as their hearts.

Roofs or Ceilings
[March 22, 1971]

In 1946, George Stigler and I published a pamphlet attacking the legal ceilings that had been imposed on rents during World War Two and were then still in effect. We argued that the ceilings, by keeping rents artificially low to those persons who were fortunate enough to live in controlled dwellings, encouraged the waste of housing space and, at the same time, discouraged the construction of additional dwellings. Hence our title, "Roofs or Ceilings."

Nationwide ceilings were subsequently abolished. However, localities were given the option to continue them. New York City—with that unerring instinct for self-destruction that has brought it to its present condition—is the only major city still controlling rents under this option.

A recent article by Richard Stone in the *Wall Street Journal*, "Shortage of Housing in New York Gets Worse Every Day," brought this ancient pamphlet vividly back to mind. At a time when there is so much talk about imposing new price controls, this cautionary tale is worth pondering.

Reports Stone. "The dimensions of the New York shortage are vast. The rental vacancy rate is below 1 percent. . . . Private building is at near-paralysis. . . . Increasing numbers of landlords simply give up, abandoning buildings they can neither afford to maintain nor sell at any price. Tenants, left with no heat, water, or electricity vacate such buildings in a matter of days. When that happens, blight swallows up whole neighborhoods, almost overnight.

"Every day there are fewer housing units available in New York City than the day before.

"New York's archaic rent-control law keeps the marginally poor whose fortune is improving from moving out of slum neighborhoods."

Others go to great lengths to find a rent-controlled apartment, including keeping "track of obituaries to divine what deaths are creating rent-control vacancies.

"Partly because of rent control, rents on private housing built since 1947—housing that doesn't come under the law—skyrocketed over the past decade. . . . After fierce public outcry, the city last summer passed a law holding annual increases to 5 percent. To no one's surprise, several major builders responded by withdrawing from the city."

Or, as we wrote in our 1946 pamphlet: "Rent ceilings cause haphazard and arbitrary allocation of space, inefficient use of space, retardation of new construction. The legal ceilings on rents are the reason there are so few places for rent. Because of the excess of demand over supply, rental property is now rationed [in New York] by various forms of chance and favoritism. As long as the shortage created by rent ceilings remains, there will be a clamor for continued rent controls. This is perhaps the strongest indictment of ceilings on rent. They, and the accompanying shortage of dwellings to rent, perpetuate themselves, and the progeny are even less attractive than the parents."

Do not suppose that this sad tale reflects anything special about housing. During World War Two, when price control was nearly universal, black markets, and rationing by chance, favoritism, and bribery developed in steel, meat, bananas—you name it. Since World War Two, there have been major crises in gold and foreign exchange—because governments have tried to fix the prices of both. When the price of the dollar was fixed too low in terms of other currencies, there was a "dollar shortage"; more recently, when it has been fixed too high, there has been concern about balance-of-payments deficits. The price system is a remarkably efficient system for bringing buyers and sellers together, for assuring that the quantities some people want to buy will match the quantities other people want to sell. Immobilize the price system and something else—if only chaos and queues—must take its place.

Would you like to see a shortage of grapefruit in New York that will get worse with every day? Let New York impose and effectively enforce a ceiling price on grapefruit below the market price. Let Washington do so, and the shortage will be nationwide. And you can substitute any product you wish for "grapefruit," provided you add the qualification that the ceiling price be "effectively enforced." That is the direction in which the well-meaning people who are talking about legal price-and-wage control are pushing us. They should be condemned to hunting for an apartment in New York.

What Is Killing the City?
[March 20, 1972]

In two remarkable columns, Stewart Alsop has explored "The City Disease" that is killing the South Bronx area of New York City (*Newsweek*, Feb. 28 and March 6). He summarized his findings as follows: "Well-intentioned and liberal-minded people (including this writer) have assumed that the way to cure conditions like those in the South Bronx is to spend a lot of money in the slums. A lot of money has been spent in the South Bronx and other New York slums. New York's expenditures for 'social services' have tripled since John Lindsay became mayor, and federal spending for social purposes has also vastly increased. All the time, the city disease has got worse—and worse and worse."

This result seems a paradox. How can it be that more spending is accompanied by worse results?

One standard explanation is that the disease has gotten worse despite the increase in spending, that it would have gotten still worse if there had been less spending, and that we need still more spending by New York City and the federal government. Though this explanation has produced a massive and continuing increase in Federal, state, and local government spending for "social services," its plausibility has worn thin as spending has mounted and the disease has continued to get worse.

A second explanation is that the fault is not with the amount of government spending but with the way government has spent the money. In housing, this explanation has led to stress on rehabilitation instead of new construction, on small-scale scattered public housing instead of gigantic housing projects, on rent supplements instead of public housing. Unfortunately, despite the great fanfare and extravagant promises that accompany each new program, still the city disease marches on.

The right explanation, I submit, is very different. Mr. Alsop is simply wrong when he says, "New York's expenditures for 'social services' have tripled." They may not have changed at all—or may even have declined. What has happened is that expenditures by the *government* of the City of New York have tripled. But where has the money come from? Primarily from the people in New York City. Where else can it come from? The money may take a detour via Albany or Washington— which will, of course, take their cut—but that only conceals, it does not change, the ultimate origin of the money. The citizens of New York City have spent more through their government and therefore have had less to spend themselves.

The total amount available for spending has not been increased by Lindsay's programs. On the contrary, it has been decreased as the deterioration of the city and ever-higher taxes have encouraged people and business to move out. Is it really a paradox that we get less for our money when government bureaucrats spend our money for our supposed benefit than when we spend our own money on our own needs?

But, you may say, government spending is for the poor; the money government spends comes from the well-to-do; hence private spending would benefit different people.

Wrong on both counts. The government program may be labeled "welfare for the poor," but that does not mean that very much of the money spent benefits the poor. Much of the money goes to buy land or buildings or services from the not-so-poor—as, most notably, in urban renewal programs—to provide amenities for the not-so-poor. Some of the rest goes to pay excellent salaries to bureaucrats. Even the part that does trickle down to the poor is largely wasted because it encourages them to substitute a handout for a wage.

As to who pays, the possibility of taxing the rich is strictly limited, especially in a city like New York. It is too easy for the rich to move. Whatever the rhetoric, the poor pay their full share of the taxes.

Government spending is the problem, not the solution. We do not need new government programs. We need to abolish the old programs and let people spend their own money in accordance with their own values. The city would then get better—and better and better.

For New York City, it is probably too late for this cure because so large a part of the voting population already consists of city employees and welfare recipients. But it is not too late for other cities to learn from New York's disease.

Prohibition and Drugs
[May 1, 1972]

"The reign of tears is over. The slums will soon be only a memory. We will turn our prisons into factories and our jails into storehouses and corncribs. Men will walk upright now, women will smile, and the children will laugh. Hell will be forever for rent."

This is how Billy Sunday, the noted evangelist and leading crusader against Demon Rum, greeted the onset of Prohibition in early 1920. We know now how tragically his hopes were doomed. New prisons and jails had to be built to house the criminals spawned by converting the drinking of spirits into a crime against the state. Prohibition undermined respect for the law, corrupted the minions of the law, created a decadent moral climate—but did not stop the consumption of alcohol.

Despite this tragic object lesson, we seem bent on repeating precisely the same mistake in the handling of drugs.

On ethical grounds, do we have the right to use the machinery of government to prevent an individual from becoming an alcoholic or a drug addict? For children, almost everyone would answer at least a qualified yes. But for responsible adults, I, for one, would answer no. Reason with the potential addict, yes. Tell him the consequences, yes. Pray for and with him, yes. But I believe that we have no right to use force, directly or indirectly, to prevent a fellow man from committing suicide, let alone from drinking alcohol or taking drugs.

I readily grant that the ethical issue is difficult and that men of good-will may well disagree. Fortunately, we need not resolve the ethical issue to agree on policy. *Prohibition is an attempted cure that makes matters worse—for both the addict and the rest of us.* Hence, even if you regard present policy toward drugs as ethically justified, considerations of expediency make that policy most unwise.

Consider first the addict. Legalizing drugs might increase the number of addicts, but it is not clear that it would. Forbidden fruit is attractive, particularly to the young. More important, many drug addicts are deliberately made by pushers, who give likely prospects their first few doses free. It pays the pusher to do so because, once hooked, the addict is a captive customer. If drugs were legally available, any possible profit from such inhumane activity would disappear, since the addict could buy from the cheapest source.

Whatever happens to the number of addicts, the individual addict would clearly be far better off if drugs were legal. Today, drugs are both incredibly expensive and highly uncertain in quality. Addicts are driven to associate with criminals to get the drugs, become criminals themselves to finance the habit, and risk constant danger of death and disease.

Consider next the rest of us. Here the situation is crystal-clear. The harm to us from the addiction of others arises almost wholly from the fact that drugs are illegal. A recent committee of the American Bar Association estimated that addicts commit one-third to one-half of all street crime in the U.S. Legalize drugs, and street crime would drop automatically.

Moreover, addicts and pushers are not the only ones corrupted. Immense sums are at stake. It is inevitable that some relatively low-paid police and other government officials—and some high-paid ones as well—will succumb to the temptation to pick up easy money.

Legalizing drugs would simultaneously reduce the amount of crime and raise the quality of law enforcement. Can you conceive of any other measure that would accomplish so much to promote law and order?

But, you may say, must we accept defeat? Why not simply end the drug traffic? That is where experience under Prohibition is most relevant. We cannot end the drug traffic. We may be able to cut off opium from Turkey—but there are innumerable other places where the opium poppy grows. With French cooperation, we may be able to make Marseilles an unhealthy place to manufacture heroin—but there are innumerable other places where the simple manufacturing operations involved can be carried out. So long as large sums of money are involved—and they are bound to be if drugs are illegal—it is literally hopeless to expect to end the traffic or even reduce seriously its scope.

In drugs, as in other areas, persuasion and example are likely to be far more effective than the use of force to shape others in our image.

Frustrating Drug Advancement
[January 8, 1973]

The title is an accurate description of the effect, though of course not the intent, of the stiffer standards for approval of drugs that Congress mandated on the Food and Drug Administration in 1962 as an aftermath of the Kefauver hearings and of the thalidomide episode.

Put yourself in the position of an FDA official charged with approving or disapproving a new drug. You can make two very different kinds of serious mistakes:

1. Approve a drug that turns out to have unanticipated side effects resulting in death or serious impairment of a sizable number of persons.

2. Refuse approval to a drug that is capable of saving many lives or relieving great distress and has no untoward side effects.

If you make the first mistake, the results will be emblazoned on the front pages of the newspapers. The finger of disapproval, perhaps even of disgrace, will point straight to you.

If you make the second mistake, who will know it? The pharmaceutical firm promoting the new drug, who will be dismissed as greedy businessmen with hearts of stone, and a few disgruntled chemists and physicians involved in developing and testing the new product. The people whose lives might have been saved will not be around to protest. Their families will have no way of knowing that their loved ones lost their lives when they did only because of the action of an unknown FDA official.

With visions of the thalidomide episode dancing in your head and the knowledge of the fame and acclaim that came to the woman who held up approval of thalidomide in the U.S., is there any doubt which mistake you will be more anxious to avoid? With the best will in the world, you will be led to reject or postpone approval of many a good drug in order to avoid even a remote possibility of approving a drug that will have newsworthy side effects.

The effect of your bias will be reinforced by the reaction of the pharmaceutical industry. Your bias will lead you to impose unduly stringent standards so that getting approval of any drug will become a far more expensive, time-consuming, and risky venture. Research on new drugs will become less profitable, and each company will have less to fear from the research efforts of its competitors. The research that is done will be concentrated on the least controversial, which means least innovative, of the new possibilities.

Granted all this, do these harmful effects of the more stringent standards outweigh the good effects of the "correct decisions" made by FDA officials? Does not the market, in the absence of such regulations, also make mistakes?

In a brilliant paper presented at a recent University of Chicago conference, Professor Sam Peltzman of UCLA explored these questions in detail. His conclusions are unambiguous: the harm done has greatly outweighed the good.

The stiffer standards had a spectacular effect on the rate of innovation. In the twelve years prior to 1962, 41.5 "new chemical entities"—that is, really new drugs—were introduced on the average each year; in the next eight years, 16.1. And their introduction was delayed by two years on the average.

Peltzman used highly imaginative techniques to assign dollar values to the benefit from suppressing harmful drugs and to the harm from suppressing or postponing the introduction of useful new drugs. His methods are too complex to describe here. I can say only that they were highly persuasive to me and to the other economists at the conference. To make sure that his results would hold up, he leaned over backward, overstating benefits from the stricter standards, and understating costs. And, of course, he recognized full well that dollar estimates are a pale reflection of the human benefit and harm in terms of lives saved and lost. But that seems the only feasible way to get a numerical measure that combines the value of comfort gained by relief of a minor distress, days gained by avoiding or shortening illness, and lives gained by curing a hitherto deadly disease.

He estimates that the 1962 drug amendments cost consumers of drugs—over and above any benefits—$250 to $500 million per year at a very minimum. This is 5 to 10 percent of the money spent annually on drugs. It is as if a 5 to 10 percent tax were levied on drug sales and the money so raised were spent on invisible monuments to the late Senator Kefauver.

To supplement this estimate, and to get some idea of the effects of regulation on the more dramatic mistakes and discoveries, Peltzman examined the costs to society of a thalidomide-type mistake, the benefits to society from a penicillin-type success (though the actual examples he uses include neither thalidomide nor penicillin), the frequency of such occurrences prior to 1962, and the areas, notably heart disease and cancer, where major discoveries are much needed for the future. He then makes the extreme assumption that *no* major innovation will be permanently kept from the market by the post-1962 procedures, that their only effect will be to delay an innovation by two years. Even with this extreme assumption, it turns out that the cost of delaying a beneficial innovation is something like ten to a hundred times the value of avoiding a thalidomide-type mistake. In human terms, the effects of the introduction of the drugs that conquered tuberculosis are dramatic. Peltzman estimates that postponing their introduction for two years would have meant about 45,000 additional deaths from tuberculosis, and twice that number of additional persons with tuberculosis, out of a much smaller population than today's.

Finally, Peltzman investigates the effect of stiffer standards on the profits of drug producers, concluding, "Drug producers as a group seem neither to have been helped nor hurt . . . the gains of reduced competition having been roughly balanced by the added costs of innovation." This is a distressing result. If the drug companies were hurt, they would have a concentrated interest to press for reform. As it is, it is "only" the general interest that suffers; the harm is widely diffused, and no one has any strong self-interest in pressing for change.

The 1962 amendments to the Food, Drug, and Cosmetic Act should be repealed. They are doing vastly more harm than good. To comply with them, FDA officials must condemn innocent people to death. In the present climate of opinion, this conclusion will seem shocking to most of you—better attack motherhood or even apple pie. Shocking it is—but that does not keep it from also being correct. Indeed, further studies may well justify the even more shocking conclusion that the FDA itself should be abolished.

Barking Cats
[February 19, 1973]

In a recent column (*Newsweek,* Jan. 8), I pointed out that approval of drugs by the Food and Drug Administration delays and prevents the introduction of useful as well as harmful drugs. After giving reasons why the adverse effects could be expected to be far more serious than the beneficial effects, I summarized a fascinating study by Prof. Sam Peltzman of UCLA of experience before and after 1962, when standards were stiffened. His study decisively confirmed the expectation that the bad effects would much outweigh the good.

The column evoked letters from a number of persons in pharmaceutical work offering tales of woe to confirm my allegation that the FDA was indeed "Frustrating Drug Advancement," as I titled the column. But most also said something like, "In contrast to your opinion, I do not believe that the FDA should be abolished, but I do believe that its power should be" changed in such and such a way—to quote from a typical letter.

I replied as follows: "What would you think of someone who said, 'I would like to have a cat, provided it barked'? Yet your statement that you favor an FDA provided it behaves as you believe desirable is precisely equivalent. The biological laws that specify the characteristics of cats are no more rigid than the political laws that specify the behavior of governmental agencies once they are established. The way the FDA now behaves, and the adverse consequences, are not an accident, not a result of some easily corrected human mistake, but a consequence of its constitution in precisely the same way that a meow is related to the constitution of a cat. As a natural scientist, you recognize that you cannot assign characteristics at will to chemical and biological entities, cannot demand that cats bark or water burn. Why do you suppose that the situation is different in the social sciences?"

The error of supposing that the behavior of social organisms can be shaped at will is widespread. It is the fundamental error of most so-called reformers. It explains why they so often believe that the fault lies in the man, not the "system," that the way to solve problems is to "throw the rascals out" and put well-meaning people in charge. It explains why their reforms, when ostensibly achieved, so often go astray.

The harm done by the FDA does not result from defects in the men in charge—unless it be a defect to be human. Most are and have been able, devoted, and public-spirited civil servants. What reformers so often fail to recognize is that social, political, and economic pressures determine the behavior of the men supposedly in charge of a governmental agency to a far greater extent than they determine its behavior. No doubt there are exceptions, but they are exceedingly rare—about as rare as barking cats.

Ralph Nader is the most prominent current example of such a reformer. In a series of valuable reports, he and his associates have confirmed dramatically what earlier studies had demonstrated less dramatically—that governmental agencies established to regulate an industry in order to protect consumers typically end up as instruments of the industry they are supposed to regulate, enabling the industry to protect monopoly positions and to exploit the consumer more effectively. These effects have probably been documented most fully for the ICC [Interstate Commerce Commission], but what is true of the ICC is true also of the FCC [Federal Communications Commission], the FTC [Federal Trade Commission], the SEC [Securities and Exchange Commission] and so on through the list of alphabetical monstrosities preying on consumers from their privileged sanctuaries in Washington.

You might expect Nader and his associates to draw the obvious conclusion that there is something innate in the political process that produces this result; that, imperfect as it is, the market does a better job of protecting the consumer than the political process. But no, their conclusion is very different: establish stronger agencies instructed more explicitly and at greater length to do good and put people like us in charge, and all will be well. Cats will bark.

This failure to grasp the inner logic of the political process means that, despite Nader's excellent intentions, despite his admirable singleness of purpose, despite his dedication and despite his high repute, he has done and will continue to do great harm to the very consumers he seeks to aid.

Chapter Eleven
Government and the Interests

The ability of special interests to get legislation enacted in their favor or to take over control of governmental bodies set up to regulate them, which is exemplified in this chapter as well as in Chapters 10 and 12, has led many social critics on both the left and the right to conclude that there is a "ruling class" that runs the government and through the government the society. On this view, the ruling class is able to use its control of government to line its own pockets at the expense of the rest of the country.

Fortunately for the chances of preserving and extending freedom, the conclusion is false. True enough, we have a mass of special-interest legislation and of regulating agencies dominated by the industries that they are supposed to regulate. True enough, the apparent beneficiaries of each such piece of legislation or of such regulating bodies are generally in the upper income groups, or at least in groups above the average. However— and here is the fallacy in the "ruling class" view—the special interests that are served are fragmented and each gets its benefits largely at the expense of other special interests. It is likely that the special-interest groups as a whole and possibly each one separately would benefit if the special-interest legislation as a whole were abolished.

Consider a simple illustration. Air fares would be roughly 60 percent of their present level if they were not controlled as they now are by the C.A.B. We know this because two states (Texas and California) are large enough to support substantial intrastate carriers that are free from C.A.B. control because they do not engage in interstate travel. (They are controlled by state bodies, but that has apparently not been very restrictive.) Their fares are about 60 percent of the controlled fares on comparable runs (compare the Los Angeles – San Francisco fare on Pacific Southwest Airlines with the Los Angeles – Reno or Los Angeles – Phoenix fares on the C.A.B. regulated carriers). This means that regulation costs air travellers 40 percent of the total amount they pay as fares to the regulated carriers.

Who benefits? Mostly no one. The profits of the airline industry have been notable for their thinness, not their abundance. Because the regulated lines cannot effectively compete on price, they compete through offering frills and extra service. As a result, their rate of use of space is decidedly lower than that of the intrastate lines, and their costs per passenger mile are much higher. Their profits are, if anything, lower, measured either relative to capital or revenue. Clearly most of the forty-cent cost to travellers per dollar of air fare simply pays for economic waste. But suppose some, say four cents, seeps through to profits.

Who travels by air? Mostly high-income people. Who owns airline stocks? Mostly high-income people. So high-income people are taking $1 out of their left pocket in their capacity as passengers to put 10 cents in their right pocket in their capacity as owners of airline stock. Smart ruling class.

The reason for this nonsense is not an all-wise, all-powerful ruling class, but precisely the same phenomenon described in the introduction to Chapter 10—the invisible hand in politics. The interests of the passengers is diffuse. Travelling is but one of many ways that the rich spend their money. The interests of the owners of airlines and their managers is concentrated. This is *the* way, or a major way, that they get their income. In the *political* process, therefore, the producer wins and the consumer is exploited. In the *economic* process, the diffused interest of the consumer receives its proper attention.

What's in a Name?
[November 20, 1967]

Consider an imaginary conversation between Roger Blough, chairman of the board of U.S. Steel, and Senators Everett Dirksen of Illinois and Vance Hartke of Indiana.

Mr. Blough: Gentlemen, I seek your assistance. The steel industry is in serious straits. Our costs are rising and our profits are falling.

Senator Dirksen: At a time like the present, when the country is faced with the grave danger of inflation, it would be most unfortunate to have steel prices rise. Yet even that would be better than to let the steel industry founder.

Mr. Blough: Unfortunately, we cannot raise our prices. We would lose too much business to steel producers in Japan and Europe. We would have to cut back sharply on our operations.

Senator Hartke: That would be serious for my constituents in Gary. What can we do?

Mr. Blough: Introduce a bill to impose an excise tax on steel.

The Senators (in unison): But surely that would hurt, not help, the steel industry!

Mr. Blough: By itself, it would. But I suggest that the proceeds from the tax be used to pay a subsidy of like amount to steel producers.

Senator Hartke: You puzzle me. Wouldn't the tax and subsidy just cancel?

Mr. Blough: Not quite. The tax would be on all steel, whether produced in this country or abroad. The offsetting subsidy would go only to domestic producers. The effect would be a higher price to domestic steel producers without the fear of inroads into our markets by foreign producers.

Senator Dirksen: What about the excess of the taxes over the subsidy? Should we use that to reduce the frightening deficit we face?

Mr. Blough: Oh, no. The proposed tax and subsidy would affect adversely the firms now engaged in importing steel. I suggest that we use the excess tax revenue to compensate them for the burden we are asking them to bear in the national interest.

Such a conversation never has taken place and never would. Mr. Blough would not make such a proposal. If he did, Senators Dirksen and Hartke would not take it seriously.

Yet the limitation on imports urged by the steel industry and sponsored by Senators Dirksen and Hartke, among others, is identical in substance to the imaginary proposal. Limiting the amount of steel that may legally be imported would enable the industry to raise prices without fear of foreign competition. It would make the price at which steel sells in the U.S. higher than the price at which it can be purchased abroad—precisely the result that the excise tax would achieve.

The recipients of permits to import steel will receive a subsidy equal to the difference between the price of domestic and foreign steel—just as under the hypothetical excise tax. Such permits will be valuable and no doubt will be bought and sold, as are currently permits to import oil and other products subject to quotas. A recipient of a permit would then be able to get his subsidy by selling the right to import steel rather than by exercising it.

The difference between the imaginary excise-subsidy and the actually proposed import quotas is political, not economic. In the one case, the subsidy by the government to the steel industry is open and aboveboard, in the other, it is disguised.

The U.S. can acquire steel by producing steel itself—or by producing other goods, selling them abroad, and using the proceeds to buy steel. If steel can be purchased at a lower price from foreign than from domestic producers, then the U.S. steel industry has failed the market test. It is best for the nation that some of the men and capital resources devoted to producing steel be devoted to more useful pursuits—perhaps producing some of the products we shall then export in return for the steel we import.

The steel industry professes to be a friend of free enterprise. In speech after speech, its leaders extol the superiority of capitalism over socialism. They stress the virtues of private initiative, free markets, competition, the discipline of profits and losses. Yet as soon as that discipline affects the wrong column of their ledgers, they run to Washington for help.

It is tempting to berate the steel industry for hypocrisy. But the real fault is with the rest of us. It is up to us to see to it that business enterprises can promote their own interests only by serving their customers, not by having the law corral customers.

How to Free TV
[December 1, 1969]

In his powerful attack on TV news coverage, Vice President Agnew accurately described the present lack of diversity, but touched only lightly on causes and cures.

The causes are not to be found in the character of the men who present the news or who run the networks. Both groups try to present the news fairly. Yet, with the best of intentions, three collections of men breathing the same intellectual atmosphere and with a strong incentive to appeal to the same audience in the same way, will inevitably present a one-sided point of view.

This narrow range of views has its origins in two related features of TV: first, the requirement of a government license in order to operate a TV station; second, the effective stifling of pay-TV for well over a decade by the Federal Communications Commission under the pressure and influence of the networks.

To see the importance of the second feature, suppose that it were made illegal for any reading matter to be sold directly to the public. Reading matter could be distributed only if it were given away to all comers, financed, as TV programs now are, by advertising, philanthropy, or government subsidy.

What would happen to our present variety of reading matter—to which Mr. Agnew referred so aptly? Would advertisers finance newspapers and magazines of the kind we now have? Perhaps a few, but surely not many, and hardly any that would take a strong, independent, and unpopular position, or that, like the *New Republic*, *National Review*, *Harper's*, *Atlantic Monthly*, would appeal to very limited audiences.

What kind of books would be published? Some time ago, I bought a magnificent collection of reproductions of Andrew Wyeth's paintings, which sells for $75. Can you conceive of an advertiser finding it in his interest to use so expensive a book with such limited appeal as a vehicle for selling his product? No, the books published would be mostly the kind that are now printed by the millions in paperback—the kind we "effete snobs" call "trash."

The books published would appeal to the masses—in this sense the advertisers could say that they were giving the public what it wants, just as the TV networks now claim. Yet the public would not get what it wants in the meaningful sense of getting everything that it was willing to pay for. It would get only those items that could be produced cheaply enough to serve as fillers between the advertisements.

This is precisely the situation in TV today. The insistence that programs must be "given away"—that is, paid for by the public through its purchase of advertised products—has led to precisely the results that it would lead to with reading matter: deadening uniformity; limited choice; low-cost, low-quality programs. It has also fostered the dominance of networks and their geographical concentration, because their special advantage is in merchandising nationwide advertising. That is why they have bitterly opposed pay-TV.

The networks have been able to maintain their monopoly position because of the requirement of a government license to operate a TV station. Without this requirement, it would have been impossible for them to have prevented the development of pay-TV on a large scale—and, for all I know, of still other alternatives to present-day commercial TV.

The FCC supposedly regulates the radio and TV industry in the public interest. But like just about every other regulatory agency—ICC, CAB, FPC, and so on through the dreary alphabet—it has in fact become an instrument of the industry it supposedly regulates. It has been used by that industry to preserve monopoly and to prevent competition. Its abolition is essential if we are to have truly free TV.

But, you will say, the number of TV channels is limited—not to three but to a fairly small number. Surely, government must decide who is to use them. That is a non sequitur. Gold mines are limited. Must the government therefore decide who is to operate them? Land is limited. That may call for zoning requirements, but does it require the licensing of the use of particular parcels to particular people? Precisely the same solution is available for the allocation of TV channels as for the allocation of land. Just as the U.S. sold much of its public land a century ago, let the FCC sell now to the highest bidder the rights now covered by a license (to broadcast at a specified frequency and power in a specified way during specified hours of the day, from a particular location). And then let it go out of business.

The owners of these rights would have private property in them, which they would protect from trespass as you and I protect our land from trespass, through the courts. They could buy and sell the rights, subdivide them, recombine them, as you and I do with our land.[1] They would have the full protection of the Bill of Rights just as the press now does.

Monopolies, if any developed, would be subject to the antitrust laws, not, as now, protected by a government agency. And they would be far

[1] The technical feasibility of this proposal is examined and demonstrated in R. H. Coase, "The Federal Communications Commission." *Journal of Law and Economics*, October 1959, and in Arthur S. DeVany, Ross D. Eckert, Charles J. Meyers, Donald J. O'Hara, Richard C. Scott, "A Property System for Market Allocation of the Electro-magnetic Spectrum: A Legal-economic-engineering Study," *Stanford Law Review*, June 1969.

less likely to develop because advertisers and networks would be denied the special privileges that they are now granted.

What kind of TV system would emerge from the free and unfettered operation of market forces? No one can say in detail. The market is most ingenious and always produces surprises. But certain things are clear. First, there would still be programs supported entirely by advertising—as giveaway newspapers are now. Second, there would be many programs supported partly by advertising, partly by fees—as many newspapers and magazines are now. Third, there would be many programs supported entirely by fees—as so many books and other publications are now. Fourth, the TV bill of fare would be far richer than it now is. It would cater to all viewers, not just those influenced by advertising. It would provide expensive programs for limited audiences as well as low-cost programs for mass audiences.

Here, Mr. Agnew, is a far better road to a cure than asking listeners to write and telephone TV stations. Give the viewer the power that makes the consumer the boss in other areas, the power to buy from whom he wants what he wants to buy. That is the way to a truly free TV.

A *Business and Society Review* Interview*
[Spring, 1972]

McClaughry: Dr. Friedman, in recent years there has been a great deal of discussion about the social responsibilities of the business corporation. Many corporate executives have made speeches about how big business should contribute to the solution of the nation's social ills. Candidates for office have reiterated the theme. What do you feel are the responsibilities of business, if any, above and beyond maximizing profits for their shareholders?

Friedman: Most of the talk has been utter hogwash. In the first place, the only entities who can have responsibilities are individuals; a business cannot have responsibilities. So the question is, do *corporate executives,* provided they stay within the law, have responsibilities in their business activities other than to make as much money for their stockholders as possible? And my answer to that is, no, they do not.

Take the corporate executive who says "I have responsibilities over

*Conducted by John McClaughry for *Business and Society Review.* Extracts reprinted with permission.

and above that of making profit." If he feels that he has such responsibilities, he is going to spend money in a way that is not in the interest of the shareholders. Where does he get that money? Perhaps from the company's employees. If he can pay his employees lower wages than otherwise, he'll have some extra money to spend. It may come from the company's customers, if he can charge them more than they would otherwise pay. Or it may come from the company's stockholders. The crucial question is: what right does the executive have to spend his stockholders' money? To spend his employees' money? Or his customers' money? Who gave him the right to decide how their money should be spent? If "socially responsive" business executives would stop and think, they would recognize that in effect they are acting irresponsibly.

Let me give you an example that has often impressed me. During the 1930s, German businessmen used some corporate money to support Hitler and the Nazis. Was that a proper exercise of social responsibility? The people who preach this hogwash talk as if everyone is always in favor of the same things, and there is no problem about which causes the money should be spent to further. But, of course, that's not the case. How the employees might want to spend the money is one thing; how the stockholders might want to spend it is another; how the customers might want to spend it is still another. The corporate executive, as long as he is hired as an agent of the stockholder, has a clear, definite responsibility to the people who hired him—to do what they want him to do.

Have you ever heard anybody suggest that the "Mom and Pop" corner grocery store should sell food below cost to help the poor people who shop there? Well, that would obviously be absurd! Any corner grocery that operated that way would be out of business very soon. The same is true on the larger scale. The large enterprise can have money to exercise social responsibility only if it has a monopoly position: if it's able to hire its employees at lower wages than they are worth; if it's able to sell its product at a higher price than can otherwise be charged. If it is a monopoly, it ought to be prosecuted under the antitrust laws. Any businessman who boasts to the public that he has been using corporate funds to exercise a social responsibility should be regarded as asking for an investigation by the Antitrust Division of the Justice Department.

McClaughry: Do you draw a distinction between corporate sponsorship of a program which has some direct effect on its own profit and loss statement and a similar type of corporate program which is only a contribution to goodwill?

Friedman: Of course. There is a big distinction. Most of the time when corporate executives talk about exercising their social responsibility, all they are doing is engaging in window dressing. This is why, in fact, there is very little actual corporate social responsibility in a meaningful sense.

Take the major business in a community. It's hiring workers in that community. It's producing products in that community. It may very well be in the self-interest of that corporation to spend money on improving conditions in that community. That may be the cheapest way it can improve the quality of the labor it attracts.

The crucial question for a corporation is not whether some action is in the interest of the corporation, but whether it is enough in its interest to justify the money spent. I think there will be many cases when activity of this kind will pay back dollar for dollar what the corporation spends. But then the corporation isn't exercising a social responsibility. The executive is performing the job he was hired for—making as much money for his stockholders as possible. The fact of the matter is that the people who preach the doctrine of social responsibility are concealing something: the great virtue of the private enterprise system is precisely that by maximizing corporate profits, corporate executives contribute far more to the social welfare than they do by spending stockholders' money on what they as individuals regard as worthwhile activity.

By innovating cheap transportation, Henry Ford probably did more to transform the character of this nation than any but a small handful of other people. Did Henry Ford build the Model T in order to exercise his social responsibility? He certainly did not. He built the Model T to make money. He made a great deal of money, but in the course of his profit-making, the community at large benefited enormously. Would the community have benefited so greatly if Henry Ford, instead of producing the best car he could and making as much money as he could, had devoted his energies to social responsibility?

McClaughry: Didn't Henry Ford hire his production workers at twice the going rate?

Friedman: He did that because he could make more money that way. In that way, he got more efficient, more productive workers. He was trying to attract people to Detroit where he was building cars—particularly people from the South. At that time, Ford announced the $5 daily wage, twice the going wage. But he didn't do it to discharge social responsibility. As Adam Smith said, "You do not owe your daily bread to the beneficence of the baker, but to his desire to pursue his own interest."

McClaughry: Is there no way, then, that the corporate executive should spend money other than to maximize the stockholders' return on their invested capital?

Friedman: Generally not. His job is to do whatever the shareholders would like to see done, and most of the time shareholders want only to make money.

Sometimes (and this is especially important in a closely held corporation because of our tax laws) stockholders may be able to achieve their own charitable purposes more cheaply through the corporation than directly. Suppose you or I owned a corporation, and we wanted to make a gift to a university or a charity. Under our present tax laws, the corporation would be permitted to deduct up to 5 percent of adjusted gross income in computing taxable income. If our corporation paid out dividends to us, on the other hand, it would have to pay them out of after-tax profits. So the corporation would have to earn roughly $2 to give me a $1 dividend which I could then give to my favorite charity. I would be permitted to deduct that from my personal income tax, so there would be no personal income tax consequences for me. That means, if I can persuade my corporation to give the gift, rather than making it myself, I can give $2 instead of only $1. In consequence, it may be perfectly appropriate, particularly in closely held corporations where there are few shareholders, for the corporation to make purely eleemosynary gifts.

Now, my solution is very simply that I do not believe such gifts ought to be deductible in computing corporate income. Of course, I go much further. I do not believe there ought to be a corporate income tax. I believe that corporations ought to be required to attribute all their earnings, whether distributed or not, to individual stockholders.

McClaughry: Would those earnings be taxable to the stockholder, even when they were not distributed?

Friedman: Yes. That would remove the only pale shadow of an excuse that there is for a special corporate income tax.

The thing that must be stressed is that a corporation really has no money. We talk as if corporations pay a tax. That's absurd. Insofar as a corporation turns tax money over to the government, either its employees are paying it, its customers are paying it, or its stockholders are paying it. We would have a much more honest, straight-forward situation if we decided whom we wanted to tax and taxed them accordingly, instead of going through this nonsensical fiction that we are getting taxes which no human being is paying.

I have come to the conclusion that the best tax would be a flat-rate tax on all income without any deductions. Through an exemption, you could avoid taxing those people with very low incomes. Our present system seems on paper to be highly graduated. In fact, it is not because there are so many loopholes. A 20-25 percent flat-rate tax on all income above roughly double our present exemptions would raise as much revenue as we are now raising from the income tax. Of course, you're not going to have it because the major purpose of the present tax structure is not to raise revenue, not to be equitable: it's to provide political plums.

Getting back to this question of corporate responsibility, let's say an executive could get away with spending half the company's income for social purposes. What would he be doing? Well, you could say he was imposing a tax of 50 percent on the shareholders' income and spending it for purposes *he* regards as desirable. If you put it that way, he is engaging in a fundamentally governmental venture for which he has never been democratically elected or chosen. He is in effect stealing this money from the shareholders and devoting it to purposes he regards as desirable. Personally, I believe that if that money is left in the hands of employees, customers, or shareholders, they will use it for more socially desirable purposes than an irresponsible corporate executive. I doubt that any company in this country is spending one percent of its income in ways that are not in fact pretty clearly and definitely in the self-interest of that corporation.

McClaughry: If you were a stockholder in a company whose management was outdoing itself in making grants to further causes they thought worthy, would you bring a stockholder's suit?

Friedman: Not necessarily. I'd probably sell my stock. I'd have made a mistake and I would rectify that mistake right away by selling my stock. If I were a large owner, I might bring suit.

Few things turn my stomach more than watching those companies' television advertising, particularly that of some of the oil companies, which would have you believe that their only purpose for being is to preserve the environment. But I really cannot blame the corporate executives for talking this nonsense. In fact, I blame them if they don't. Given the attitude of the public-at-large, one way for an enterprise to promote its profits is to profess to be socially responsible. How can I blame the corporate executive? He's performing his duty to me as a stockholder. If he talks this kind of nonsense in his executive capacity, I can't object.

What I do object to is not what these businessmen do in their corporate capacity, but what so many of them do in their private capacity. Businessmen are affected by the intellectual environment in which they live. Good businessmen often regard themselves as philosophers. They go around in their private capacity talking the same kind of arrant nonsense that it may be profitable for them to talk in their business life. Businessmen should not confuse their personal feelings with their jobs. Sometimes, I think that businessmen as individuals have a suicidal instinct. There is nothing that would, in fact, destroy the private enterprise system more than a real acceptance of the social responsibility doctrine.

McClaughry: What about a chemist who makes napalm or a toy manufacturer who produces unsafe toys? Should they divorce their personal feelings from their jobs?

Friedman: If a chemist feels it is immoral to make napalm, he can solve his problem by getting a job where he doesn't have to. He will pay a price. But the ultimate effect will be that if many, many people feel that way, the cost of hiring people to make napalm will be high, napalm will be expensive, and less of it will be used. This is another way in which the free market does provide a much more sensitive and subtle voting mechanism than does the political system.

. . .

McClaughry: How does your argument relate to another topic of current interest—safety?

Friedman: What's the "right" number of accidents for Consolidated Edison to have? Now that seems like a silly question. All accidents are bad. But let's suppose for a moment that Con Ed does have an accident. One of its trucks hits your car. You have a case against them and they will have to pay damages. Well, that's part of their operating expense, and it has to be recouped from their customers. Suppose it costs them less to avoid a certain number of accidents than it does to pay for damages in these accident suits. Well, that would reduce the price they have to charge their customers. Obviously it's in their interest—and their customer's as well—to avoid these accidents. On the other hand, suppose it costs Con Ed more to avoid additional accidents than it does to pay damages—and it well might. To avoid all accidents, they might have to do all their work at night, give instructions that their trucks should never go faster than 2 MPH, and so on. You can see by this that Consolidated Edison must have the "right" number of accidents, that number where the cost of avoiding an additional accident would be more than the damages paid the victim.

Well now, what is the difference between this situation and the pollution case? There's only one: in the pollution case, it is often impossible to identify the individual victims and to require person-by-person compensation. In Consolidated Edison's case you can identify the victims clearly. In the U.S. Steel case, you can identify the victims as a group, and *all* the costs fall back on U.S. Steel. Therefore, in a single-company town like Gary, U.S. Steel has a private interest in maintaining the right level of pollution, because an extra $100 spent to reduce pollution would add less than $100 to the welfare of all of the people in the city of Gary. Under the circumstances where you cannot identify the victim, however, it is highly desirable to take measures to see that costs are imposed on the consumer. There is only one person who can pay the costs, and that's the consumer. If the people whose shirts are dirtied by Consolidated Edison could bring suit, Con Ed would have to pay the cost of cleaning their shirts—which is to say, Con Ed's customers would. If it were cheaper to stop polluting than it was to pay those costs, Con Ed would do so.

In those cases where you can determine what costs are being imposed on people other than the customer, the least bad solution seems to me to be a tax. Let's consider an industrial enterprise which pollutes a river. If you can calculate roughly that by putting in the effluent, an industry is causing a certain amount of harm to people downstream, then the answer would seem to be to tax it, roughly equal to the amount of harm it has imposed. This provides the right incentive. If it's cheaper for the corporation to put the effluent in the water and pay the tax than it is not to pollute or to clean up the river, then that is what should be done.

McClaughry: You mention Consolidated Edison. Does a large corporation—in this case, a regulated monopoly corporation—have a particular responsibility above and beyond efficient operation? Con Ed presumably bought Big Allis, its supergenerator, because it produced power at a rate cheaper than some combination of smaller generators. Every so often Big Allis conks out, and the result is poor service to consumers who have no recourse other than to put in their own generators. And radical decentralization of the system is not practical anymore. Is there any reason why Con Ed's management should have decided to buy two or three small generators instead of Big Allis?

Friedman: Yes, of course. They would have done so if in fact they thought it would provide their customers with better service at a lower price. The feature you are talking about fully enters into Consolidated Edison's calculations if they calculate correctly. Even electricity is not without substitutes. You can heat a house with electricity, with oil, with gas.

It's like the case before: you don't have to have 100 percent mobility. It's the margin that counts. There are some things like TV sets for which it is difficult to find substitutes. However, even there if service is unsatisfactory, TV sets will be less attractive until service is more attractive. Fewer sets will be bought, people will go to the theater or movies instead. So there are substitutes all along the line.

McClaughry: One of the problems that has become a national issue in the last decade has been helping the "hard core" unemployed participate in the economic system. In New York City, a number of the large banks cooperated to hire some 60,000 new employees—a great many of them Negroes and Puerto Ricans—to keypunch bank statements. There is reason to believe that someday new equipment that can read directly from the printed checks will enable the banks to completely dispense with the keypunch operation. In such a situation, technology will put most of these people out of work. Does the government have a responsibility to help these people find new productive labor?

Friedman: First, were the banks who did this exercising a social responsibility? I doubt it. It was probably the cheapest way for them to get labor, and it was obviously sensible for them to advertise it as a socially responsible action. But the people who have these jobs are presumably better off than if they didn't have them. They accepted the jobs voluntarily. Nobody forced them. I don't believe that anyone has any responsibility of the kind you are talking about.

What does it mean to say that government might have a responsibility? Government can't have a responsibility any more than the business can. The only entities which can have responsibilities are people. Should some people be taxed to provide these particular individuals with some kind of retraining? In my opinion, the answer is no.

As a citizen, I am willing to tax myself to assist people who have low incomes. But I want to do so regardless of whether the reason for their plight is that they happen to be sick, or that they happen to be trained for an industry for which there is no more demand, or that they happen to be old. That is why I have long been in favor of getting rid of our present

welfare system and our whole range of subsidization programs and instituting instead a single negative income tax which would provide an income floor to prevent people from becoming destitute. Beyond that, I
would not like to see us do anything.

Let's go back to the problem of the hard-core unemployed. Before we
start looking for solutions, we ought to ask what has caused the problem.
The answer is that most hard-core unemployment has been produced by
governmental measures. Let me list the main ones: a major source of so-
called hard-core unemployment is the minimum-wage rate, a governmental requirement that employers must discriminate against people who
have little skills. . . .

Another cause of unemployment is government support and assistance
to trade unions. The greatest denial of employment rights almost surely
occurs in the skilled construction trade. A much larger number of people
would be employed at fairly decent wages were it not for the trade
unions' restrictive policies, policies which are in large part possible because of the assistance of federal, state, and local governments. To be specific, on the federal level the Davis-Bacon Act essentially established
union wage rates as minimum-wage rates. In addition, there are the special immunities which trade unions have been given under various labor
acts. On the local level, there are the building codes and the frequent failure to enforce the law against violence and the destruction of property
when they occur in the course of a labor dispute.

The American Medical Association, in my opinion the most powerful
"trade union" in the United States, derives its power entirely from the
government. If not for the fact that the government says only people who
are licensed may practice medicine, and that the licensing arrangement is
in the hands of organized medicine, as is inevitable if licensing exists, the
AMA would be far weaker. It is a clear case of a government-granted
monopoly. Nonlicense, permitting people to practice medicine without a
license, would be a far superior arrangement. I am personally convinced
that the unlicensed practice of medicine would result in a vastly higher
standard of medical practice and much more readily available medical
facilities.

A third cause is the defective governmental system of education. In
many cases, low-income people in slum areas receive terrible schooling
and training. The way to solve that problem is to give the parents the
money to buy schooling for their children wherever they can in the pri-

vate market. They'd do a lot better than they do now at public, government schools.

Fourth, the welfare arrangements that we have adopted are harmful to their supposed beneficiaries. They have in many cases made it more profitable to be on welfare than to be employed. They have also made it very difficult for people to get off welfare and into jobs.

McClaughry: Let's turn for a moment to a recent issue that commanded a great deal of national attention—the plight of Lockheed Aircraft. Some 60,000 jobs were reputed to be in jeopardy if the Lockheed corporation went under. As you know, the government, by a very narrow vote in Congress, has agreed to provide a $250 million loan guarantee to keep the present management of Lockheed managing, Lockheed operating, and employees drawing paychecks. How would you have handled the situation?

Friedman: I am opposed to the government guarantee of the Lockheed loan because I believe it is an undesirable interference with free enterprise. A free enterprise system is a profit-and-loss system, and the loss part is at least as important as the profit part. What provides and assures the proper use of resources in a free enterprise system is that if a firm doesn't use resources properly, it goes broke. And if you say that every time it goes broke, it is going to be bailed out by the government, then there is no effective mechanism for weeding out the inefficient enterprise.

In this particular instance, however, Lockheed may have had a case. Part of the corporation's difficulties stemmed from the very unfavorable contract settlement made on the C5A. Lockheed was required to absorb a loss of close to $200 million. I can well imagine that there is a case for the renegotiation of that contract, and maybe the government should have paid Lockheed more for the C5A. But, two wrongs don't make a right. You ought not try to offset a mistake of that kind by asking the government to guarantee loans to private enterprises.

McClaughry: What about guarantees such as those made by the Federal Housing Administration, a government agency?

Friedman: The total volume of FHA-insured loans outstanding is absolutely incredible—over $68 billion! There is no reason why the government should subsidize people.

McClaughry: Isn't it more a question of absorbing risk? The home ownership subsidy didn't come until 1968.

Friedman: Then people were able to borrow at a lower rate than they otherwise could have because of the government guarantee. Why should some taxpayer subsidize another taxpayer to enable him to buy a house?

McClaughry: Because if a person who wanted to buy a home and was such a poor risk that the interest rate would be exorbitant would have no option open to him.

Friedman: If he is indigent, our general program for assisting indigent people ought to help him. But I don't see why we ought to have a program to help people who are such poor risks they can't borrow money. What justification is there for it? Why should some citizens have taxes imposed on them to enable other citizens to borrow money more cheaply?

McClaughry: As a matter of fact, in the FHA 203 program, the original program, the insurance mortgage premium cost paid by the home buyers had produced not a loss to the taxpayers, but a tremendous reserve.

Friedman: That is not correct because you are not looking at the full cost to the taxpayer. If the government guarantees a collection of assets, it thereby raises the interest rate it must pay on its own debt. There is a certain market for government-guaranteed debt. The larger the amount of government-guaranteed debt you try to float, the further you have to go to tap people who don't want to buy that kind of debt. To put it more obviously, the interest rate that the government pays depends on the volume of its obligations. If the government guarantees FHA loans, we have to include in the cost to the taxpayer the effect of the increase in the rate of interest the government pays on its other debt.

McClaughry: What kind of benefits would flow from the abolition of the FHA and Small Business Administration loan-guarantee systems?

Friedman: People who now do not have guaranteed loans would be able to borrow at a lower rate of interest. There is only a fixed pool to go around. None of these programs *creates* funds to be loaned. There is a certain total amount of savings which can be loaned. If more of it goes into government-guaranteed loans, less of it is available for other purposes. That means the price charged in other areas is higher. By guaranteeing FHA or SBA loans, you make it more expensive for GM or Consolidated Edison to borrow to put up a new plant.

McClaughry: Do you believe then that under these programs the government is channeling resources to the impecunious and away from the relatively affluent?

Friedman: Not at all. It is channeling resources to those people who are entitled to such guarantees, and they are mostly far from impecunious. Most of the government-guaranteed loans do not go to the poor. The

Small Business Administration guarantees a large volume of loans to what they call "small businesses," but since the loans are on the order of $200, $300, $400 thousand and more, they are obviously going to what are, in an absolute sense, rather large businesses. When General Motors or Consolidated Edison obtain lower interest rates from their banks, who benefits? Primarily the customers who buy their services.

You mustn't identify a large corporation with rich people. Henry Ford founded a very large corporation. Who was the main beneficiary? The poor. His contribution was to provide a car which relatively poor people could buy, but he headed a rich corporation. Now, if you had made it more difficult for him to borrow to finance his activity, would that have hurt the rich or the poor? Clearly, it would have hurt the poor.

McClaughry: A lot of voices are being raised these days that say big business has reached the point where it has become unwieldy and inefficient and there ought to be radical deconcentration or decentralization of the large manufacturing enterprises. How do you feel about that?

Friedman: The questions are, what has produced these large concentrations, and what are the most effective measures to deconcentrate? The most effective single thing we could do to increase the amount of competition in American business would be to eliminate tariffs. The next most effective step would unquestionably be to change the corporate tax system. Under our present arrangement, income that is not distributed is not taxed under the personal income tax. Also, capital gains are taxed at a lower rate than other income. Both have the effect of making it profitable to create large agglomerates. It is very undesirable for a corporation to pay out its entire income because those payments become subject to the personal income tax. The alternative is to invest it, but if I don't have the opportunity to invest it in my own enterprise the only way I can invest is to buy other enterprises. Consequently, a major force that has been producing conglomerates and large enterprises has been these aspects of our present tax laws. The tax reform I mentioned earlier, which would require corporations to attribute unearned income to their stockholders and their stockholders to report it on their personal income tax, would be one of the most effective things we could do.

Another measure would be to get rid of government regulations. We ought, by all means, to abolish the Interstate Commerce Commission and the other regulatory commissions. We ought to auction off TV and radio licenses to the highest bidders and put the FCC out of business. The three television networks, which are conglomerates, grew by the grace of the

FCC and the fact that the FCC has not been willing to permit pay TV. Now cable TV is beginning to undermine the networks. Unfortunately, the FCC is trying to regulate cable TV and is going to stifle it.

The fourth step toward reducing economic concentration is vigorous antitrust enforcement, but I think that is much less important than the others.

McClaughry: But if the big corporations are growing larger through government benefits, immunities, favors, and privileges, won't they seek to perpetuate them for their own self-interest?

Friedman: They are acting in the self-interest of each corporation separately, but the end result may be harmful to business enterprises collectively. This is why I said earlier that businessmen often have suicidal impulses. Look at what is going on now in the area of wage and price control. It's absolutely insane. If there is one thing you can be sure of, it is that if you have wage-price control, it will end up primarily price control—not wage control. After all, the businessmen don't have the votes; the trade unions and the workers do. And yet you have businessmen all over the country coming out in favor of price and wage control. If this country becomes a collectivist socialist country, I don't believe it will be because the socialists will win at the ballot box. It will become so because of wage-price control, because if you seriously control prices, you have to ration goods and you have to allocate labor. All these businessmen profess to be free enterprisers. The truth of the matter is that the biggest enemies of free enterprise are businessmen, and they always have been.

McClaughry: Do you see any signs that the American public may be rebelling at this continued stream of subsidies to large corporations?

Friedman: No, I don't really see any such signs. I do see some of the American public getting fed up with paying as large a portion of their income as taxes as they do now, but I don't believe that is especially directed against subsidies.

And here again, the large companies don't benefit. Most of the large subsidies help nobody. It is just money thrown away. What is the effect of a subsidy? It is to induce more people to enter a different industry than would have otherwise—all ultimately making the same profits they would have made otherwise. So, you must distinguish between the fact that the government is giving a subsidy and the idea that anyone benefits from it.

McClaughry: Adam Smith once said that the public good is nothing more than the sum of all the private goods. Yet you seem to be saying that the sum of all the private goods of businessmen as seen by them does not add up to anything that is good for anyone. Was he wrong?

Friedman: No. First of all there are two different propositions. The sum of all the private goods is the public good, but the sum of what all the people *think* to be in their private good is not necessarily the public good. Also, Adam Smith's invisible hand requires the right framework. If people are required to compete, then individuals acting separately in their own self-interest will act jointly in the public interest through the market.

Now, under *political* arrangements, it is not true that people separately pursuing their self-interest will promote the public interest. In fact, it is quite the opposite. There is Adam Smith's invisible hand in economics and there is an invisible hand in politics which works in the opposite direction. The social reformers who seek through politics to do nothing but serve the public interest invariably end up serving some private interest that was no part of their intention to serve. They are led by an invisible hand to serve a private interest.

McClaughry: The ICC, for example?

Friedman: Right. It was the railroads which were a major factor in promoting the passage of the Interstate Commerce Act. But the railroads could not have done it without the well-meaning reformers.

The same is true right now. Those businessmen who are promoting wage and price control would never be able to succeed if it weren't for the fact that they are getting support from well-meaning reformers who talk about wage-price control to promote what they regard as the public interest. The Lockheed people couldn't have gotten their government aid if they hadn't had the support of the well-meaning reformers who said, "Oh, my God, we can't lose those 60,000 jobs."

McClaughry: Some thirty years ago, Joseph Schumpeter wrote that capitalism was in an oxygen tent. Do you think that is true today?

Friedman: That's a very, very hard question to answer. You have to make a sharp distinction between the world of affairs and the world of ideas. Friedrich Hayek's *Road to Serfdom,* published in 1944, reflected the way I and other people who felt the way I did looked at the world at that time. If you had asked us then about the health of capitalism and free enterprise twenty-five years later, I think we would have said it would be closer to its deathbed than it actually is now.

The interesting thing about it is that at that time it looked as if the world at large were on the road to central planning. In point of fact, we went very little further down that road. In Britain, central planning came to a screeching halt with the failure of the control of the engagements order. There is less central planning in Britain now than in 1946. In Germany, the dramatic reversal from the Nazi central planning to Erhard free enterprise is an economic miracle. In the United States, we've had a lot of intervention, but it hasn't gone in the direction of central planning. Indeed, in that respect we are much better off now than most of us thought we would be twenty-five years ago.

I hasten to add this does not mean that the governments have gotten smaller. Governments continue to grow in size, but it has come primarily through engaging in redistributive programs, transfer programs—like social security, welfare, medicare—rather than through expanding their direct control over business enterprise. So in the world of affairs, I think capitalism is in far better shape than Schumpeter thirty years ago or Hayek twenty-five years ago would have thought.

In the world of ideas, however, that is not true. For a time it looked as if there were a reaction against collectivism in the direction of individualism. But more recently we've started once again to move in the direction of ideas which are predominately anticapitalist and toward a collectivist society. We must be very careful here and distinguish between the slogans people utter, the objectives they state, and the means by which they want to achieve those objectives. People who regard themselves as radical fill the air with their desire to do their own thing, get rid of the establishment and centralized control, and so on. But when you ask them how they are going to do it, the answer is always by giving government more power. They say there are mean, nasty people running things in Washington, in business, and in universities. On the other hand, they say good people like themselves exist, and if they were running things, everything would be fine. So the objectives people aim for are all individualist, but the means by which they hope to achieve those objectives are all totalitarian and collectivist.

McClaughry: Would you say that the movement toward collectivism has been largely among intellectuals?

Friedman: Yes I would, and this is a real puzzle. In some ways you'd think it would be the other way around. Intellectuals, of all people, ought to value freedom of speech, freedom of thought. In fact they do value them in intellectual areas for themselves. But their attitude in general is that they want freedom for themselves, but control over everybody else.

The second reason you would think intellectuals would be different is that the argument for collectivism is really simple-minded. It says that if there is an evil it is because a bad man did it, and the way to correct it is to put a good man in power. On the other hand, the argument made for individualism is very subtle and sophisticated. It claims that if you let individuals pursue their own self-interests, they will be led by an invisible hand to pursue the social interest more effectively than if they are organized to pursue it directly.

Intellectuals in general tend to mouth all kinds of slogans about social responsibility, about the vicious capitalists who are grinding the poor under their heels, deliberately polluting the streams, and so on. This is especially true of mass media—newspaper writers and reporters, magazines, TV, and radio. There are some exceptions, but I think that the people who write, talk, and produce for those agencies are overwhelmingly collectivists in their thinking—modern liberals, if you want—in favor of more power for government.

It really makes you think. If you ask any of these people what they think about current government programs, they will agree that they are terrible. Everything the government has done is terrible. What is the answer to the problem? More government. Take public housing. It has failed—so we ought to have more and bigger public housing. The welfare program has done a great deal of harm. What ought we do? We ought to have more and bigger welfare programs. I heard Mayor Hatcher of Gary, Indiana, on TV. He was talking about unemployment. He didn't mention that some of that unemployment in Gary might be attributable to the high wages the steel union had negotiated. No, not a word about that. What was his answer? He was going to Washington to get more federal money.

McClaughry: Why do you think these attitudes are so popular among intellectuals?

Friedman: Schumpeter gave one answer. He said that a free enterprise society, by its success, creates a large number of intellectuals who, by their nature, feel they don't have the power they are entitled to. They become frustrated and repressed, and thus dissatisfied with the existing system. I think there is a good deal of truth to that. But, of course, that doesn't argue that intellectuals are collectivists. It only argues that they would be against the status quo; that they would be free enterprisers in a collectivist world and collectivists in a free enterprise world.

However, that's hard to observe because the potential free enterprisers in a collectivist world wouldn't be permitted to talk. The only place we'd hear the intellectuals speaking freely would be in a free enterprise society. I haven't seen any public announcement of the formation of a Russians for Capitalist Action. You don't have a capitalist party in the Soviet Union, but there is a Communist Party here.

If you ask why so many intellectuals are collectivists, I think the fundamental reason is very different. I think it's in their own self-interest, in a double way. First, in a collectivist society, intellectuals have more power than they do in a free enterprise system. In the 1930s, the New Deal created an enormous number of jobs that didn't exist before for intellectuals. I had one myself, so I am speaking from personal experience. There has been a "drang nach Washington" since the New Deal which intellectuals everywhere recognize as having improved their personal status. Second, it is much easier to sell simple-minded, collectivist ideas than it is to sell sophisticated, free enterprise ideas. Take our topic—social responsibility. Why does this nonsense fill the air? Because it is simple-minded and easy to sell. Because listeners don't have to go through a complicated thinking process.

Trying to sell people on the idea that although there are things that are wrong, if you try to make them better, you'll make them worse, is a lot harder than selling them the idea that the way to solve a problem is to elect a good man and have the government do something. Consequently, there is a better market for collectivist intellectualism than there is for free enterprise individualism.

Now, you'll say to me, doesn't that cut both ways? Why am I a free enterpriser then? Oughtn't I be in that market? Well, it's not quite so easy to say. There is a much bigger market for Fords than there is for Checker Marathons. There is a much bigger market for collectivist intellectuals than there is for free enterprise intellectuals, but there is some market for free enterprise intellectuals. In fact, my impression is that there is a larger demand for free enterprise intellectuals than there is a supply. Although there is only one quarter of the demand for free enterprise intellectuals, I think there is only one-tenth of the supply. That is the real puzzle.

Who Represents Whom?
[October 14, 1974]

As I sat for a day and a half at the summit conference on inflation, I kept asking myself: who are these people on the ballroom floor or temporarily on the podium presenting brief statements? What do the labels like ECONOMISTS, LABOR, HEW that designated where we were supposed to sit really mean?

Labor: This was a large group. It was prominently represented on the podium. At the end of the meeting, President Ford announced the creation of a White House Labor-Management Committee, consisting of eight representatives of labor, eight representatives of business.

The people who spoke from the podium and the labor members of the committee are all officials of labor *unions*. Yet only about one-fourth of all U.S. workers are members of labor unions. Who speaks for the great majority of American workers?

Labor-union officials would no doubt claim that all workers have common interests and that in speaking for union members they are speaking for all workers. Partly true but mostly false. Different unions are in conflict one with the other. The unionized sector is in conflict with the non-unionized sector. High wages obtained by any one union mean fewer jobs in the trade involved, hence more competition and lower wages for other jobs. Higher wages for union members as a whole mean lower wages for non-unionized workers.

Business: The eight business members of the Labor-Management Committee are all from *big business*. So were most of the delegates who represented business on the podium, though a few represented organizations of small businesses. Yet there are nearly 10 million independent business enterprises in the U.S.—excluding some 3 million farmers. Who speaks for the great majority of American businessmen?

Again, the interests of executives of big business and of proprietors of small ones are far from identical.

Consumers: Establishing organizations purporting to represent consumers has become a growth industry. Executives of a number of such organizations spoke from the podium—each bemoaning the "under-representation" of "the" consumer. But I suspect that, taken all together, the membership of such organizations is a tiny minority of all consumers.

The poor, the elderly, the minorities: Speaker after speaker expressed concern for this group, always described as especially hard-hit by inflation. For the most part, each speaker then proceeded to urge that measures in the interest of his special group were also in the interest of "the poor, the elderly, the minorities." A few spokesmen were explicit representatives of these groups. Their intentions were admirable, but their proposals—as judged by this delegate representing only himself—would do more to strengthen the organizations employing them than to benefit the disadvantaged they claim to serve.

Enough of this catalogue. I do not offer it in criticism of the summit itself, or its organizers, or the participants, but only as a striking illustration of an inherent defect of the political mechanism. The summit was a "town meeting of the air." It did give a wide range of interests an opportunity to express their feelings and to display their thoughts. It did bring forth a bewildering variety of proposals for governmental action.

But it also brought out the vital difference between the political market and the economic market.

In the political market, we do not decide for ourselves, but only for all of us. If we vote for something, but are in the minority, we do not get it. If we vote against something and are in the minority, we get it. In most matters, our individual vote is as a grain of sand; it therefore seldom pays us to vote with care. To be effective on an issue that affects us with special force we must act as an organized pressure group. These are the facts of political life, and no amount of rhetoric can eliminate them. That is why governmental action benefits special-interest groups at the expense of one another and of the "silent majority."

In the economic market, each of us can decide for himself. Within the limits of our income, we can be sure that what we vote for with our dollars we get. If we choose to buy something, we get it. If we choose not to buy it, we do not. Our votes will not be wasted, and it pays us therefore to vote with care. That is why the economic market is so far the only mechanism available that provides real individual democracy.

Chapter Twelve
Government and Education

Some years ago, when Charles E. Wilson, former head of General Motors, was testifying before Congress in connection with confirmation for a high government post, he remarked, "What is good for General Motors is good for the United States." My colleagues in the universities sneered at this remark, pointed to it as showing how small-minded, how self-interested, how blind our business leaders are. Simultaneously, they and their colleagues were trooping down to Washington testifying in favor of "federal aid" to higher education, i.e., government subsidies. One after another in effect said, "What's good for higher education is good for the country." Never did I see one even smile when he said it, or recognize in any way any inconsistency between his sneers at Mr. Wilson and his testimony in Washington.

All of us—you and I not excepted—are far more aware of our own interests than that of other people's. We all know that what is good for us is good for the country. That is why the "devil" theory of special-interest legislation is wrong. The men who urge Congress to pass laws that you and I regard as benefiting their special interests seldom do so out of devil motives. They are generally completely sincere when they urge that the measure is in the public interest. As the Bible says, we see the mote in the other man's eye, not the beam in our own.

As you have read my animadversions against special interests in prior chapters, you have probably been sympathetic to my view in most cases because the special interests I have been inveighing against are not yours. In this chapter, I come closer to home for many readers, particularly those who are college students or on college faculties.

I believe one of the great scandals in the United States is government subsidization of higher schooling. There is no other policy I know of which so clearly and on so large a scale imposes costs on low-income people to provide subsidies to high-income people. Some academic people have recognized the evil and spoken out against governmental subsidy. But their number is pitifully and shamefully small. A larger number have recognized the evil without speaking out against it or have proposed that it be solved by still larger governmental expenditures so that still more extensive subsidies to youngsters from low-income families would offset the subsidies to youngsters from high-income families. (This is in effect the recommendation of the Carnegie Commission on Higher Education headed by Clark Kerr, former president of the University of California.) But most have simply been smugly self-righteous, taking exactly the same stand as the oil industry people who defend oil-import quotas, the chemical producers who defend tariffs, and so on *ad nauseam*.

The items in this chapter offer alternatives to the present relation between government and schooling: at the level of higher schooling, loans to students to repay costs rather than subsidies, scholarships at institutions chosen by the student rather than direct provision of schooling by state institutions; and at the level of elementary and secondary schooling, a voucher plan that would enable parents to choose schools for their children.

These proposals are still very poor bets. They go against the narrow self-interest of most teachers and educational administrators—at least as they are likely to view that self-interest—and hence are likely to be viewed unfavorably by intellectuals as a class. Yet the growing dissatisfaction with the present system at all levels and by many different segments of our society offers some hope for change.

On the university level, a number of universities, notably Yale, have been experimenting with plans for extending loans to students to be paid back out of future earnings rather than granting scholarships along lines that I first proposed in a 1955 article and then later in *Capitalism and Freedom*. The distinctive feature of these loans is that the amount to be paid back would not be a fixed, unchangeable dollar sum but an amount depending on the success or lack of success of the individual student in later life. On the elementary and secondary level, two experiments on vouchers are now underway as noted in "The Voucher Idea," reprinted here from the *New York Times*.

"Free" Education
[February 14, 1967]

Gov. Ronald Reagan has stirred up a hornet's nest by proposing that students who attend state colleges and the University of California be required to pay tuition of $150 to $250 a year in addition to present student fees of $90 to $275 a year. Professors and students have risen almost as one man in protest at such an outrageous suggestion. Make the students pay for their own schooling? Preposterous. "Free" education is an ancient tradition in California, and this is one tradition that even the campus rebels are disposed to defend with all their might and main—after all, their pocketbooks are at stake.

Unfortunately, low-income taxpayers and youngsters not in college are much less effective than students and professors in presenting their case to the public. "Free" tuition is highly inequitable to them. In addition, it lowers the quality of higher education. Governor Reagan's proposal is long overdue and unduly modest, not only for the state of California, but for other states as well.

The cost of higher education to the state of California is roughly $2,000 per student per year. The youngster admitted to a state school automatically gets a scholarship of that amount. By reason of this subsidy, he can expect to earn a higher income for the rest of his life than youngsters of equal ability who do not go to college. He will repay a small part of the subsidy himself—in the form of taxes on the increase in his income. But the greater part of the subsidy is paid by the rest of the taxpaying public, including his fellow citizens who are not able to take advantage of the "free" education.

Despite the rhetoric to the contrary, state colleges and universities serve mainly the well-to-do. For California, more than half the students in 1963 came from the top quarter of families—whose incomes exceeded $10,000 a year. At the other end of the scale, only 5 percent or so of the students came from the 18 percent of the families with incomes less than $4,000. Yet, the idealistic students march in the name of social justice.

It is eminently desirable that every youngster, regardless of his or his parents' income, social position, residence or race, have the opportunity to get higher schooling—*provided he is willing to pay for it either currently or out of the higher income the schooling will enable him to earn.* There is a strong case for providing generous *loan* funds to assure opportunity to all. There is a strong case for disseminating information about the availability of such funds and for urging the underprivileged to take advantage of the opportunity. There is no case for subsidizing those who get higher schooling at the expense of those who do not.

California in effect says to its high-school graduates: "If you are in the top half or so of your class, you automatically qualify for a scholarship of $2,000 a year—provided you attend a state-run school. If you are so foolish as to go to Stanford or Claremont, let alone Harvard or Yale or Chicago, not a penny for you." If California is going to give scholarships, it would be far better to give them to the youngsters directly and let them decide which schools to attend—as under GI educational benefits. State-run institutions would then finance themselves by tuition fees and would compete on more even terms with private institutions. If they were more attractive to students, they would flourish; if not, they would decline.

The need to compete for students would force colleges to be more responsive to student interest. Berkeley is justly famed for the quality of its research faculty—not for the quality of undergraduate teaching. As California is demonstrating, state schools have developed to a high pitch the art of appealing to the legislature and influencing public opinion—that is the way now to get funds—while all the time demanding independence from political influence. Far better that they develop to a high pitch the art of schooling youngsters—that would make them truly independent of politics.

When the smog clears, perhaps California will have shown other states how to broaden educational opportunity, raise the quality of college training, and simultaneously relieve the budget—all by exploiting the insight that people value what they pay for and will pay for what they value.

"Public" Education
[March 13, 1967]

"Does money bring happiness?" is a recurrent theme in movie, short story, and novel. Yet the corresponding question is seldom asked about government expenditures. It is simply taken for granted that more government spending means more of whatever the spending is for.

Take the debate over the financing of higher education in California. Educators from all parts of the country have not hesitated to proclaim without detailed study that the proposed cuts in state appropriations jeopardize the quality and quantity of higher education in California. Apparently they regard this proposition as in a class with the proposition that two plus two equal four. Yet, while California is at or near the top of the country in per capita *government* expenditures for higher education, it appears to be backward in the quality and quantity of higher education— despite the many boasts to the contrary.

In the *Financial Barrier to Higher Education in California,* a study prepared for the California State Scholarship Commission and published in 1965, well before the present furor, Edward Sanders and Hans Palmer point out:

—Dropouts are massive. "Only 27 percent of the first-time freshman enrollees graduated four years later"; in the U.S. as a whole, 54 percent do.

—"A smaller percentage of the number of high-school graduates actually complete a four-year program than in the U.S. as a whole"—23 percent of high-school graduates receive a bachelor's degree in California, 28 percent, in the U.S. as a whole.

—"California appears to be considerably less successful than the remainder of the nation in bringing students from low-income groups into college."

Perhaps California educators should take a brief recess from patting themselves on the back and grapple with these depressing facts—or, if they are wrong, refute them.

Could it be that California lags in higher education because of—and not despite—its leadership in *government* spending? After all, the "public" is served not only by government schools but also by private schools, ranging from junior colleges to major universities like Stanford and the University of Southern California.

The government financing of "free" state schools has starved private schools. How easy would you find it to sell books or houses or cars if the government were giving them away? It is a tribute to the quality of the private schools and the generosity of private donors—as well as to the defects of state schools—that the private schools account for as much as 12 percent of total enrollment in California institutions of higher learning, 16 percent of full-time enrollment, and 26 percent of bachelor's degrees.

Though large government spending may reduce private spending, must it not raise total spending? Clearly, it would, if government simply gave individuals money to spend on schooling but did not itself run schools.

However, once government runs schools, it is by no means certain that even total spending, let alone total results, will be higher. We are all more reluctant to vote taxes on ourselves for general benefits than we are to pay directly for benefits we ourselves receive. Yet once tax-supported facilities are available "free," we are also reluctant to spend "our own money" for private alternatives. Many a parent might be willing to spend an extra sum to get better schooling for his child—but if he dispenses with "free" schools, he must pay not only the extra cost but the whole cost. Thus, paradoxical as it may seem, total spending on higher education in California might be larger today than it is, if government spending were smaller. And even if total spending were not larger, total *results* would almost surely be better if the smaller government spending were directed more toward encouraging and aiding the poor to take advantage of educational opportunities and less toward providing facilities for the well-to-do.

The right question—not only in education but in many other areas as well—is: how can the community get the most—in quality and quantity—for the money it spends? *Not*, how can the taxpayer, legislature, and governors be persuaded to increase government appropriations?

Police on Campus
[April 14, 1969]

The disruption this winter at my university—the University of Chicago—was handled brilliantly and effectively by president Edward Levi and the administration, *given the attitude of the faculty*. But this attitude undermines our defenses against the intolerant radicals who are seeking to destroy all universities. We must do some drastic rethinking if we are to preserve the university as the home of reason, persuasion, and free discussion.

At Chicago, nonviolent passive resistance by the university plus the steady, undramatic application of university disciplinary procedures finally brought a sit-in at our administration building to an end without force and violence and without any concession by the university to the "demands" of the students. But the cost in damage, vandalism, and interruption of vital university functions was enormous—all because fewer than 5 percent of the students permitted themselves to be inveigled into the adoption of coercive tactics.

President Levi's approach was the right one because of the widespread belief among the faculty that the university is a sanctuary and that calling on the civil authorities—i.e., the police—must be a very last resort. Given this attitude, the use of police on campus can only divide, fragment, and embitter both faculty and students.

In the Middle Ages in Europe, universities were very nearly city-states and did provide sanctuary against often hostile external political units. More important for the U.S., the university has regarded itself, and has been regarded by students and parents of students, as *in loco parentis*, and hence as having an obligation to control its "children" within the family. Neither of these reasons for the faculty attitude is any longer valid. A more relevant reason is that the university can perform its true function only if it is a community whose members share common values and have a common commitment to free and untrammeled inquiry. The need to use outside force to maintain discipline undermines this sense of community and hence should be avoided—provided that it can be avoided without tolerating modes of discourse (confrontation, force, coercion) that are fundamentally inconsistent with the basic values of the university.

Whatever the desirability of avoiding outside force, I have become increasingly impressed with how ineffective university disciplinary procedures are for offenses such as trespass, destruction of university property, and interference with the civil rights of others. If a student were to break and enter my apartment, I would, if I could, call the police at once. If he were arrested and convicted, it would never occur to me to submit him to a university disciplinary procedure.

Should it be different for a student who breaks and enters a dean's office? In that case should we, who are ill-equipped and ill-trained for the job, turn ourselves into police officers, force ourselves into the student mob, get fellow professors to identify the participants, pass out summonses, and then use suspension or expulsion or the like to punish such offenses? I believe not.

The university is part of the community at large. We should tend to our business—which is to teach the young and to conduct scholarly analysis. We should rely on the civil authorities to protect us from coercion by other people, whether that coercion takes the form of seizure of property or interference with the civil rights of other students or faculty. If this coercion interferes seriously with the university's task we may also want to deny persons committed to such tactics access to the university—not to punish them, but to preserve the university.

If this distinction between the proper domain of the university and of the civil authorities were widely accepted by the faculty, it might be possible to nip incipient disruptions in the bud by calling in the police at once. Indeed, if it were widely accepted, the occasion for calling in the police would be unlikely to arise.

As it is, we have the worst of both worlds. Time and again, unwillingness to have the police on campus has permitted a disruption to grow to a scale that has made mass force and violence inevitable when police were finally called—Columbia, San Francisco State, and Berkeley bear tragic testimony. Thanks to wise leadership and an eventually united faculty, the University of Chicago was able to avoid that outcome—this time. Next time—who knows?

The Ivory Tower
[November 10, 1969]

Moratorium Day was marked by attempts to get universities, as institutions, to take a stand on the war in Vietnam. These attempts have met with surprising success. A few universities officially suspended classes on October 15. Many others approved the suspension of classes by individual faculty members. Some faculties have voted to take a political position on the war—most notably, at Harvard. Seventy-nine college presidents signed a public letter expressing disagreement with our policy in Vietnam.

The actions and the statements have typically been accompanied by a disclaimer that they involved the taking of a political position by the university as an institution. For example, the letter of the college presidents starts with the admirable sentiment, "We speak as individuals. . . . The universities and colleges which we serve take no positions as institutions on the Vietnam war; these are pluralistic communities where men speak for themselves alone on off-campus issues." But why then a statement signed only by *college presidents?* Why do these men not issue statements as individuals; or add their names to statements signed by citizens from varied walks of life? However sincere the college presidents are in their protestations, the very fact that college presidents and only college presidents signed the statement cannot help but give the impression that their institutions as institutions have taken a political position.

This is a dangerous trend. If continued, it will destroy the university as the home of free inquiry and the uninhibited search for truth. This conclusion has nothing to do with the merits or demerits of the position taken by the faculties and the presidents on the particular issue of Vietnam. The basis for the conclusion was stated lucidly by my colleague Prof. George J. Stigler of the University of Chicago, in an unpublished memorandum written some years ago in connection with very different issues.

> The university [wrote Professor Stigler] is by design and effect the institution in a society which creates discontent with existing moral, social, and political institutions and proposes new institutions to replace them. The university is, from this viewpoint, a group of philosophically imaginative men freed of any pressure except to please their fellow faculty, and told to follow their inquiries wherever they might lead. Invited to be learned in the institutions of other times and places, incited to new understanding of the social and physical world, the university faculty is inherently a disruptive force. . . .
>
> The instrument of criticism and dissent is the individual faculty member, not the university in some group sense. . . . This *individualization* of the university is the feature which allows universities to have so privileged a position in society: a professor may become an unmitigated nuisance, or even, with great luck, a serious threat to powerful political or social groups in the population, but the university as a community is no part of this professor's school or party. In fact, if the university is properly staffed with active and independent minds, some of this profes-

sor's colleagues will deny the validity of his ideas and many will deny the primacy or significance or applicability of them. . . .

Should the university as an institution enter moral, social, or political movements, it then becomes an instrument of oppression against the individual professor. If the university endorses idea X, any opponent of idea X in the university community has been censured. It matters not whether X is a nearly universal moral conviction—such as that the dignity of man must be defended—or the most transitory and partisan endorsement of a man or scheme. If there were an absolutely certain truth, the university community could endorse it with small cost; however, the very first of these certain truths has yet to be determined.

The university as an institution discharges its moral responsibility to society when it provides the conditions for free inquiry, and it violates this responsibility when it sacrifices freedom of inquiry to more immediate goals. . . .

I place no weight on the objections on grounds of cost or expediency to the intervention by the university as an institution in moral, social, and political movements. . . . A university is dedicated to the costly and inefficient enterprise of discovering and improving knowledge. The one, the grave complaint against institutional intervention in social movements is that it constitutes a rejection of the paramount moral goal of a university.

Homogenized Schools
[February 28, 1972]

How a question is asked often determines the answer. For example, if you were asked, "Should parents be permitted to spend their income on better schooling for their children?" you would almost surely say "yes." If you were asked, "Is it fair and just that children who happen to live in low-income communities should receive poorer schooling than children who live in wealthy suburbs?'' you would almost surely say "no"—and that is what courts have said recently in California, Texas, and New Jersey in declaring local financing of public schools unconstitutional. Yet clearly the two answers are contradictory. If all children must receive the same schooling, how can parents spend more on their children's schooling?

The contradiction suggests that it may be worth exploring the implications of the courts' decisions.

If it is wrong for different communities in a state to spend different amounts per child on public schooling (or in some other sense provide unequal schooling), how can it be right for different states to do so? For different countries? Even if we stop at our own borders, the courts' decisions clearly imply federal financing of schools to assure equal expenditure per child throughout the land. "Control by local school boards of local schools" brought hearty applause from Congress when President Nixon said it in his State of the Union address. But it will be a slogan without content if Washington pays the bill.

Parents could escape a homogenized school system by sending their children to private schools. But surely that would be inconsistent with the courts' answers to the second question. If private schooling is permitted, an obvious escape from the courts' decisions is to starve the governmental school system and encourage private schools. The courts would surely treat that, and properly, as an evasion of the law, just as they did the many attempts to set up private schools in the South that followed court orders to public schools to integrate. Equal spending on schooling per child therefore logically implies the prohibition of private schools—and indeed this answer has been reached by some of the more "advanced" educational reformers.

But why stop with schooling? If it is wrong for different children to have different amounts spent on their schooling, how can it be right to have different amounts spent on their food? Housing? Clothing? Etc.?

Translating into practice the appealing negative answer to the second question therefore implies seeking the complete equalization of conditions of life—a homogenized society. This is a road that we have been trying to travel for some time. We have not gotten very far, because, fortunately, the ingenuity of men in pursuing their own interests and the interests of their spouses and children keeps defeating the attempts of clumsy bureaucrats egged on by egalitarian sentiment. Yet we have already paid a high price in freedom and efficiency for the attempts.

What is wrong with traveling this road? Is not the vision of a society in which the law requires that all children receive the same amount of schooling, housing, feeding and clothing an inspiring and desirable vision?

It certainly is not. Such enforced egalitarianism can be obtained only on a low level. What gain equality at zero? If I cannot use extra income to improve the lot of my children, why should I seek extra income? Even more, if my children (and by extension I myself) will have the same level of living whatever I do, why should I work? If there is no carrot to encourage effort, there will have to be a stick. Enforced egalitarianism also means forced labor; it also means a slave state. It is a horrible, not an inspiring, vision.

Of course, taking one step down this road does not condemn us to travel it to its bitter end. Socialism is not like pregnancy. We can be, as we are, a little or even more than a little socialist without going all the way. Yet it is the ideal that animates our actions. If the ideal is false, perhaps we should reconsider the steps that we have taken, or are prepared to take, in its name.

There is all the difference in the world between the more fortunate among us giving of our substance in order to establish a minimum standard below which no disadvantaged person or child shall be forced to live, and trying to legislate uniformity of condition. The difference is between freedom and slavery.

The Voucher Idea*
[September 23, 1973]

A fable may dramatize the true source of the nation's present discontent with our public schools: suppose that, fifty or seventy-five years ago, the U.S. had adopted the same institutional arrangements for the distribution of food as it did adopt for elementary and secondary schools. Suppose, that is, that the retail provision of groceries had been nationalized, that food was paid for by taxes and distributed by government-run stores. Each family would be assigned to a store, as it is now assigned to a school, on the basis of its location. It would be entitled to receive, without direct

*The New York Times Magazine

payment, a collection of foods, as its children are entitled to receive a collection of classes. It would be able to choose among foods, as its children choose among subjects. Presumably this would be done by giving each family some number of ration points and assigning point prices to various foods. Private grocery stores would be permitted (just as private schools are), but persons shopping in them would be taxed for the support of the public stores just the same.

Can there be any doubt what retail food distribution would be like today if this system had been in effect? Would there be supermarkets and chain stores? Would the shelves be loaded with new and improved convenience products? Would stores be using every device of human ingenuity to attract and retain customers?

Suppose that under such a system you were unhappy with your local grocery. You could not simply go to a different store unless you were able and willing to pay twice for your groceries, once in taxes and again in cash. No, you would have to work through political channels to change the elected or appointed Grocery Board, or the mayor, or the governor, or the president. Obviously this would be a cumbrous inefficient process. And suppose you had different ideas from your neighbors about the kind of service you wanted? What then? You would have to find a neighborhood of likeminded people to which you could move.

Of course the well-to-do would escape all this by patronizing the few luxury establishments that would arise to cater to them. They would willingly pay twice for their food, just as they now pay twice for the schooling of their children. (I do not blame them. It is right and proper that parents should deny themselves in order to purchase the best products they can for their children's bodies or minds. I blame only those well-meaning persons who, while sending their own children to private schools, self-righteously lecture the "lower classes" about their responsibility to put up with government-supplied pablum in the "public interest.")

Consider the producer rather than the consumer. The supermarket is a modern invention that has contributed enormously to the well-being of the masses. What would the inventor have done—if he had existed at all—in the hypothetical world of government grocery stores? In the actual world, all he had to do to try out his idea was to use his own capital, or persuade a few people to venture some capital, and set up shop. In the hypothetical world, he would have to launch a successful political campaign to persuade a local grocery board, an entrenched civil service, and harried legislators that his idea was worth trying. Obviously, innovations would come primarily from the few private stores serving the well-to-do.

Ask yourself what activities in the U.S. have participated least in the technological revolution of the past century. Is there any doubt that schooling, mail service, and legislative activity head the list? Grocery stores would be on the list, too, if they had been government-owned.

Schooling is not groceries. Yet the many and important differences do not invalidate the comparison. The delivery of mails is not the same as the delivery of schooling, yet both are inefficient and technologically backward for the same reason: they are conducted mostly by government agencies enjoying an effective monopoly. The delivery of groceries is not the same as the production of hi-fi equipment. Yet both are highly efficient and technologically progressive for the same reason: they are conducted mostly by private enterprises operating in a competitive market.

The same contrast applies to schooling itself. As Adam Smith wrote nearly 200 years ago, "Those parts of education, it is to be observed, for the teaching of which there are no public institutions, are generally the best taught." That is equally true today: music or dance, secretarial skills, automobile driving, airplane piloting, technical skills—all are taught best when they are taught privately. Try talking French with someone who studied it in public school, then with a Berlitz graduate.

As the fable suggests, the way to achieve real reform in schooling is to give competition and free enterprise greater scope; to make available to children of low- and middle-income parents, particularly those living in slums, a range of choice in schooling comparable to that which the children of upper-income parents have long enjoyed. How can the market be used to organize schooling more effectively? The most radical answer is to put schooling precisely on a par with food: eliminate compulsory schooling, government operation of schools and government financing of schools except for financial assistance to the indigent. The market would then have full rein.

A slightly less radical answer is to put schooling on a par with smallpox vaccination or getting a driver's license: require every person to have at least a minimum level of schooling, as he is required to be vaccinated or to take a driving test before he is granted a license—but let the schooling be obtained privately and at the parents' expense. Again, except for the indigent.

These solutions have much to be said for them as ways to further both freedom and equal opportunity. However, they are clearly outside the range of political feasibility today. Accordingly, I shall discuss a more modest reform—one that would retain compulsory schooling, government financing and government operation, while preparing the way for the gradual replacement of public schools by private schools.

The City of New York now spends about $1,500 per year for every child enrolled at public elementary and secondary schools. Parents who send their child to a private school therefore save the city about $1,500. But they get no benefit from doing so. The key reform would be for the city to give such parents a voucher for $1,500 to pay for schooling their child (and for no other purpose). This would not relieve them of the burden of taxes; it would simply give parents a choice of the form in which they take the schooling that the city has obligated itself to provide.

To widen still further the range of choice, parents could be permitted to use the vouchers not only in private schools but also in other public schools—and not only in schools in their own district, city or state, but in any school anywhere that is willing to accept their child. This would involve giving every parent a voucher and requiring or permitting public schools to finance themselves by charging tuition. The public schools would then have to compete both with one another and with private schools.

Today the only widely available alternative to a local public school is a parochial school. The reason is that only churches have been in a position to subsidize schooling on a large scale and only subsidized schooling can compete with "free" schooling. (Try selling a product that someone else is giving away!) The voucher plan would produce a much wider range of alternatives. In the first place, choice among public schools themselves would be enormously increased. The size of a public school would be set by the number of customers it attracted, not by politically defined geographical boundaries. Parents who organized nonprofit schools, as a few pioneers have, would be assured of funds to pay the costs. Voluntary organizations—ranging from vegetarians to Boy Scouts to the Y.M.C.A.—could set up schools and try to attract customers. And, most important, new sorts of private schools would arise to tap the vast new market—perhaps Mom-and-Pop schools like Mom-and-Pop grocery stores, perhaps also highly capitalized chain schools, like supermarkets.

But why require parents to spend the voucher in a single school? Why not *divisible* vouchers? Let part be spent for the core school, and the rest for mathematics lessons, music lessons, or vocational training purchased from another source. One does not buy all one's groceries at a single store. Why should one buy all of a child's schooling at a single school?

Let us examine in detail some problems with the voucher plan and some objections that have been raised to it:

1. *The church-state issue.* Parents could use their vouchers to pay tuition at parochial schools. Would this violate the First Amendment? Whether it does or not, is it desirable to adopt a policy that might strengthen the role of religious institutions in schooling?

On June 25, 1973, the Supreme Court struck down by a six-to-three majority laws in New York and Pennsylvania that provided for reimbursing parents for part of the tuition paid to nonpublic elementary and secondary schools. The majority held that the laws "have the impermissible effect of advancing religion." The minority (in three separate dissents) urged that "government aid to individuals generally stands on an entirely different footing from direct aid to religious institutions" (Chief Justice Burger); that "preserving the secular functions of these schools is the overriding consequence of these laws" (Justice White); and that the court has failed to "distinguish between a new exercise of power within constitutional limits and an exercise of legislative power which transgresses those limits" (Justice Rehnquist).

To this nonlawyer, the tuition-reimbursement plans appear to be at least kissing cousins of the voucher plan that I have outlined. However, as I read the decisions, two differences might lead the court to rule favorably on a full-fledged voucher plan: the voucher plan would apply to all parents, not simply those with children in nonpublic schools; and it would grant the same sum to all parents not, as in the particular tuition-reimbursement plans struck down, a sum much smaller than the per-pupil cost (a point that Justice Powell referred to explicitly in the majority decision).

Whatever the fate of a full-fledged voucher plan, it seems clear that the court would accept a plan that excluded church-connected schools but applied to all other private and public schools. Such a restricted plan would be far superior to the present system, and might not be much inferior to a wholly unrestricted plan. Schools now connected with churches could qualify by subdividing themselves into two parts: a secular part reorganized as an independent school eligible for vouchers, and a religious part reorganized as an after-school or Sunday activity paid for directly by parents or church funds.

The constitutional issue will have to be settled by the courts. But it is worth emphasizing Justice Burger's point that the vouchers would go to *parents, not to schools.* Under the G.I. Bill, veterans are free to attend Catholic or other religious colleges, and, so far as I know, no First-Amendment issue has ever been raised. Recipients of Social Security and welfare payments are free to contribute to churches from their government subsidies, with no First-Amendment question being asked.

Indeed, I believe that the penalty now imposed on parents who do not send their children to public schools produces a *real* violation of the spirit of the First Amendment, whatever lawyers and judges may decide about the letter. The penalty abridges the religious freedom of parents who do not accept the liberal, humanistic religion of the public schools, yet, because of the penalty, are impelled to send their children to public schools.

In practice, the voucher plan might well reduce the role of parochial schools by eliminating their privileged position as the only effective alternative to public schools for most people. In the first instance, parochial schools would benefit, but soon they would encounter far greater competition than they do today. However, I hasten to add that my advocacy of the plan in no way hinges on whether this conjecture is correct.

2. Financial cost. A second objection to the voucher plan is that it would raise the total cost of schooling—because of the cost of paying for children who now go to parochial and other private schools. This is a "problem" only if one neglects the present discrimination against parents who send their children to nonpublic schools; universal vouchers would end the inequity of using tax funds to school some children but not others. And current laws impose the responsibility on the state to school *all* children, not just children now in public schools. Moreover, there are two offsetting considerations: first, growing financial difficulties are forcing many nonpublic schools to close, which also raises governmental costs; second, under a voucher plan, parents who now send their children to nonpublic schools might be more favorable to higher public expenditures for schooling.

There would, however, be a real problem of finding enough money to begin with. One way to meet it is to make the amount of the voucher less than current expenditures per public-school child. Take present total ex-

penditures on schooling, divide by the number of eligible children and let
the resulting sum—or some amount between that sum and present expenditures per public-school child—be the amount of the voucher. If
$1,500 is now spent per public-school child in New York, $1,300 spent
in a competitive school would provide a far higher quality of schooling.
Witness the drastically lower cost per child in parochial schools. (The
fact that élite, luxury schools charge high tuitions is no counterargument,
any more than the $7.25 charged at the "21" Club for its Twenty-one
Burger means that McDonald's cannot sell a hamburger profitably for
25 cents.)

The net effect of a compromise plan, making the voucher somewhat
less than the current average cost, would be: (a) to require public
schools to economize somewhat; (b) to give parents of children who
now attend a public school the alternatives of keeping them there or
transferring them to any other school, public or private, at no financial
cost if the school's tuition is $1,300 or less, or at a cost equal to the ex-
cess of the school's tuition over $1,300; (c) to enable parents of chil-
dren who now attend a parochial school to keep them there if they
wish, relieved of the tuition they have been paying (almost invariably
less than $1,300), or to take advantage of any of the other alternatives
available to parents of public-school children; (d) to relieve parents of
children now attending élite private schools of $1,300 of the annual
cost of schooling their children, as a partial offset to the school-tax payments they will continue to have to make.

3. *The possibility of fraud.* How can one assure that the voucher is
spent for schooling, not diverted to beer for papa and clothes for mama?
The answer is that the voucher would have to be spent in an *approved*
school or teaching establishment. True, this does mean some government
regulation of the schools, but of course private schools are regulated to
some extent now, to assure that attendance at them satisfies compulsory
schooling requirements. Compared to current regulation of public
schools, the government requirements in a voucher plan would be a mere
trifle.

A more subtle problem is the *kind* of schooling for which the vouchers
may be used. The major justification for both compulsory schooling and
government financing of schooling is the so-called "neighborhood effect"—i.e., the assertion that schooling benefits not only the children and
their parents but also the rest of us by promoting a stable and democratic

society. But do all kinds of schooling contribute to responsible citizenship? Where should the line be drawn?

The voucher plan does not create this problem. It simply makes it more visible. Much that is taught today in public schools cannot readily be justified as conferring benefits on the community at large. I regard it as a virtue of the voucher plan that it forces us to face this issue rather than evade it.

4. *The racial issue.* Voucher plans were adopted for a time by a number of Southern states as a device to avoid integration. They were ruled unconstitutional. Discrimination under such a plan can be easily prevented by permitting vouchers to be used only in schools that do not discriminate. However, a more difficult problem has troubled some students of vouchers. This is the possibility that a voucher plan might increase racial and class separation in schools, exacerbate racial conflict and foster an increasingly segregated and hierarchal society.

I believe that it would have precisely the opposite effect—that nothing could do more to moderate racial conflict and to promote a society in which black and white cooperate in joint objectives, while respecting each other's separate rights and interests. Much objection to forced integration reflects not racism but more or less well-founded fear about the physical well-being of children and the quality of their schooling. Integration has been most successful when it has been a matter of choice not coercion.

Violence of the kind that has been rising apace in public schools is possible only because the victims are compelled to attend the schools that they do. Give them effective freedom to choose and students—black and white, poor and rich, North and South—will desert in droves any school that cannot maintain order. Let schools specialize, as private schools would, and the pull of common interest will overcome the pull of color, leading, I believe, to far more rapid integration than is now in process—in fact, not on paper.

The voucher scheme would completely eliminate the busing issue. Busing would occur, and might indeed be increased, but it would be wholly voluntary—just as the busing of children to music and dance classes is today.

I have long been puzzled that black leaders have not been the most vigorous proponents of the voucher plan. Their constituents would benefit from it most; it would give them power over the schooling of their children, eliminate the domination of both the citywide politicians and, even more important, of the entrenched bureaucracy. Black leaders themselves frequently send their children to private schools. Why do they not help others to do the same? My tentative answer is that vouchers would also free the black man on the street from domination by his leaders, who correctly see that control over local schooling is a powerful political lever.[1]

5. *The economic-class issue.* The question that has perhaps divided students of vouchers more than any other is their likely effect on social and economic class structure. Some have argued that the great value of the public school has been as a melting pot in which rich and poor, native and foreign-born, black and white have learned to live together. This image had much validity for small communities and still does. But it has almost none for large cities and their suburbs. In them, the public school has fostered residential stratification, by tying the kind and the cost of schooling to residential location. Most of the country's outstanding public schools are in high-income enclaves—Scarsdale or Lake Forest or Beverly Hills. Such schools are better regarded as private tax shelters than as public schools. If they were, in the strict sense, private, their cost would not be deductible in computing federal income tax. But the cost is deductible as local taxes because the high-cost and high-quality school is nominally public.

Elementary schools would probably still be largely local under a voucher plan. But even they might be less homogeneous than they are now, because of the indirect effect of the voucher plan in making residential areas more heterogeneous. And secondary schools would almost surely be less stratified. Schools defined by common interests—one stressing, say, the arts; another, the sciences; another, foreign languages—would perforce attract socially and economically more heterogeneous clienteles from a wide variety of residential areas.

One feature of the voucher plan that has aroused particular concern is the provision that parents may "add on" to the voucher; that is, if the voucher is for, say, $1,300, a parent could add another $500 to it and send his child to a school charging $1,800 tuition. Some fear that the result might be even wider differences in school expenditures per child than

[1] Some black educators have supported the voucher plan. In his recent remarkable book *Black Education, Myths and Tragedies,* Thomas Sowell concludes: "Voucher systems are no panacea. All that can be claimed for them is that they offer important benefits not obtainable under the existing institutional structure, without making the other problems any worse. In the world as it is, that is a very large advantage."

now exist, because low-income parents would not add to the amount of the voucher while middle-income and upper-income parents would supplement it extensively.

This possibility has particularly worried Christopher Jencks and his associates at the Center for the Study of Public Policy in Cambridge, Mass., who conducted an O.E.O.-financed study of vouchers. In their 1970 report, "Education Vouchers," they assert, on the basis of the most casual empiricism, that "an unregulated market would redistribute resources away from the poor and toward the rich." Being confirmed egalitarians, they respond by proposing first that the voucher be larger for children from low-income families than for others; second, that voucher schools be required (among other things) to "(a) accept a voucher as full payment of tuition; (b) accept any applicant so long as it had vacant places; (c) if it had more applicants than places, fill at least half of these places by picking applicants randomly."

I have great sympathy for the proposed "compensatory" voucher. For a variety of reasons, costs of schooling are greater in slum areas than elsewhere, so that vouchers of equal dollar amount would not purchase equal schooling. In addition, I share the motives of those who believe that taxpayers should be willing to help the children of the poor. Moreover, with few exceptions, governmental expenditures benefit disproportionately middle- and upper-income groups, so compensatory vouchers would only help to redress the balance. As a realist, however, I believe that it is a mistake to recommend a compensatory voucher. In the first place, the political facts that account for the present bias in government spending will also pervert compensatory vouchers. In the second place, equal per-child vouchers, while falling short of the ideal, would be a great improvement over what now exists.

The proposed restrictions on voucher schools are not justified in principle from the point of view even of confirmed egalitarians like Jencks, let alone of persons like myself who regard freedom as the primary social goal, though welcoming, as a desirable by-product, the tendency for a free society to foster equality of both opportunity and outcome. Equality surely should refer to the *whole* of the income or wealth of families. Can the egalitarian say, it is all right for the well-to-do to spend any income that the tax collector leaves them on riotous living, but they must be penalized (by being denied a voucher) if they try to spend more than the publicly specified sum on schooling their children?

The very poor would benefit the most from the voucher plan. For the first time, poor parents would have a real opportunity to do something about their children's schooling. Social reformers, and educational reformers in particular, often self-righteously take for granted that the poor have no interest in their children or no competence to choose for them. This, I believe, is a gratuitous insult. The poor have had limited opportunity to choose. But U.S. history has amply demonstrated that given the opportunity, they will often sacrifice greatly, disinterestedly, and wisely for their children's welfare. Even the poorest are capable of scraping up a few extra dollars to improve the quality of their children's schooling, although they could not replace the whole of the present cost of public schooling.

In the middle classes, there is now much private expenditure on schooling, but most of it goes for music, dancing, golf, and similar skills that supplement the public school. The voucher plan would enable people to spend their own money as well as the voucher on what they regard as most valuable.

The net effect, I believe, would be a larger total sum spent on schooling, with that sum, if anything, more evenly divided. But this, too, like Jencks's opposite conclusion, is a judgment, not a documented finding. Fortunately, we do not need to rely on casual empiricism. The current experiment in the Alum Rock school district in San Jose, California, goes even further than Jencks by restricting the use of the vouchers to public schools. A proposed experiment in New Hampshire is designed to go in the other direction, toward an unrestricted voucher—though unfortunately the recent Supreme Court decisions have induced New Hampshire to exclude parochial schools. The results of these experiments may provide some solid evidence by which to judge the likely outcome of unrestricted vouchers. [1]

6. *Doubt about new schools.* Is this not all a pipe dream? Private schools now are almost all either parochial schools or élite academies. Will the effect of the voucher plan not simply be to subsidize these, while

[1] One feature of the Jencks report that is both surprising and depressing is that although the study was designed to develop voucher experiments, the authors were content to accept their own casual empirical judgment about the effect of unrestricted vouchers on equality and to foreclose any test of it in their proposed experimental design. If, as they believe, the effect of vouchers on the dispersion of amounts spent on schooling is so crucial, ought not experiments be designed to furnish tested evidence on this point?

leaving the bulk of the slum dwellers in inferior public schools? What reason is there to suppose that alternatives will really arise?

My grocery fable perhaps suggests the answer. The absence of alternatives when there is no market does not mean that none would arise when there is one. Today, cities, states, and the federal government spend about $50 billion a year on elementary and secondary schools. That sum is about a third larger than the total spent annually in restaurants and bars for food and liquor. The smaller sum surely provides an ample variety of restaurants and bars for people in every class and place. The larger sum, or even a minor fraction of it, would equally provide an ample variety of schools. It would offer a vast market that would attract a host of entrants, both from the public schools and from other occupations. In the course of giving occasional talks on the voucher plan, I have been enormously impressed by the number of persons who have come to me afterward and said something like: "I have always wanted to teach [or run a school] but I couldn't stand the educational bureaucracy, red tape, and general ossification of the public schools. Under your plan, I'd love to try my hand at starting a school."

7. *The impact on public schools.* It is essential to separate the rhetoric of the professional public-school bureaucracy from the real problems. Both the National Education Association and the American Federation of Teachers claim that vouchers would "destroy the public-school system" which has been the foundation and cornerstone of our democracy. Claims like this are never accompanied by any evidence that the public-school system is in fact, under current conditions, achieving the great results claimed for it—whatever may have been true in earlier times. Nor is it ever made clear why, if the public-school system is performing so magnificently, it need fear competition from nonpublic, competitive schools.

The real problem arises from the defects, not the virtues, of the public schools. In small, closely knit communities where public schools, particularly elementary schools, are now reasonably or highly satisfactory, I doubt that even the most comprehensive voucher plan would have much effect. The public schools would remain dominant, perhaps improved by the threat of potential competition. But elsewhere, and particularly in the urban ghettos where the public schools are failing so dramatically, most parents would doubtless try to send their children to other schools.

Difficulties would arise from a possible exodus of quality pupils from some public schools. The parents who are most concerned about their children's education are likely to be promptest in transferring them, and even if their children are no smarter than those who remain, they will be highly motivated to learn and will have favorable home backgrounds. Such a sorting-out process goes on now, but, it can be argued, the voucher plan will greatly accelerate it, so that many public schools will be left with "the dregs," society's rejects, and will become, by virtue of the well-documented effect of the students on a school, even poorer in quality than now.

As the private market took over, the quality of all schooling would rise so much that even the worst, while it might be *relatively* lower in the scale, would be better in *absolute* quality. And many of today's rejects are rejects only because the schools are so poor. As store-front academies and similar institutions have demonstrated, many "rejects" perform admirably in a school that evokes their enthusiasm instead of their antipathy.

Nonetheless, it is possible that, at least for a time, some children who remain in public schools will get even poorer schooling than they do now. This raises the moral dilemma that we are all familiar with: are we justified in imposing poorer quality schooling on some children to leaven the schooling of others? It is easy to answer "yes" for other people's children, almost impossible to be so saintly or so diabolical—I do not know which—as to say "yes" for one's own children.

I am comforted in my own negative answer by three considerations. First, the possibility is purely hypothetical; it has neither been demonstrated by experiment nor rendered probable by any persuasive indirect factual evidence. Second, I am convinced that at worst the phenomenon would be temporary. Third, the children who would be benefited most are from the very same social and economic groups as those who, it is feared, would be harmed.

There is no doubt what the key obstacle is to the introduction of market competition into schooling: the perceived self-interest of the educational bureaucracy. The role of this interest group is nothing new, as demonstrated by a fascinating study by British economist Edward West on the development of compulsory and government-financed schooling in New York State (*Journal of Law and Economics,* October, 1967). West demonstrated that teachers and public officials who wanted higher pay and more job-security spearheaded the pressure that led to full assumption of financing by the government, which came with the Free School

Act of 1867, and compulsory schooling, which came later. On the present situation, let me quote an eloquent, if bitter, judgment by Kenneth B. Clark:

> It does not seem likely that the changes necessary for increased efficiency of our urban public schools will come about because they should. . . . What is most important in understanding the ability of the educational establishment to resist change is the fact that public school systems are protected public monopolies with only minimal competition from private and parochial schools. Few critics of the American urban public schools—even severe ones such as myself—dare to question the givens of the present organization of public education . . . . Nor dare the critics question the relevance of the criteria and standards for selecting superintendents, principals and teachers, or the relevance of all of these to the objectives of public education—providing a literate and informed public to carry on the business of democracy—and to the goal of providing human beings with social sensitivity and dignity and creativity and a respect for the humanity of others.
>
> A monopoly need not genuinely concern itself with these matters. As long as local school systems can be assured of state aid and increasing federal aid without the accountability which inevitably comes with aggressive competition, it would be sentimental, wishful thinking to expect any significant increase in the efficiency of our public schools. If there are no alternatives to the present system—short of present private and parochial schools, which are approaching their limit of expansion—then the possibilities of improvement in public education are limited.

Let me give the last word to my great master. Before there was a United States of America, Adam Smith wrote:

> Were there no public institutions of education, no system, no science would be taught for which there was not

some demand; or which the circumstances of the times did not render it either necessary or at least fashionable to learn. . . . Were there no public institutions for education, a gentleman . . . could not come into the world completely ignorant of everything which is the common subject of conversation among gentlemen and men of the world. . . .

The public can facilitate [the] acquisition [of the most essential parts of education] by establishing in every parish or district a little school, where children may be taught for a reward so moderate, that even a common laborer may afford it; the master being partly, but not wholly paid by the public; because, if he was wholly, or even principally paid by it, he would soon learn to neglect his business.

Chapter Thirteen
Monopoly

Since the two columns in this chapter which deal with the Post Office were published, a much-ballyhooed "reform" has been effected. The Post Office is no longer a government department; it is now a separate corporation, the Post Office Service, but still a monopoly, still a government organization. And, as I suggested that it would be in the second column, it has remained "high-priced and inefficient." Postal service continues to deteriorate and deficits to mount.

Both governmental monopoly, like the Post Office, and private monopoly, like the New York Stock Exchange or A. T. & T., are undesirable; but of the two evils, governmental monopoly is much the worse because it tends to be less efficient. In Britain, both mail and telephone are governmental monopolies; in the United States, mail is a governmental monopoly and telephone a private monopoly. Mail service is better in Britain than in the United States (because the British civil service is more efficient than that of the United States) but phone service is worse. A nice, almost controlled experiment.

More important, while there are some cases, of which telephone is probably one, where technical considerations enforce monopoly, most private monopoly reflects governmental assistance and support in the form of exclusive franchises or a governmentally administered cartel, as in banking, radio, TV, airlines, railroads, and so on; or special immunities, such as those granted to trade unions; or licensure requirements, as in medicine, dentistry, law, barbering, and so on; or tariffs and quotas. Hence, the problem of monopoly, as a matter of policy, is largely a problem not of getting government to enact legislation against monopoly but of keeping government from enacting and enforcing legislation strengthening and preserving monopoly.

A favorite parlor question of mine in economic discussions is to say to my partner in conversation: "Suppose you could get one law and only one law enacted for the sole purpose of stimulating competition. What law would you enact?" The answers typically center on strengthening antitrust laws, occasionally on eliminating regulatory bodies, but hardly ever do I get what almost everyone agrees is the correct answer after he hears it: a law abolishing all restrictions on foreign trade, i.e., enacting free trade. Foreign competition would do far more to promote domestic competition than a manifold multiplication of the budget of the antitrust division of the Department of Justice.

The three columns in the chapter touch on only a few monopoly issues. Some columns in other chapters (notably those on oil, steel, and TV) could as well have been included in this. Yet even so, I confess that the problem of monopoly is far from adequately treated in this book.

The Post Office
[October 9, 1967]

Complaints on postal service sent to the postmaster general are directed to the wrong address—that is like berating a dog for barking instead of purring. The Post Office is both a monopoly and a government bureau—so it should occasion no surprise that it is costly, inefficient, and backward.

Even Postmaster General O'Brien has recognized this fact. He has proposed that the Post Office be converted into a nonprofit government corporation. But that would change only the form, not the substance. As a monopoly, it would still be costly; as a government organization, it would still be inefficient and backward.

There is a simpler, more modest, yet more effective solution. Let Congress simply repeal provisions of the present law which prohibit private persons from competing with the U.S. Post Office (presently, private persons may provide mail service, but only if the letters also carry U.S. stamps).

The tyranny of the status quo leads most of us to take it for granted that the postal service must be a government monopoly. The facts are very different. There have been many private ventures—including the storied Pony Express, which failed when the telegraph line (also private) reached California and provided an even faster service. Many others succeeded—which was precisely what led postal officials to foster, over many decades, a succession of congressional enactments to outlaw private mail delivery.

It will be objected that private firms would skim the cream by concentrating on first-class mail and especially local urban delivery—on which the Post Office makes a substantial profit—while leaving to the Post Office the mail on which it loses money.

But this is an argument for, not against, competition. Users of first-class mail are now being overcharged (taxed is the word we use in other contexts) to subsidize the distribution of newspapers, periodicals, and junk mail. Similarly, local delivery subsidizes mail for remote areas.

If we want to subsidize the distribution of such material, we should do so openly and directly—by giving the originators of such mail a subsidy and letting them buy the services of distributing it as best they can. And we should finance the subsidy in accordance with the general canons of taxation, not by a special levy on the users of first-class mail.

Nonetheless, the argument is politically powerful. It explains why many a newspaper and periodical—even some staunch defenders of free markets in other connections—will defend the Post Office's monopoly. They will defend it because they favor subsidizing dissemination of information and educational matter—but doubt that they can persuade the public to do so directly and openly. They will be overimpressed by the importance of the subsidy to their pockets—because they will not allow fully for the improvements that competition would bring. It would be expensive for them to pay the full cost of the present inefficient delivery service—but the cost will be cut sharply by the more efficient service that would spring up.

In any event, I see no reason myself why readers of newspapers and periodicals, and distributors of junk mail, should not bear the full cost of distribution, whatever it may turn out to be—and I, for one, hope that it does not turn out to be so low as to encourage still more junk mail.

One obstacle to introducing competition is a lack of imagination. Our minds are not fertile enough to envisage the miracles that unfettered enterprise can accomplish, in mail service as in other areas—rapid delivery within a city by pneumatic tubes and between cities by facsimile wire, much more extensive use of traveling post offices instead of monuments to the political pull of the postmaster general and the local congressman, and so on *ad infinitum*.

A more important obstacle to introducing competition is the nature of the political process. Competition would benefit the general public. But the general public has no effective lobby. It would benefit men and women who would find new business and employment opportunities. But few of them have any idea that they would be benefited, so they have no effective lobby. Competition might harm postal employees and big users of subsidized mail. As concentrated special-interest groups, they are well organized and do have an effective lobby. Their special interest, not the general interest, is therefore likely to shape the course of postal legislation. An oft-told tale.

The Public Be Damned
[August 5, 1968]

A presidential commission has just made official what you and I have long known from experience. The Post Office "each year . . . slips further behind the rest of the economy in service, in efficiency, and in meeting its responsibilities as an employer."

The commission recommended that the Post Office be converted from a government department to a nonprofit government corporation. That might improve matters some, but since the Post Office would still be a monopoly and a governmental organization, it would remain high-priced and inefficient. A far better solution is one I suggested many months ago (*Newsweek*, Oct. 9, 1967)—simply repeal the present provision making it illegal for private enterprise to provide mail service. Competition would quickly set modern technology to work in the transmission of mail, and simultaneously lower the cost to the consumer. The government system would have to shape up or ship out.

But neither the one proposal nor the other will be adopted. The facts of political life that make this prediction a near-certainty were brought home to me when I was writing my earlier column on the Post Office. Why not, I thought, use it to persuade a congressman to introduce a bill to repeal the present prohibition on private delivery of mail? That would have started desirable legislation on its way, made the column more topical, and given the congressional sponsor some publicity. So I spoke to a number of friends in Congress.

All were favorable to the substance of the bill, yet none was willing to introduce it. As one congressman said to me, "Can you suggest any unions we might conceivably persuade to testify in favor of it?" I could not do so.

Strong pressure groups will oppose changing present arrangements: the postal unions that have become experts in lobbying before Congress; the users of third-and fourth-class mail, who fear that the subsidy they now enjoy would be threatened if Congress no longer finances postal deficits.

No strong pressure groups will favor the proposed changes—which serve only the widespread general interest of the public. If the proposed changes were made—if, for example, private competition were permitted—pressure groups would emerge. Enterprises that succeeded in the new business and their employees and customers would become such groups. But these are only potential, not actual.

A congressman has limited time and influence. It is wise for him to husband that time and influence to promote measures that have some chance of being adopted, or, at least, of bringing him some political support. What can he gain by the purely quixotic gesture of sponsoring a bill to introduce competition into the postal service? Only the active hostility of present special interests. True, many more persons would be benefited than would be harmed and the aggregate benefit would greatly exceed any transitional harm. *But,* and it is a big but, the few persons who believe that they would be harmed will be aware of that fact, and each will expect significant harm, so it will pay them to fight the bill. Most persons who would benefit will not be aware of that fact. Even if they were, the benefit to most would be small. Hence, they are unlikely to devote much effort to promoting the bill—or even to have their vote influenced by its introduction. Their vote is likely to be determined by the matters with respect to which they are members of special interest groups.

Many citizens regard it as a paradox that a democratic government, supposed to promote the general welfare, should enact so many measures that promote special interests. It is not a paradox. It is the result to be expected when government engages in activities that have concentrated effects on small groups and widely diffused effects on the rest of the citizens. A majority rules in a political democracy, but the majority that rules is typically a coalition of special interests—not a majority promoting the general interest.

In the heyday of nineteenth-century capitalism, William H. Vanderbilt, a railroad tycoon, is said to have remarked, "The public be damned" to an inquiring reporter. That may have been his attitude but it was never an accurate description of how private enterprise behaved. Competition saw to that. Enterprises that damned the public did not survive for long. But however accurate it may have been then, today the phrase fits Washington to a T.

Customers Go Home
[August 26, 1968]

You are in a business that is booming. Customers are pounding at your door. Sales records are being set every month. Profits are soaring.

How do you react? You close up shop for one day a week and tell customers to stay home. Impossible? Not at all. That is precisely what firms dealing in securities have been doing some months now. Business is so good, they claim, that they need to shut down one day a week to keep up with the paper work.

Perhaps the most surprising thing about this surprising performance is that it has elicited so little comment about how surprising it is. The financial writers all take it for granted that it is an understandable and natural, if regrettable, response to an upsurge of stock-market activity.

It is anything but. In an industry with as many firms as there are in the securities business, such a concerted shutdown would generally be unstable, unnecessary, and illegal. It would be unstable because it would pay each firm separately to keep open precisely on the day on which other firms closed down. The firms that first opened for business would force the rest to do the same. It would be unnecessary because the firms would respond to the increase in custom either by hiring more help or by raising prices. Either would be more profitable than slamming the door in customers' faces. It would be illegal because it would violate antitrust laws.

The concerted shutdown is a clear sign that there exists an effective monopolistic agreement to restrain trade in the securities industry. The existence of such a monopoly, not anything special about the process of buying and selling securities, explains how the industry can get away with a four-day week.

The shutdown is not the only evidence of monopoly. The standard schedule of rates for buying and selling securities, recently the subject of extensive investigation by the SEC, is another. The high price of seats on the New York Stock Exchange is a third. On the London market, where seats are not so tightly limited in number, the price of a seat is nominal.

Monopoly is harmful to the public, whether private, as in the securities industry, or governmental, as in the Post Office. Both mean unnecessarily high prices to the consumer. Both are departures from free enterprise.

But there are important differences. Private monopolists have a far stronger incentive than governmental monopolists to be efficient. Each firm dealing in securities will try to keep down its costs in order to keep up its profits. The civil servants administering the Post Office have a private interest in wheedling from Congress as large a budget as they can.

Private monopoly is also more subject to erosion than governmental monopoly. Competition will make itself felt in one way or another whenever the monopoly price is far above the competitive price. The recent stock-market hearings offer a dramatic example. The commission charged on large purchases and sales is clearly exorbitant. As a result, firms executing such orders have been able to get the business only by agreeing to "give up" part, often a large part, of their commissions to other firms designated by the customers—clearly an indirect form of price-cutting. In addition, a third market has developed in which large traders deal directly, bypassing the organized exchanges. A less dramatic but more pervasive example is competition among firms to provide "free" services to customers in the form of investment information and advice, attractive lounges with tickers, and so on.

The Post Office has not been forced in the same way to cut the rate for first-class mail even though the present rate is well above the competitive price. And it certainly has not felt impelled to compete by offering better service. Its legal monopoly on carriage of mail is a far more effective deterrent to competition than any private agreement can possibly be.

Indeed, one can go even farther. Private monopolies seldom last long unless they can get governmental assistance in preserving their monopolistic position. In the stock market, the SEC both provides that assistance and shelters the industry from antitrust action—as the ICC does for railroads and trucking, the FCC for radio and television, the CAB for airlines, and so on through the dreary governmental alphabet. Remove this assistance and, while private monopoly will not disappear, it will be greatly reduced in scope and importance.

Chapter Fourteen
Central Planning vs.
Free Enterprise

This chapter covers a wide range of specific issues—from the mode of governing the West Bank of the Jordan to federal relief to individuals damaged by floods. Their common theme is the widespread bias against the free market and in favor of central planning, despite the clearly superior performance of the market. This theme has been present in many of the earlier chapters of this book, but in most of these it has been a minor theme. In these columns, it is the major theme.

This general bias against the free market is a puzzling phenomenon, particularly on the part of intellectuals. I have often noted that the two groups that threaten the free market most are businessmen and intellectuals, but for opposite reasons. The businessman is in favor of free enterprise for everyone else but not for himself—he's always a special case, urging that governmental assistance, protection, and subsidy for him are necessary to serve the national interest. The intellectual is just the other way. He is strongly in favor of free enterprise for himself but not for anyone else. He wants no central government planning bureau to tell him what to write, what research to engage in, what to teach. No, he believes in free speech, a free press, and academic freedom. But when it comes to other people, that's a different story. Then he will tell you about the necessity of having central direction to avoid the wastes of competition and duplication of effort and to assure that resources are employed in accordance with the "right" social priorities.

Why is it that intellectuals do not see the inconsistency? Is it only their expectation (which, incidentally is doomed to be disappointed) that in a centrally planned society they will be in the driver's seat? Is it their tendency to overestimate the power of deliberate direction because cerebration is their specialty and to underestimate the power of voluntary cooperation? Is it the subtlety of the argument for a free market by comparison with the simplicity of the argument for passing a law to remedy a supposed ill? All these play a role, I believe, but even together they do not seem to me to offer a satisfactory explanation for the persistent faith in the virtues of central direction despite the enormous accumulation of evidence, particularly in recent decades, that collectivism is the road to tyranny, inequality, and misery; and that a free market is the only feasible road to freedom and plenty.

Resolving this puzzle is of the greatest importance. The free society badly needs, and certainly deserves, the support, not the hostility, of intellectuals.

Politics and Violence
[June 24, 1968]

There is no simple, widely accepted explanation for the increasing violence that is disfiguring our society. That much is clear from the public soul-searching renewed by the tragic assassination of Robert Kennedy.

This soul-searching has touched on many plausible contributing factors—from the malaise over Vietnam and racial unrest to the boredom produced by affluence. But it has neglected one factor that underlies many specific items mentioned. That factor is the growing tendency, in this country and throughout the world, to use political rather than market mechanisms to resolve social and individual problems.

The tendency to turn to the government for solutions promotes violence in at least three ways:

1. It exacerbates discontent.
2. It directs discontent at persons, not circumstances.
3. It concentrates great power in the hands of identifiable individuals.

1. The political mechanism enforces conformity. If 51 percent vote for more highways, all 100 percent will have to pay for them. If 51 percent vote against highways, all 100 percent must go without them.

Contrast this with the market mechanism. If 25 percent want to buy cars, they can, each at his own expense. The other 75 percent neither get nor pay for them. Where products are separable, the market enables each person to get what he votes for. There can be unanimity without conformity. No one has to submit.

For some items, conformity is unavoidable. There is no way that I can have the size of U.S. armed forces I want while you have the size you want. We can discuss and argue and vote. But having decided, we must conform. For such items, use of a political mechanism is unavoidable.

But every extension—and particularly every rapid extension—of the area over which explicit agreement is sought through political channels strains further the fragile threads that hold a free society together. If it goes so far as to touch an issue on which men feel deeply yet differently, it may well disrupt the society—as our present attempt to solve the racial issue by political means is clearly doing.

2. *If a law, or action by a public official, is all that is needed to solve a problem, then the people who refuse to vote for the law, or who fail to act, are responsible for the problem.* The aggrieved persons will naturally attribute to malevolence the failure of others to vote for the law, or of civil servants to act.

A specific problem often can be resolved by a law—generally one that imposes costs on some to benefit others. But along this road, there is no end to demands. These will inevitably call for more than the total of the nation's resources—however ample they may be.

Circumstances—the fact that resources are limited—make it impossible to meet all demands. But to each citizen it will appear—often correctly—that he is being frustrated by his fellow men, not by nature. Men have always reached beyond their grasp—but they have not always attributed failure to the selfishness of their fellow men.

France is today a striking example—of both escalating demands and the personalizing of discontent.

3. *Political power is not only more visible but far more concentrated than market power can ever be.* The Kennedy family is a harrowing example. Joseph P. Kennedy amassed a fortune of hundreds of millions of dollars. Yet he never had power of a kind to tempt anonymous assassins. Two sons have been assassinated, one at the pinnacle of political power, the other at the beginning of a great political career.

To put it objectively, had the Kennedy fortune never been amassed, the effect on the history of the world would have been trivial—except that it would have been more difficult for the sons to pursue political careers. The assassination of the two sons may well change the history of the world.

A free and orderly society is a complex structure. We understand but dimly its many sources of strength and weakness. The growing resort to political solutions is not the only and may not be the main source of the resort to violence that threatens the foundation of freedom. But it is one that we can do something about. We must husband the great reservoir of tolerance in our people, their willingness to abide by majority rule—not waste it trying to do by legal compulsion what we can do as well or better by voluntary means.

Because or Despite?
[October 28, 1968]

"Nixon's whole campaign," wrote James Reston in the *New York Times* recently, "now is directed to this 'new class' of workers who have moved into the middle class *as a result of* the welfare state and planned economy policies the Republicans have held against Roosevelt for more than a generation." (My italics.)

"As a result of" or "despite"? Reston has much company in taking the first for granted. Indeed, this view is so widely held that it will seem to most readers sheer perversity on my part to question it.

There is no doubt that the condition of the ordinary man improved greatly in the past thirty-five years, There is no doubt that a vast array of legislation was adopted in that period with the announced aim of improving the condition of the ordinary man. Is it not obvious that the first must be the consequence of the second?

Far from it. We all know that intentions are hardly a reliable guide to results. We all know that the mere fact that one event precedes or accompanies another does not demonstrate that the one causes the other—*post hoc, ergo propter hoc* is the label for a logical fallacy, not a valid method of reasoning. In the past thirty-five years, there have also been two great wars, a sharp rise in juvenile delinquency, an explosive growth in the fraction of the world's population living under communism. Shall we say then that these events are responsible for the improvement in the condition of the ordinary man in the U.S.?

To justify his statement, Reston would at least have to show that a comparable improvement in the condition of the ordinary man has never occurred in the absence of "a welfare state and planned economy policies." He clearly cannot do so.

Consider, for example, the experience of the U.S. between the Civil War and the First World War. During this interval, nearly half a century, the U.S. had neither a welfare state nor planned economy policies. The U.S. came about as close to a laissez-faire, free-enterprise society as one could hope to observe in practice. The only significant exception was that tariffs were imposed on imports of goods. But people could come freely—immigration was unrestricted.

Yet the conditions of life of the masses of the people improved enormously—including the condition of the millions on millions of immigrants who streamed to the U.S. The overwhelming majority of immigrants were impecunious when they came, most with few skills and little wealth beyond the clothes on their backs. History records few if any examples of a comparable transformation of poverty-stricken millions into prosperous workers and an affluent middle class. This remarkable performance owed much to wise governmental policy—the policy of noninterference—but owed nothing to either welfare state or planned economy policies.

The conclusion suggested by this sweeping comparison of historical episodes is confirmed by a detailed examination of the legislation enacted since 1933. Much of that legislation has interfered with productive efficiency while helping hardly anyone—agricultural price-support programs, legislation to regulate business, foreign-exchange controls, for example. Much of the rest, though enacted in the name of welfare, has in fact imposed heavy burdens on persons in the lower-income classes and yielded benefits primarily to persons in the middle- and upper-income classes—public housing, urban renewal, governmental financing of higher education, for example. Still other legislation has directly increased poverty or converted transitory poverty into permanent dependence—legal minimum-wage rates, the special immunities of labor unions, and direct relief, for example. And all of the legislation has involved much sheer waste.

The condition of the ordinary man has improved greatly in the past thirty-five years—as it did in the prior thirty-five years and in the thirty-five years before that. The improvement has throughout, in my opinion, been a product of the enormous opportunities provided to all by a competitive free-enterprise system—the most effective machine yet developed for eliminating poverty and raising the standard of life of the masses. The recent improvement has occurred despite a mass of ill-considered and mischievous legislation. It will continue even if that legislation is retained. But it would proceed more rapidly and its benefits would be spread wider if that legislation were repealed.

Invisible Occupation
[May 5, 1969]

On a recent visit to Israel, I toured the west-bank territory occupied during the 1967 six-day war. Much to my surprise, there was almost no sign of a military presence. Israeli soldiers were conspicuous only by their absence. The Jordanian Arabs were peacefully going about their business. I had no feeling whatsoever of being in occupied territory.

We crossed and recrossed the frontier between Israel and the west bank without encountering any soldiers and without noticing any obvious barriers to free movement. Traffic in Jenin, one of the major cities in the west-bank territory, was being directed by a Jordanian policeman wearing a gun on his hip. Even Israeli civilian administrators were few and far between. Governmental functions were being carried out by the prewar Jordanian civil servants.

The absence of a military presence and the continuity of administration are deliberate. At the outset of the occupation, Moshe Dayan, the charismatic general and minister of defense, laid down a policy of laissez-faire—if I may appropriate that much abused economic term to describe a related political phenomenon. Intervention by Israeli authorities was to be held to a minimum—and even that minimum was to be exercised as far as possible by consultation with the appropriate local groups rather than by order.

This wise policy involved almost literal laissez-faire in the economic sphere—and is possible only because it did. Jordanian money is permitted to circulate alongside Israeli money. West-bank farmers may grow whatever they wish and may sell their produce at any price they can command not only in the west bank but also in Jordan itself, so there is active trade across the Jordan River. An agricultural extension service manned by several hundred Jordanian civil servants, plus a literal handful of Israeli experts added after the war, has been galvanized into greater activity and has been extremely effective, so that agricultural output is growing rapidly. To a casual observer, the area appears to be prospering.

The major interferences with economic laissez-faire are restrictions on the export of farm products to Israel and on the movement of labor. Restrictions on exports have been imposed because Israel has adopted a governmental policy of supporting the prices of some farm products (we are by no means the only country that goes in for such foolishness). The importation of these products into Israel from the west bank would tend to force down the fixed prices or require the accumulation of additional surpluses. Restrictions on the movement of labor partly have a similar rationale—preservation of union wage rates—and partly the valid justification of reducing social tension and the danger of disruptive activity.

These restrictions encourage the west bank to sell to Jordan rather than to Israel. As a result, Israel exports more to the west bank than it imports from the west bank and the west bank exports more to Jordan than it imports from Jordan. Jordan thereby gets foodstuffs and other items partly in return for pieces of paper (Jordanian currency) hoarded by west-bank residents. In effect, Israel is indirectly giving the equivalent of foreign aid to Jordan!

Another surprising consequence is that the military, who generally favor running things by direct orders coming down a chain of command, are in Israel the strongest supporters of free markets and nonintervention. They see by example that the anonymous market frees them from burdensome tasks and eliminates much potential conflict. They see that the elimination of barriers to the movement of goods, men, and capital would foster the economic integration of the west bank with Israel without requiring political integration.

Here, on a scale sufficiently small to be readily comprehensible, is a striking illustration of the general principle that the free market enables people to cooperate in some areas to their joint benefit while permitting them to go their own way in other areas of their life. This principle explains why the nineteenth century, when laissez-faire was the ruling philosophy, was an era of international peace and economic cooperation while the twentieth century, when the key words are central planning and government intervention, has been marred by recurrent international strife and discord. Marx to the contrary notwithstanding, trade unites and politics divides.

Up in the Air
[July 28, 1969]

This column was begun in a jet that had crossed the Atlantic in six hours but had now been circling Kennedy for an hour, stacked up awaiting permission to land.

What waste. A multimillion dollar jet, a marvel of modern technology, manned by a highly skilled and highly paid crew, occupied by nearly 200 passengers, many spending highly valuable time, serviced by a pleasant and attractive complement of hostesses, guzzling fuel as it circled aimlessly high in the sky. The cost was easily thousands of dollars an hour.

How is it that this waste occurs, not only occasionally, which is no doubt unavoidable, but regularly, so that experienced travelers, let alone the airlines, regard it as a routine matter? How is it that the large financial return from eliminating the waste is not an effective prod?

As I sat in the plane, I reflected that the airplane manufacturers seem to be able to turn out these marvelous mechanical miracles in ample number to meet the demand of the airlines for them. The airlines seem to be able to acquire the highly skilled flight crews in ample number (with a real assist, it is true, from the military services, which train most of them). They seem to be able to hire sufficient stewardesses to woman the cabins. Occasionally, a plane is delayed by mechanical trouble, but the airlines generally have been able to acquire the skilled maintenance and ground men to service the planes, so this is seldom a bottleneck. I have heard no stories of planes being delayed by the inability to get ample airplane fuel, or meals to feed the passengers, or liquor to befuddle them.

How is it that it has been possible to attend to all these matters—and yet not to arrange things on the ground so that planes can generally be landed promptly and without delay? Is it somehow inherently more difficult to arrange space for landing planes than to build them and operate them in the air? That seems very dubious indeed.

I believe the answer to the puzzle is much simpler. Every other activity described is mostly private and highly competitive—private enterprise builds the planes, private (or where governmental, highly competitive) airlines fly them, private firms produce and supply the fuel for man and machine. The airports, on the other hand, are a socialized monopoly—financed and run by government. As a result, there is no effective way that the waste involved in airport delays can be converted into effective pressure to eliminate them. The pressure must make its convoluted way through the FAA, the administration, Congress, and local governments.

There is no reason why this need be so. In the heyday of free enterprise, the railroads built and almost wholly financed their own terminals—even when they were "union" terminals servicing a number of lines—and still operate them. Why should airlines not be required to provide their own landing facilities—not necessarily directly but perhaps by paying fees to other private enterprises that run the airports? The airlines doubtless initially welcomed federal subsidization of landing facilities. I wonder whether they now think they really got a bargain?

President Nixon has proposed a vast expansion of landing facilities to be financed by user charges but to continue to be operated by governmental agencies. The method of finance is the right one. The cost of landing facilities should be borne by those who use them. The method of operation is the wrong one. The right solution is to move toward private operation as well as finance.

Many a reader will regard my explanation as too pat—as simply a knee-jerk reaction of an economic liberal (in the original sense of that much-abused term). Maybe so—but I urge them to see whether the shoe does not fit, not only here but elsewhere. Where are the long lines of frustrated drivers? At the doors of the automobile dealers selling cars produced by private enterprise—or on the highways and city streets provided by government? What are the problems plaguing education? A shortage of high-quality desks, chairs, and other educational equipment, including books, produced by private enterprise—or the inefficient organization and conduct of public schools? Where is technology backward and primitive? In the privately run telephone industry (albeit the existence of monopoly does occasionally produce delay and inefficiency)—or in the governmentally run Post Office?

Development Fashions
[December 21, 1970]

Recently I spent a week in a "developing" country. (A euphemism used to avoid the invidious designation of "underdeveloped." In U.N. language, countries are classified as either "developing" or "developed" despite the fact that most of the "developed" countries are developing faster than the "developing" countries. Semantics, where is thy sting?)

The country I visited is very different in resources and political background from other underdeveloped countries that I have visited. Yet the governmental policies that it is following to foster economic development are identical. I was able to reel them off without being told. Just as every female, whether her legs are slender and beautiful or fat and dumpy, was driven by fashion to hike up her dress, so every "developing" country, regardless of its specific characteristics, is driven by fashion to adopt a uniform set of governmental policies.

Here is a partial list of what every well-dressed "developing" country must have these days.

1. *An international airline.* Hardly a country is so underdeveloped that it does not have a fleet of U.S.-built jet aircraft, often indeed flown by U.S. or other foreign pilots, to show its name in the international airports of the world. Ghana Airways, Korean Air Lines, Turkish Airlines—the list goes on and on. Almost all lose money—but then what woman fusses about the price tag if she can get the money from her husband or father or uncle?

2. *A steel plant for countries that happen to have readily available supplies of ore and fuel may make economic sense.* But every "developing" country wants this symbol of industrialization, regardless of whether it makes sense. Egypt's steel mill is the modern equivalent of Egypt's ancient pyramids—a monument to proclaim the glory of her rulers. The major difference is that the maintenance costs of the modern monuments are far higher than of the ancient monuments—each year, Egypt spends about twice as much in producing steel at home as it would cost to buy it abroad.

3. *Auto-assembly plants.* The cheapest way for most underdeveloped countries to get automobile transportation would be to import the secondhand cars that are a drag on the U.S. and European markets. But this would be demeaning. India, as I once put it, is too poor to afford secondhand cars. So "developing" countries impose high tariffs on secondhand cars, or sharply restrict their import by quotas, in order to induce Ford or American Motors or Fiat or Rootes to set up a local assembly plant producing new cars. The resulting prices for secondhand and new cars strike an American as fantastic (some years ago, after selling an old Buick in

the United States for $22, I priced the same model in no better condition in Bombay at $1,500).

A South American expert has estimated that his country would save money if it paid the employees at a local Ford assembly plant their current salaries to stay at home and imported directly from the U.S. the cars now being produced locally.

In 1963, I estimated that the annual cost to India of getting its motor transportation by producing new cars locally instead of by importing new and used cars amounted to more than one-tenth of the foreign aid India was then receiving each year from the U.S.

Free trade in ideas, like free trade in goods, fosters standardization, though neither in ideas nor goods does this go so far as to eliminate all variety—as witness this column.

This tendency toward standardization is greatly reinforced by the jet experts who propagate the current orthodoxy in the economics of development with all the zeal of religious missionaries of an earlier and simpler age. The new missionaries come bearing gifts in the form of "development loans" at low interest rates or outright grants called "foreign aid." The gifts strengthen the government sector relative to the private sector and enable government officials to follow policies and undertake projects that would be politically unacceptable if the people at home had to pay the costs. That is why foreign aid is very far indeed from an unmixed blessing for the ordinary people in the underdeveloped countries.

Women seem to be staging a successful revolt against the fashion experts who decreed the midi. Who would have believed it possible? Maybe the badgered citizens in the underdeveloped countries of the world will yet be inspired to do likewise and to liberate themselves from their fashion experts. That will be the day!

Federal Flood Relief
[September 4, 1972]

In an earlier and simpler age, a disaster such as Hurricane Agnes would have been met by local resources, insurance, and charitable contributions. Today, it is taken for granted that the federal government should be the major source of emergency assistance and should also compensate the victims for the greater part of their material damage. I have encountered literally no questioning of this assumption. Yet, the change is by no means an unmixed blessing.

Look at it first from the viewpoint of the victims. For many years, governments at all levels have absorbed roughly a third of their total income, and most of that has gone to the federal government. Up to now, they may well say, we have not gotten our money's worth. If we had been relieved of that burden, we would be better able to meet the present disaster. As it is, we regard our past taxes as insurance payments, and the compensation we are now getting is no more than our just due.

Clearly, they have a real case. But what of the rest of us? The House overwhelmingly voted $1.6 billion in aid despite, as one paper put it, "warnings that much of the money could be wasted by fraudulent claims." The action was lauded as a sign of generosity. So it is, but at whose expense? Not a word in the papers about that. Would we be willing privately to contribute that much? To compensate every victim, regardless of his own resources? There is no way of knowing. Is that a fair sum in view of the implicit insurance contract envisioned by the victims? Again, there is no way of knowing.

But these are only the surface issues. The real issues go deeper. What effect do these arrangements have on the character and efforts of the participants? On the use of our human and natural resources?

One adverse effect is clear. The rest of us are encouraged to avoid personal involvement. We can sympathize casually, and then go about our business. After all, Big Brother is taking care of the victims. He is doing it with our money, so we can feel righteous, but the connection is so remote that we have no sense of individual participation. Surely, nothing has done so much over the years to destroy a sense of human community, of individual responsibility for assisting the less fortunate, as the bureaucratizing of charity.

The victims are affected as well. Help extended to them on a personal basis would stimulate a reciprocal feeling of obligation. It would strengthen their self-reliance. Help extended by government produces resentment and weakens self-reliance. Rugged individualism has been the motor of progress. Are we sure that we have a substitute?

As to the use of resources, people choose their residence partly on the basis of the likelihood of floods and other natural disasters. The resulting higher demand for "safe" locations than for "unsafe" locations raises the value of "safe" land and lowers the value of "unsafe" land. "Safe" places have a higher density of settlement than they would otherwise, but those who do settle in the "unsafe" places have the compensation of a lower price of land or of lower rents.

Let government (i.e., other people) assume full financial responsibility for losses. People will still prefer "safe" places, since many losses cannot be compensated for. But the preference will be less. The added density of settlement in "unsafe" places will produce a distorted use of resources. It will soon become obvious that people cannot be permitted to choose freely their place of residence (or other aspects of their way of life) if government pays a large part of the bill. Acceptance of government financial responsibility for losses inevitably means an extension of government control over behavior.

You may answer that all this is nit-picking; that people do not choose their residence primarily on the basis of the chance of a flood of a kind that occurs once in a hundred years, that the immediate problem is the distress of the victims of the flood and that only the federal government has the resources to assist them.

Largely true, yet it misses the point. Given the general arrangements that we have adopted, the flood victims clearly qualify for federal relief. But are we wise to continue and to expand such arrangements? Can human dignity, individual freedom, and personal integrity survive an indefinite extension of the area of our lives for which Big Brother assumes responsibility?

Chapter Fifteen
The Oil Crisis

Excuses must be distinguished from reasons. The excuse for the oil crisis that hit the world after the Arab-Israeli War in October 1973 was political: the Arab countries were unshielding the "weapon" of oil to induce other countries to put pressure on Israel to make concessions to the Arab nations and the Palestinian refugees. The reason, I believe, was very different: to exploit the monopoly position of an oil cartel that has been developing now for some years. The excuse furnished window dressing for the naked exercise of monopoly power. It also furnished some of the cement required to hold the cartel together.

The initial success of the cartel was dramatic. The price of oil was tripled and quadrupled in brief order. This success produced widespread panic throughout the oil-consuming countries. There is a strong tendency for all of us—but particularly for politicians and journalists—to have a short time perspective and to extrapolate into the indefinite future what is happening today. That is why each crisis gets overblown, gets treated as the worst or best or greatest from time immemorial.

For an economist, it was obvious that the initial success could not last. It is a key proposition of economics that nothing can influence price except as it affects the quantity demanded or the quantity supplied. The mere pronouncement by OPEC (Organization of Petroleum Exporting Countries) of higher prices was unimportant. What was important was their decision to cut production below the level that they had earlier planned to produce. How much a given cut in production affects prices depends on what economists call the "elasticity" of demand by consumers and of supply by other producers. The cut in OPEC production must one way or another be offset either by a cut in consumption or by an increase in production by other suppliers. The more elastic demand is—that is, the larger the percentage reduction in quantity consumed for each 1 percent rise in price—the smaller will be the price increase required to achieve the necessary cut in consumption. Similarly, the more elastic is the supply from other sources—that is, the larger the percentage increase in quantity supplied for each 1 percent rise in price—the smaller will be the price increase required to achieve an offsetting expansion in other production.

Here is where a second key proposition of economics enters in: both demand and supply tend to be more elastic, the longer the time allowed for adjustment. In the immediate aftermath of a cut in supply such as that engineered by the oil cartel, it is difficult for consumers and for other producers to adjust. It takes time to change prior arrangements, to shift for example from one method of heating to another, or from large cars to small cars, or to drill new wells, explore new fields. As time elapses, the possibilities of adjustment become larger and larger. The result is that every cartel seems to be much more successful at its outset than it can continue to be. The cut in production by the OPEC cartel quadrupled the price initially—because it took a very large inducement to produce a corresponding cut in consumption. But as consumers adjusted, and other sources of supply expanded, the price inevitably eased off and it would have required bigger and bigger cuts of production to keep prices up. This process is still at work. The price of oil is now (June, 1974) much below its crisis level, but it is still far higher than precrisis, or than it will be a year from now.

This tendency for the power of a cartel to decline is reinforced by a third key economic proposition: the more successful the cartel, the greater the pressure on it not only from a reduction in consumption and an increase in noncartel supply but also from within the cartel. The members of a cartel have conflicting interests. Each is anxious for the others to cut production while he expands production to profit from the high prices. The process has been very evident in the oil cartel. Libya, Iran, Iraq, and some other members of OPEC have been vociferous in demanding ever higher prices while themselves producing all out to benefit from the high prices. They have been able to succeed so far because they have been able to persuade Saudi Arabia and Kuwait to bear the whole of the cut in production. But the cuts required by Saudi Arabia and Kuwait will become larger and larger, and their willingness to undertake them smaller and smaller, as the downward pressure on prices from cuts in consumption and alternative supplies increases. The cartel will break up—as just about every other such cartel in the past has—long before Saudi Arabia and Kuwait output approach zero. It is instructive that in recent OPEC meetings, Saudi Arabia has been pressing for lower prices, the other cartel members for higher prices. This reflects primarily self-interest, hardly at all concern for the interests of the consuming countries or a desire to contribute to slowing worldwide inflation, or even the Harvard education of Saudi Arabia's Sheik Yamani—to mention the factors that are prominently referred to in newspaper accounts of the dispute within OPEC.

These considerations explain why, in my opinion, the "energy crisis" was greatly exaggerated, why it will disappear from our major concerns, and why the price of oil will return to a level much closer to its pre-October 1973 price than to the peak prices reached shortly thereafter.

The danger is that our panic reaction to the "oil crisis" will produce unwise governmental measures that will convert a temporary oil crisis into a permanent one. The final four of the five columns in this chapter deal with the immediate panic reaction that produced extensive controls over the distribution of oil. Fortunately, coupon rationing of ultimate consumers was avoided but not rationing and allocation of oil at prior levels of distribution. Some of this too is now in the process of being dismantled, as bureaucratic inefficiency has reinforced the more ample supplies of oil. But so long as the Federal Energy Office exists, in one guise or another, neither the controls nor the harm they do will disappear.

Perhaps the more serious long-run danger is that, in the name of "Project Independence," we shall adopt a long-run policy that will foist high cost oil on consumers indefinitely, insulate U.S. oil producers from foreign competition, and subsidize heavily their domestic operations. This danger is the key message of the first column in this chapter, "Oil and the Middle East" (June 26, 1967), written seven years ago after the Six Day Arab-Israeli War but no less pertinent today.

Oil and the Middle East
[June 26, 1967]

Few U.S. industries sing the praises of free enterprise more loudly than the oil industry. Yet few industries rely so heavily on special governmental favors.

These favors are defended in the name of national security. A strong domestic oil industry, it is said, is needed because international disturbances can so readily interfere with the supply of foreign oil. The Israeli-Arab war has produced just such a disturbance, and the oil industry is certain to point to it as confirmation of the need for special favors. Are they right? I believe not.

The main special favors are:

1. *Percentage Depletion:* This is a special provision of the federal income tax under which oil producers can treat up to 27.5 percent of their income as exempt from income tax—supposedly to compensate for the depletion of oil reserves. [1] This name is a misnomer. In effect, this provision simply gives the oil industry (and a few others to which similar treatment has been extended) a lower tax rate than other industries.

2. *Limitation of Oil Production:* Texas, Oklahoma, and some other oil-producing states limit the number of days a month that oil wells may operate or the amount that they may produce. The purpose of these limitations is said to be "conservation." In practice, they have led to the wasteful drilling of multiple wells draining the same field. And the amount of production permitted has been determined primarily by estimates of market demand, not by the needs of conservation. The state regulatory authorities have simply been running a producers' cartel to keep up the price of oil.

3. *Oil Import Quotas:* The high domestic prices enforced by restriction of production were threatened by imports from abroad. So, in 1959, President Eisenhower imposed a quota on imports by sea. This quota is still in effect. [2] Currently, it is slightly more than one million barrels a day (under one-fifth of our total consumption).

Foreign oil can be landed at East Coast refineries for about $1 to $1.50 a barrel less than the cost of domestic oil. The companies fortunate enough to be granted import permits are therefore in effect getting a federal subsidy of this amount per barrel—or a total of about $400 million a year.

These special favors cost U.S. consumers of oil products something over $3.5 billion a year (Gilbert Burck, *Fortune*, April 1965). This staggering cost cannot be justified by its contribution to national security.

The following points indicate the basis for this judgment:

1. Restricting imports may promote the domestic industry, but why

[1] [This rate was reduced in the Tax Reform Act of 1969 to 22 per cent.]
[2] [It has more recently been ended as a result of the 1973–74 oil crisis.]

pay a $400 million subsidy to oil importers? A tariff of $1.25 a barrel would restrict imports just as much—and the U.S. government rather than the oil importers would get the revenue. (I do not favor such a tariff but it would be less bad than a quota.)

2. Oil from Venezuela—after the U.S., the largest oil producer in the world—is most unlikely to be cut off by international disturbances threatening our national security. Yet it too is covered by the import quota.

3. Restrictions on domestic oil production at least have the virtue that domestic production could be expanded rapidly in case of need. But such restrictions are an incredibly expensive way to achieve flexibility.

4. The world oil industry is highly competitive and far-flung and getting more so. The Mideast crisis has left large oil-producing areas undisturbed. Moreover, the Arabian countries themselves cannot afford to refuse to sell for long.[3] Only World War Three is likely to produce severe disruptions of supply—and then the emergency is likely to be brief.

5. If all the special favors to the oil industry were abandoned, prices to the consumer would decline sharply. Domestic production also might decline—but then again, if the industry were freed of all the artificial props that raise costs and stifle initiative, production might rise rather than decline. In either event, a vigorous and extensive domestic industry would remain, protected by the natural barrier of transportation costs.

If domestic output did decline, we might want to insure against an emergency by stockpiling oil, paying for holding reserve wells in readiness, making plans for sharp reductions in nonessential consumption, or in other ways. Measures such as these could provide insurance at a small fraction of the $3.5 billion a year the U.S. consumer is now paying.

The political power of the oil industry, not national security, is the reason for the present subsidies to the industry. International disturbances simply offer a convenient excuse.

Why Some Prices Should Rise
[November 19, 1973]

"When the price of a thing goes up," wrote the British economist Edwin Cannan in 1915, "a good many people . . . abuse, not the buyers nor

---

[3] [The recent embargo is only a partial contradiction. It was poorly enforced, and the cartel that conducted it is, in July 1974, showing signs of strain.]

the persons who might produce it and do not do so, but the persons who are producing and selling it, and thereby keeping down its price. . . . It certainly would appear to be an extraordinary example of the proverbial ingratitude of man when he abuses the farmer who does grow wheat because other farmers do not. . . . But have we not all heard the preacher abuse his congregation because it is so small?"

This ancient article, from which I have taken my title, has been brought to mind by the oil crisis.

Time and again, I have castigated the oil companies for their hypocrisy, for loudly proclaiming their allegiance to free enterprise yet simultaneously undermining free enterprise by seeking and getting special governmental privilege (percentage depletion, prorationing of oil, import quotas, etc.). Yet we shall only hurt ourselves if we let resentment at their past misdeeds interfere with our adopting the most effective way to meet the present problem.

The current oil crisis has not been produced by the oil companies. It is a result of governmental mismanagement exacerbated by the Mideast war. The price of natural gas at the wellhead has been held down for years by government edict. Since August 15, 1971, the price of retail gasoline and of fuel oil has been held down by the successive phases. The result has been to encourage consumption and discourage both current production and the expansion of capacity. It took the Mideast war to bring these evil effects of price-fixing to a boil.

If all Mideast oil is shut off, we shall have to do without some 10 percent of our present oil supplies. That is no tragedy. It means going back to the rate of consumption of 1970 or 1971—when no one thought we had a catastrophic shortage of fuel.

The most effective way to cut consumption and encourage production is simply to let the prices of oil products rise to whatever level it takes to clear the market. The higher prices would give each of the 210 million residents of the U.S. a direct incentive to economize on oil, to find substitutes for oil, to increase the supply of oil.

How much will the price have to rise? No one can tell. But if consumption must be cut by 10 percent, it is hard to believe the price would have to rise by more than, say, double that percentage. A 20 percent rise in oil and gasoline prices would not be nice—but consider the alternative.

The only alternative is exhortation backed by compulsion: artificially low prices accompanied by governmental rationing. This method induces each of us to oppose the general interest rather than to further it. Our separate incentive is to wangle as much as we can from the rationing authorities. And they can have only the crudest criteria to know how to distribute the limited supplies. They have no way to know whose "need" is genuine and whose is artificial—even if we put to one side, as experience warns us we cannot, special influence, corruption, and bribery.

Two hundred and ten million persons each with a separate incentive to economize; or 210 million persons dragooned by men with guns to cut down their use of oil—can there be any doubt which is the better system?

But, you will say, rationing by price hurts the poor relative to the rich. What of the poor man with his old jalopy as the only way to get to work? The answer is straightforward. If high oil prices impose special problems on some, let us provide funds to mitigate their problem. Let us not impose compulsion and waste on 95 percent to avoid special measures for 5 percent.

Note that what is called for is higher prices for oil products *relative* to other products —*not general inflation*. Only some prices should rise.

The oil problem offers a particularly clear illustration of how the price system promotes both freedom and efficiency, how it enables millions of us to cooperate voluntarily with one another in our common interest. It brings out equally why the only alternative to the price system is compulsion and the use of force.

It is a mark of how far we have gone on the road to serfdom that governmental allocation and rationing of oil is the automatic response to the oil crisis. This will not prevent higher prices, which will in fact do the job—but you may be sure that the rationing authorities will take the credit.

The Inequity of Gas Rationing
[December 10, 1973]

There is wide agreement that the most efficient solution for the energy-and-oil crisis is to let the free market reign—to let prices rise to whatever level is necessary to equate the amount people want to buy with the amount available. Higher prices would give each of us a private incentive to conserve energy, would give producers an incentive to add to the supply, and would assure that energy was used for purposes valued most highly by purchasers.

The one argument against this traditional free-market solution is that it is "inequitable." Any solution requires that we use less energy than we would like to use at present prices—that is precisely why we have a crisis. Any solution will therefore "hurt" all of us. But it is maintained that the free market imposes the burden disproportionately on the poor, that government rationing would avoid this "inequity" and hence should be adopted, despite all its defects—waste, bureaucracy, black markets, and corruption.

The argument has a strong emotional appeal. But it has no rational basis.

Consider one scheme for rationing gasoline that has been proposed: give each family coupons entitling it to purchase a specified number of gallons a week at present prices, but then permit it to purchase additional gasoline at free-market prices. Since my concern is with equity, let me waive all questions about the feasibility of assuring that coupons would be honored and about the effects on production incentive. Suppose the allotment per family is fifteen gallons per week, that every family uses its allotment, that the fixed price is 45 cents a gallon and that the free-market price, in the absence of rationing, would be 75 cents a gallon *for the same total amount of gasoline* (I shall discuss below the reason for this condition). The scheme is then precisely equivalent to sending each family in the United States a check for $4.50 a week (30 cents times fifteen gallons), financing the payment by a tax on the oil industry, and letting the free market distribute the gasoline. Is there anyone who would favor such a national dividend, distributed regardless of need? If there be such a person, would even he favor having its size determined solely by the price of gasoline? If the scheme is bad when stated in its naked form, how can concealing it in ration coupons make it good?

Or consider another variant: distribute coupons covering all gasoline that will be available (say twenty gallons per week), fix the price at 45 cents a gallon, but permit the coupons to be sold in a "white" market. Assuming the same facts as in the preceding paragraph, the price of the coupons would be 30 cents a gallon. The scheme would be precisely equivalent to imposing a tax of 30 cents per gallon on gasoline and using the proceeds to send each family in the United States a check for $6 a week (30 cents times twenty gallons). Again, stated nakedly in that way, does the scheme really have any appeal?

Note that I have considered the least inequitable schemes. Alternatives that would prohibit the sale of coupons or that would allocate coupons on the basis of number of cars or "normal" mileage driven rather than equally to all families are equivalent to sending *larger* checks to high-income than low-income families.

Because of my emphasis on "equity," I have omitted a major defect of these rationing schemes—the defect that required me to assume *the same amount of gasoline*. Both schemes would reduce the incentive of producers to add to the supply and would therefore mean *less* gasoline than under the free market.

The effect on production is important both in the current emergency and in the longer run. Suppose that shortages in any commodity or service are always met by taxes designed to absorb the increase in price. What incentive would that give private enterprise to provide excess capacity to meet such a possibility? As it is, the prospect of occasional bonanzas makes it profitable for enterprises to maintain greater productive capacity and larger inventories than are required under normal circumstances. With that prospect eliminated, the government would itself have to provide such reserves—a task it has hardly demonstrated the competence to perform.

The free-market solution is not only more efficient, it is also more equitable. True "equity" calls for making provision for special hardship cases. It does not call for raining government checks on all and sundry.

Why Now?
[December 31, 1973]

"Running Out of Everything" was *Newsweek*'s cover headline some weeks back. It dramatized the fact that, for the first time since World War Two, the U.S. had begun to experience major shortages not only of petroleum products, but of a wide range of other items.

Of the many attempts to explain this state of affairs that I have seen in the media, not one faces up to the crucial question: Why now? Why did shortages not emerge in 1968 at the height of the Vietnam war, or in 1958, or for that matter in 1938 or 1928? What is different about 1973?

The Mideast war is one obvious answer. The Arab boycott it unleashed has exacerbated the shortage of crude oil. But an energy shortage was well on its way before the Mideast war broke out. Government allocation of fuel was already on the way. And none of the other shortages owes anything to the Mideast war.

One popular answer—particularly for the energy crisis— is that consumption of energy has been increasing rapidly. But that has been going on for decades. Why should it have produced shortages only now?

The response is typically that we are running short of reserves of fossil fuel—that there are only ten or fifteen years of proven oil reserves, for example. But that too has been true for decades. In the 1920s, scare stories were being written about the danger that we would run out of oil because the then proven reserves would last for only ten or fifteen years. In the interim, consumption of crude oil has multiplied manyfold—and so have proven oil reserves. The fact is that it does not pay to find and prove more than about fifteen years' oil reserves at any time.

But this time, it is said, we are short of refining capacity. Perhaps so, but why now? How is it that until now, refining capacity was able to keep up with demand, but in the years 1971 to 1973 it was not?

The greedy, selfish oil interests? If, as is frequently charged, they have conspired to create a shortage profitable to themselves, why have they been so slow? They are no more powerful now than they have been for many years. Why did they wait so long before squeezing the hapless consumer? And how do they make profits by having no oil to sell? By full-page advertisements urging consumers to economize on fuel? This is simply the irrational search for a devil.

The answer to "Why now?" is straightforward—yet I know from bitter experience how hard it is to persuade anyone other than an economist that so simple an answer can be correct. Nineteen seventy-three is different from other peacetime years because, for the first time since World War Two, the U.S. has had extensive price and wage controls. The key to today's shortages is the price freeze ordered by President Nixon on August 15, 1971.

Has fuel oil been especially short? August 15, 1971, was summertime. It will surprise no one that fuel-oil prices are generally lower in the summer than in the winter. The result of freezing prices at summertime levels was to make gasoline more profitable to produce than fuel oil. Has pipe been hard to get for drilling new wells? As it happened, the controlled prices for pipe and flat steel made it more profitable to produce flat steel.

I am not enough of an expert—no one is—to know the million and one places where prices fixed by bureaucrats on the basis of arbitrary rules and accidental starting points have created distortions and shortages. Some have been dramatic, like the beef shortage and the destruction of baby chickens. But most have not been. They are hidden in the interstices of an incredibly complex production system that cannot operate without the enormous efficiency of a market-price system to adapt changing demands to changing supplies. And many have been overcome by millions of citizens who found ways to avoid or evade the price controls.

I know that it is hard for you to believe that so seemingly simple a matter as price fixing can produce so complex a phenomenon as widespread shortages. But then, I find it hard to believe that an automobile engine is a complex matter until I start probing around in its innards when it stops functioning on a dark road in the early hours of the morning.

At any rate, if this is not the answer, what is? In what other respect—pervasive enough to produce the pervasive effect we see—is 1973 different from earlier peacetime years?

FEO and the Gas Lines
[March 4, 1974]

As I write this in Chicago, lines are forming at those gas stations that are open. The exasperated motorists are cursing; the service-station attendants are fuming; the politicians are promising. The one thing few people seem to be doing is thinking.

How is it that for years past, you and I have been able to find gas stations open at almost any hour of the day or night, and have been able to drive up to them with complete confidence that the request to "fill up" would be honored with alacrity and even with a cleaning of the windshield? To judge from the rhetoric that pollutes the air these days, it must have been because there was a powerful Federal Energy Office hidden somewhere in the underground dungeons in Washington, in which an invisible William Simon was efficiently allocating petroleum products throughout the land, riding herd on greedy oil tycoons lusting for an opportunity to mess things up and create long lines at their gas stations.

Of course, we know very well that the situation is precisely the reverse. The lines date from the creation of a real Federal Energy Office run by a very visible, able, and articulate William Simon. Which is the cause and which the effect? Did the lines produce the FEO or the FEO the lines?

After the Arabs cut output, Germany imposed no price controls on petroleum products. It did initially restrict Sunday driving but soon removed that restraint. The price of petroleum products jumped some 20 or 30 percent, but there were no long lines, no disorganization. The greedy consumers found it in their own interest to conserve oil in the most painless way. The greedy oil tycoons found it in their own interest to see to it that petroleum products were available for those able and willing to pay the price.

Other European countries, like the U.S., imposed price controls. And, like us, they had chaos.

The Arab cut in output can be blamed for higher prices, but it cannot be blamed for the long lines. Their creation required the cooperation of shortsighted governments.

The world crisis is now past its peak. The initial quadrupling of the price of crude oil after the Arabs cut output was a temporary response that has been working its own cure. Higher prices induced consumers to economize and other producers to step up output. It takes time to adjust, so these reactions will snowball. In order to keep prices up, the Arabs would have to curtail their output by ever larger amounts. But even if they cut their output to zero, they could not for long keep the world price of crude at $10 a barrel. Well before that point, the cartel would collapse.

The effects of consumer and producer reactions are already showing up. The European countries that introduced rationing and restrictions on driving have eliminated them. World oil prices are weakening. They will soon tumble. When that occurs, it will reveal how superficial are the hysterical cries that we have come to the end of an era and must revolutionize our energy-wasting way of life. What we have been witnessing is not the end of an era but simply shortsightedness.

At home, unfortunately, our problems will not be over so soon. The panicky FEO forced oil companies to shift so much production to heating oil that we face a glut of heating oil but a paucity of gasoline. The FEO's allocations among states have starved some, amply supplied others. Its order that refineries operating at high levels must sell oil to those operating at low levels sounds fine. In practice, however, it reduces the incentive for the recipients to buy oil abroad and produces a wasteful use of oil at home.

We have the worst of both worlds: long lines and sharply higher prices—indeed, higher than I believe they would have been without the waste resulting from FEO controls.

Is rationing the solution? Far from it. It is the problem. We already have rationing of producers and distributors. Coupon rationing of final consumers would simply be the hair of the dog that bit you.

The way to end long lines at gas stations is to abolish FEO and end all controls on the prices and allocation of petroleum products. Within a few weeks, your friendly dealer would again be cleaning your windshield with a smile.

How can thinking people believe that a government that cannot deliver the mail can deliver gas better than Exxon, Mobil, Texaco, Gulf, and the rest?